Secondary Art Education:

An Anthology of Issues

Bruce E. Little, Editor

Douglas County Comprehensive High School
Georgia Southern University

National Art Education Association
1916 Association Drive
Reston, Virginia 22091

1990

About NAEA . . .

Founded in 1947, the National Art Education Association is the largest professional art education association in the world. Membership includes elementary and secondary teachers, art administrators, museum educators, arts council staff, and university professors from throughout the United States and 66 foreign countries. NAEA's mission is to advance art education through professional development, service, advancement of knowledge, and leadership.

©1990 The National Art Education Association, 1916 Association Drive, Reston, VA 22091-1590.

ISBN 0-937652-53-9

Contents

Preface
Bruce E. Little   v

1   The Discipline of Art
    Harlan Hoffa   2

2   Art Criticism and Social Integration of the
    Disciplines of Art
    Tom Anderson   11

3   The Period of Transescence and Its Relevance
    for the Secondary Level Art Education Program
    Andra N. Johnson   21

4   Forms of Instruction Used by Art Teachers
    with Pre-Adolescents
    Mary Stokrocki   35

5   Are Art Teachers Prepared to Teach the NAEA
    Essential Components?
    Adelaide Rusch and **William J. Thomas**   47

6   Grading Student Artwork: A Plan for
    Effective Assessment
    Carole Henry   61

7   Environment of Middle and Secondary Art
    Classrooms: Becoming Aware of, Designing, and
    Implementing Changes in the Furniture, Facilities,
    and Spaces
    Antonia Araca   69

8   The Art Classroom as a Behavior Setting
    Frank D. Susi   93

9   Sketchbooks
    Roberta W. Rice and **Sue Ellen McNeil**   107

10   Computers in Art Education
Deborah Greh   125

11   Health Hazards in Secondary Art Education
Sally Hagaman   143

12   Recurring Themes: A Program for Interdisciplinary
Learning
Arnold Amster   151

13   Teaching Exceptional Students in the Regular High
School Art Classroom
Robert D. Clements and **Claire B. Clements**   163

14   Preparing to Teach Art to Secondary Students from
All Cultural Backgrounds
Enid Zimmerman   185

15   The Role of the Researcher in Secondary Art
Education
Linda S. Bradley   201

16   Theory-Practice Schisms of the 1990s
Karen A. Hamblen   211

17   New Approaches to Secondary School Art Education —
A Program for the Artist of the Future
George Szekely   223

18   The Next Generation: Initiative or Inertia in
Secondary Art Education
Guy Hubbard   243

Preface

Editor

No publication of this type could hope to address all of the important issues impacting upon art education today. Less likely still is the possibility that such a publication could hope to adequately reflect the myriad opinions held by thoughtful professionals on each of these issues. With that in mind, the articles contained herein attempt to provide only a sampling of the individual perspectives which art educators hold regarding some of the important issues facing contemporary art education. The contributing authors represent not only the diversity of opinion found in the profession, but also the varied professional populations involved in teaching art. Articles are included by classroom teachers, college professors, and researchers alike. Viewpoints are expressed by newly emerging leaders, "rising stars" and the sage voices of art educators, whose long and distinguished careers have enriched our profession significantly. It is my hope that this publication will reflect the multiple voices which speak for and through art education, for it is in this diversity that our profession's greatest strength can be found.

At the inception of this anthology I was a high school art teacher in a community just outside of Atlanta, Georgia. I remember many conversations with colleagues from the ranks of the elementary, middle, and high school art teachers, confirming the value of much of our professional literature. Yet, most still wished for information that directed itself to their immediate classroom concerns and that was expressed in a language that was more accesible to the classroom teacher. (Certainly not a new problem, as Karen Hamblen so aptly points out in her article within this same publication.) With this expressed concern in mind, I made the decision, where it seemed appropriate, to encourage authors to maintain their scholarly integrity while writing in a style that would be more appealing to the classroom teacher. The reader will, therefore, note a diversity of styles contained within the anthology. Some are very formal in their scholarly presentation while others are more relaxed, but no less informative or helpful. Stylistic purists will no doubt disapprove, but art education is comprised of many voices, each of a different timbre and resonance. I have chosen to allow them to speak, each in his or her own way.

The authors included in this anthology certainly speak for themselves with eloquence and do not need me to clarify their statements, however it seems that a brief statement of what the reader can expect to find in this volume is in order. I would, therefore, direct your attention to the following very brief comments on each article, simply as an overview.

Through the device of an imaginary conversation between a high school art teacher and the school's principal, Harlan Hoffa examines multiple ways of knowing about art. He further suggests that art education experiences which emphasize only one way of knowing about art to the exclusion of others impoverishes the art experiences of the larger population of students it seeks to serve and may place the future of art education in peril.

Tom Anderson argues that the study of art criticism, as well as all the disciplines of art, should convey to students that art is reflective of the lifeways of a civilization and as such is imbued with and instructive of the personal and social values of its creators.

The nature of the learner in grades six through eight and the manner in which the art curriculum can serve the unique needs of the middle school student are discussed by Andra Johnson in her article on "Transescents". And Mary Stockrocki allows us to go with her as she visits and observes the inner workings of six middle school art classrooms where she examines the forms of instruction most frequently used with art students at this age level. Stockrocki's research findings will ring true and clear to other middle school teachers through her depiction of very real classroom situations.

Adelaide Rusch and William J. Thomas conclude that most teachers need not add new components of art history, criticism, and aesthetics to their art programs. They suggest instead that teachers examine closely the content of their existing programs for activities, from which instructional ideas focusing on each of the four DBAE components can be "excavated".

An experienced art teacher, Carole Henry shares insights and classroom tested techniques for assessing student achievement. She provides a method through which the art teacher can even evaluate such difficult and subjective qualities as creativity and originality.

Antonia Araca proposes, in her article, an index method for analyzing the physical spaces in which art teachers provide instruction. The index also provides strategies for redesigning the classroom environment to meet the increasingly complex needs of today's art students. Frank Susi also examines the physical setting of the artroom, focusing on the instructional environment as a resource which, if manipulated appropriately by the teacher, can increase the effectiveness of instruction and promote more positive and productive student behavior.

Authors Roberta Rice and Sue Ellen McNeil endorse the use of the student sketchbook as uniquely supportive of the aims of a discipline based art education approach. The use of a sketchbook, which contains both visual and verbal images, records the internal as well as the external world of the student. They stress the many benefits to be derived from student participation in this very distinctive artform.

The almost dizzying array of newly emerging technologies, which impact on education in general and art education in particular, can be overwhelming. Although, as Deborah Greh points out, computers have made their way into art classrooms over the past decade, there remain some legitimate concerns about the real contributions this technology can make to the art curriculum. Greh addresses many of these concerns based upon her own extensive experience of teaching art to young people through the use of the computer.

Sally Hagaman provides extremely important and clearly usable information related to the legal and health risks to which students and art teachers are exposed in the classroom.

Enabling students to grasp the complex interrelationships which exist among literature, history, and art is a formidable, yet worthy educational endeavor. Arnold Amster describes a high school program which, over the course of a decade, has provided for students just such an enabling experience. Overcoming the logistics of staffing, scheduling, and budgetary concerns, among others, the "Recurring Themes" program has engaged academically committed students in an intensive interdisciplinary experience to which the response has been overwhelmingly positive.

Providing truly meaningful instruction to the diverse populations of exceptional students mainstreamed into the art class can be a true challenge for the art teacher. Robert and Claire Clements combine their considerable expertise to suggest many concrete and useful ways in which the teacher and non-disabled peers can ease the transition and full participation of these exceptional students in the art program.

How are we to adequately and equitably educate our art students when they come from such divergent cultural backgrounds? And how can we resolve the difficulty that arises from the fact that curricula and even the strategies used to teach them are infused with culturally imbedded assumptions which may not hold true for our students from different cultures? Enid Zimmerman addresses these questions among others as she lends her insights into this difficult and complex issue which promises to provide an even greater challenge to us as we enter the next century.

Linda S. Bradley calls upon art education researchers to provide practitioners with more research into the dynamics of the high school art program and the students it serves. In her article she outlines a few critical concerns which she believes need to be addressed. Differences among the theories espoused by researchers and the actual practices of teachers in the classroom remain widespread, and occur for many reasons. Karen Hamblen suggests that this may not be as unhealthy a situation as some might think.

George Szekely provides the reader with a truly innovative look at an experimental art education program which places responsibility on the students for making their own creative discoveries, rather than relying on art teacher directed solutions. Szekely challenges the "who?", "what?" and "why?" of art education, and whether you agree or disagree with his approach, you will no doubt respect the creativity that went into developing the program.

Finally, Guy Hubbard looks into his crystal ball and predicts major changes in the way the business of art education will be carried out in the future. He proposes that such factors as economic shifts, the increasingly diverse student population, dropouts, new technologies, and an aging and dwindling teacher population will all impact dramatically upon the art programs of the Twenty-First century.

Assembling a publication of this type is an undertaking in which many people take part and deserve recognition. Many thanks must first go to those who have agreed to share their professional insights with the rest of us. So, to the contributing authors I express my gratitude for their patience and cooperation during the many months required to complete this task. Additionally, thanks are in order to those who participated in the reviewing process: Patrick Taylor, Virginia Carnes, and Jane Rhoades. Thank you, also to Tom Hatfield and his staff at the NAEA Office for their tireless effort and expertise in taking this document to press. A special thanks must also go to three of my own teachers, whose special attention to their students' needs has provided me with a standard of excellence that I strive for in my own teaching: Don Carmichael, Hugh Williams, and Paul Edmonston. My final thanks go to my art students at Douglas County High School, who have provided me with so much joy as a teacher and are a constant reminder of why we continue to struggle to provide quality art education experiences in the nation's schools.

1

The Discipline of Art

HARLAN HOFFA

The Pennsylvania State University

It is clear that many art teachers look at what the Getty Center for Education in the Arts calls Discipline Based Art Education as the chimera of the decade. Dictionary definitions of "chimera" include "an imaginary monster compounded of incongruous parts", "an illusion or fabrication of the mind", and an "unrealizable dream." The term, Discipline Based Art Education, which the Getty Center for Education in the Arts coined, is certainly a "fabrication of the mind" — not in the sense of its being falsehood but, rather, as an assemblage of ideas. It is, nevertheless, a concept which some art teachers might find "incongruous". And to the cynics, the doubters, the iconoclasts, and the nihilists in the profession, Discipline Based Art Education may, indeed, seem to be an "illusion" if not a "monster." Even to the carriers of the flame, the true believers and the searchers after art education's very own Holy Grail, DBAE must seem like a hope that has yet to be fulfilled — though, most assuredly, not one they would call an "unrealizable dream." Chimera, indeed!

There can be no doubt that the prospect of teaching art history, art criticism, and aesthetics along with art production as advocated by DBAE has scared the bejezzus out of many teachers. And not without good reason, because for the last half century art teachers have been told that they should be artists as well as teachers, state certification standards have emphasized studio art courses out of all proportion to the attention they paid to art history or art criticism, and the art rooms in even the best of schools are equipped like multi-purpose studios. The concept of the "artist-teacher" has, in short, been indelibly tattooed onto the brain pan of art teachers for decades. The artist has been the singular role model that art teachers have held for themselves, and it has been the one that they have worked to implant in the minds of their students. The underlying (if unspoken) premise has been that, since artists obviously know a great deal about art, art teachers and art students

1

should — to the best of their abilities — try to think and act like artists when they set about the teaching and the learning of art. Such a premise is not unique to the arts, and, in fact, many of the reforms in science education that resulted from the Sputnik scare in the 1950's were based on modeling the behavior of science teachers on that of professional scientists. Moreover, one need be neither artist nor scientist to recognize that imitation is at the core of learning ranging from a baby learning to say "Mama" to dressing for success at the workplace.

The problem, therefore, is not in the acceptance of the artist as someone whom art teachers and their students should try to emulate. The problem, instead, has been in their acceptance of artists as the *only* role model, as if to say that artists alone know everything that is worth knowing about art. The scope of what is knowable in art has been severely and unnecessarily limited by that approach, and, at the very least, it sends some very strange messages about what is worth knowing about the world of art. Imagine, if you will, the following dialogue between a high school principal (the questioner) and a high school art teacher (the questionee).

Question: Do artists know anything about art?
Answer: Of course they do!
Question: Do artists know everything about art?
Answer: Of course not!
Question: Is what artists know about art the most important thing to teach to high school students?
Answer: Sometimes the answer is "yes", at least for students who hope to become artists. Sometimes it is "no", especially if teachers believe that even students who have no desire to be artists should still know something about art.
Question: Should all students be expected to know something about the arts in the same way that they are all expected to have some knowledge about math or literature or history?
Answer: If the arts are ever to take their place along side those other subjects — and they ought to — the answer has to be an unqualified "yes".
Question: If, as you say, knowing something about the arts should be an important part of general education for all students, what should they be expected to know? How to draw a knee cap? How to pull a six inch cylinder on a potter's wheel? How to tell an etching from an engraving? The characteristics of a Doric or a Corinthian column? The significance of the Bauhaus? The difference between a print and a reproduction?

2

Answer: Maybe some of that; probably a lot more. It is pretty unclear what all students should know about art.

Question: Whaddaya mean, unclear?

Answer: I mean that there may have to be a different kind of art education, one that calls for a broader approach to what "knowing" means in art.

Question: I do not understand. You crazy artists all talk in circles.

Answer: What I am saying is that there are ways of knowing about art that go beyond knowing how to lay on the paint. For the majority of students, who may become audiences for art rather than its producers, knowledge that deals with information about art will certainly be more useful than developing a lot of artistic skills that they may never use again. And it is also more important from a numerical point of view because the number of people who look at art and who make judgments about it are greater by far than the number who make art in the first place. It may also be more important from an epistemological point of view because though art teachers, by definition, teach art, they do not very often ask questions about what "knowing" in art really means.

Question: How does anyone — student or teacher — know when he or she knows anything about art? Is it possible to measure that kind of knowledge? To judge it? To evaluate it? If so, how so? If not, why not? How in the world is it possible for anyone to teach art without even wondering what it means to "know" art?

Answer: I am not sure that that is a real problem because, though not many art teachers worry about the nature of artistic knowledge, they teach art anyway. They are probably a lot like that legendary bumble bee who continued to fly because it did not know that, aerodynamically, it was impossible. The point is not whether knowing the epistemology of art is absolutely necessary for all art teachers, but whether they could do their jobs better if they knew more about "knowing" and what that means. The easy way would be for them to just go on as they always have and leave questions about the nature of art to aestheticians and questions about the realm of knowledge to epistemologists. Discipline based art education — that chimera of the '80's looming on the western horizon — has made such a choice difficult, however, because it opened a Pandora's Box of questions that many art teachers may wish had never been raised in the first place.

So much for fiction. The point is that teachers of art, like teachers of anything else, are answerable to their school administrators and to the community whose taxpayers support the educational enterprise. Beyond

3

that, however, art teachers are also answerable to broader professional mandates that are rooted in what society as a whole expects from the arts and in what art teachers demand from themselves as representatives of the art world in the narrowly prescribed community of their schools. In that sense, art teachers serve many masters: those of the arts, those of the schools, those of society as a whole, and those which have developed out of their own professional history and ethos.

A hundred years ago or so, as the schools were struggling under the double burden of providing skilled workers for emerging industries while at the same time accommodating wave after wave of immigrants from the culturally diverse nations of central and southern Europe, drawing was taught as a kind of "manual training" for the next generatiom of factory workers. It is not without reason that the organizations from which the National Art Education Association developed were called "drawing and manual training associations", that Walter Smith's drawing exercises were as rigid and prescribed as they were, or that he moved from England to Massachusetts at the urging of a group of industrialists rather than an invitation from either school people or artists. What was taught in those years was, in fact, not art at all as we know it today but merely drawing, and, if the results had failed to meet the needs of factory owners, those drawing classes would almost certainly have disappeared in short order. Art teachers in the latter third of the 19th century were, by that reckoning, an adjunct to the industrial world, and they were, in no uncertain terms, answerable to it as well as to the educational system of which they were a nominal part. Later, in the afterglow of Sigmund Freud, art teachers became quasi-therapists, and during World War II they became propagandists; in each instance with tacit obligations to worlds beyond their own. A couple of decades ago the magic word in art education was "creativity", and that, too, was motivated, at least in part, by the need to play catch-up with the Soviets as a post-Sputnik shock wave swept the nation. Once again art teachers found themselves trying to meet educational goals that were only marginal to the discipline of art, and, once again, art teachers jumped on the passing band wagon as if their very lives depended on it. And, to some extent, perhaps they did so because for more than a century the teaching of art in American schools has been justified on the basis of non-artistic goals and purposes of one sort or another. It is not surprising that that history has resulted in a kind of split professional personality among art teachers. In David Riesman's terms, they were "inner directed" by their commitment to the arts but "other directed" by their need to cloak that commitment under

4

a constantly changing set of ulterior goals and objectives. Eat your heart out Polonius; art teachers have not always been "to thine own self true."

The first break in that pattern was the artist-teacher movement which put a premium on the artistic competence of teachers but, at the same time, resulted in their isolation — if not their alienation — from what was happening elsewhere in their schools as art rooms became sanctuaries for self determination rather than places where the subject of art was taught and learned. Along with the obvious advantage of teaching artistic values for their own sake, however, the artist-teacher movement carried some undesirable baggage with it as well. It made the art room a special place for special students — which was good for the talented minority — but it also made it seem foreign, and perhaps even forbidden, to the majority of students who had no desire to model their behavior on that of artists. Equally damning, it presented the subject of art to students from one undeniably credible but, nonetheless, restrictive point of view — that of the artist.

The remaining question is whether what the Getty Organization now calls Discipline Based Art Education is simply one more band wagon trundling its way through our professional landscape, or is it something notably different?

Like the artist-teacher movement, DBAE is based on the assumption that art education is important because art is important and not for any instrumental purposes that art may be called upon to serve. Unlike the artist-teacher movement, however, it equates art history, art criticism, and aesthetics with the conventional emphasis on art production. The problem with such a broad based approach for many art teachers is that it seems to have changed the rules of the game in the middle of their careers. Teachers who earned their spurs as artist-teachers are now being told that they must teach something that their educational background or previous experience never prepared them to do. They may feel, quite justifiably, that they know too little about art history, only a smidge about art criticism and nothing at all about aesthetics, but, even so, they are now expected to teach such material in order to more fully represent the discipline of art. Small wonder that some of them are angry, fearful, or, at the very least, cynical. It is, after all, not their fault that they were educated to do something quite different. They finished their bachelor's and perhaps their master's degrees in art education according to their college's requirements, and they did whatever was necessary to meet their state's teacher certification standards, only to be told that that is no longer enough. It is the kind of put-down that few of today's art teachers have ever experienced — though perhaps it is comparable to the trauma that an earlier generation of art teachers once faced when they were told that the only way to be a respectable teacher was to be an artist as well.

The underlying question is whether discipline based art education (as a concept rather than as the title of the Getty initiative, hence written in lower case letters) is shimmer or chimera. If DBAE is nothing more than a flicker on the landscape of art education, a passing fancy, an aberration that will soon disappear into history, teachers can ignore it and wait until it goes away if they so choose. If, on the other hand, what DBAE stands for is to be a permanent feature of art education for decades — as the artist-teacher movement has been — those who ignore it do so at their own peril.

Discipline based art education as we now know it is, for all practical purposes, the creation of the Getty Center for Education in the Arts. The ideas that gave it life were born in the writings of Manuel Barkan thirty years earlier, but they were nurtured by the silver spoon of the Getty Center only in the 1980's, and those resources gave it a currency that Barkan could never have imagined. In that sense it is comparable to other now historical events in art education that range from the Owatonna Project (supported by the Carnegie Foundation), to the Arts in Education Program (supported by the JDR 3rd Fund), to Cemrel's Aesthetic Education Program (supported by the U.S. Office of Education). Each of those projects died an untimely death when external funding ran dry, and, though they have entered the folklore of art education, none of the innovations that those programs undertook has yet risen from the dead. No town except Owatonna tried to infuse itself with the arts; no independent curriculum development projects have taken up where Cemrel left off; and no one worked at bridging the gap between art education and school administrators after the JDR 3rd program went belly up.

A question, therefore, arises about whether discipline based art education will survive the inevitable end of its support by J. Paul Getty's estate. The odds would seem to be against it if the precedents noted above continue to prevail, but DBAE may have more going for it than the largess of an outside patron would suggest.

The Getty Center has recruited a cadre of energetic, well respected, highly capable, very articulate advocates for DBAE that would make the twelve

Apostles seem faithless by comparison; they have produced a continuous flow of elegant and eloquent publications; they convene selected "taste-makers" in art education at fairly regular intervals; and they willingly — even eagerly — participate in the conventions and other affairs of the National Art Education Association. In short, the advocates of discipline based art education have woven themselves into the political fabric of art education in ways that their predecessors never succeeded in doing. The prospect is that the substance of discipline based art education — if not the specific label — will continue to be a factor in art education for many years to come, with or without the support of the Getty Center for Education in the Arts. Moreover, there are sound professional reasons for teaching more art history, art criticism, and even aesthetics, regardless of such external imperatives, which range from pressing the boundaries of "knowing" in art, to the steadily increasing size and sophistication of arts audiences in recent years, to the number of colleges and universities who are mandating arts courses as a graduation requirement for all students. The conventional hands-on approach to art teaching is obviously not appropriate to those demands, and the bottom line — though not necessarily the last word — is that today's artist-teachers are likely to be under increasing pressure to deal with the discipline of art in all of its dimensions rather than only those of manipulating media, nurturing the creative impulse, or fostering individual expression. The remaining question is what to do about it.

There are some things that any art teacher could do to provide more in the way of art history, art criticism, and aesthetics for their high school students. And, sad but true, there are others of monumental importance about which they can do little or nothing. Art teachers have only a small voice in controlling the art education curricula at colleges and universities, they have little influence on their state teacher certification standards, and they are in no position to redesign their art rooms or to restock the libraries and audio-visual collections in their schools. Yet, without differentiated curricula and certification standards and without the necessary instructional resources, no real change in what is taught as art can possibly take place. Teachers do, however, have some control over their own professional destinies, and it is fully within their power to take additional courses in art history or aesthetics, to participate in in-service workshops, and to retool themselves by the simple expedient of reading everything they can lay their hands on that will add to their fund of knowledge about art history, art criticism, and aesthetics. Moreover, state, national, and regional art education associations can add their collective voice to those of individual teachers to assure that art education curricula are revised, that certification standards are differentiated to provide a two-track system for art education (studio and art history/criticism), and that more appropriate instructional facilities and resources are available.

Such suggestions are so self evident that they seem almost gratuitous, but there are two additional steps that any teacher with the wit and the will can make if he or she is sufficiently motivated. The first of these is to set aside all prior conceptions about what is involved in the teaching and learning of art and to look afresh at the various ways that art can be known. Indeed, it means questioning the very nature of "knowing" in art. The model of the artist will certainly hold up under such scrutiny, but so, too, will several others — the art historian, the art critic, and the aesthetician among them. And, most assuredly, art education will be better, stronger, and more central to the broader mandate of schooling with those added dimensions. The second step that art teachers can take — and, indeed, must take if they are to deal effectively with art history, art criticism, and aesthetics — is to look at the subject of art in much the same way that teachers of other subjects view their disciplines. In short, art teachers should look at art as a discipline to be mastered rather than as some kind of magical experience that has more to do with metaphysics than with academics.

That much, at least, art teachers can do for themselves, but, though necessary, it is also insufficient to the need. If the arts are to be remade into an academic discipline in the secondary school curriculum which has the same rigor and intellectual demands as literature or history, foreign language study, or science, several other parts of the educational enterprise must also be mobilized to that intent and purpose. For example, teacher education programs at colleges and universities should consider the possibility of a separate and distinct curricular track in art history and art criticism to complement the art studio emphasis that now dominates art education. In order to accomplish that goal, however, it will also be necessary to revitalize — perhaps even to popularize (without diluting) – what is taught as art history on most campuses. Lessons from Kenneth Clark, Robert Hughes, and other television evangelists of art might be brought into play in this regard as well as the literary styles of critics such as John Canaday or others who write for the popular press rather than those whose audiences are limited to esoteric "little journals". The intent of using such models would not, of course, be to reduce art history and art criticism to the lowest possible common denominator but, rather, to overcome some of the exclusivity and elitism that colors much of what is now written and spoken about such topics.

All of that would be quite meaningless, however, if the state certification standards for art teachers were not modified to permit the graduates of such programs to teach or if, upon graduation and certification, the needed instructional resources were unavailable in the schools.

If art is, in fact, to attain its full measure of academic respectability as a discipline, a complete re-design of the infra-structure of art education will be needed. The most critical aspects of that re-designing process, in addition to in-service training for the current population of art teachers, are: first, curriculum revision in art teacher training institutions; second, changes in state certification standards; and, third, the development and distribution of text books, films, video cassettes, and slide collections that are specific to adolescent audiences and interests. None of the above will be quick or inexpensive or easy to sell to those who will be involved in light of the ponderous bureaucracies that are involved. It is, nevertheless, necessary to begin the process because art education in America's secondary schools can no longer survive by catering only to the special interests of the few while ignoring the needs of the many. The needs of that ninety to ninety-five percent of high school students who never pass through the art room door are, to be sure, quite different from those of the talented minority, but they are no less real on that account. High school art teachers — and, indeed the whole art education community — can no longer afford the luxury of ignoring that large population of students and their needs if they hope to survive into an indefinite future where the only certainty will be even tighter budgets for what seems to be the marginally academic subject that art has been for the past one hundred years. Giving lectures to large classes, grading essays and exams, and organizing endless trays of slides may not give art teachers the same jollys as one-on-one studio instruction or giving demonstrations to small groups of like-minded students, but those are not the only two alternatives. The third possibility — and a very real one it is — could be the elimination of high school art programs entirely unless they play a more active role in the education of all students. There are, in short, both good reasons and real reasons for putting the discipline of art back into art education, and the time to begin, most assuredly, is now.

2
Art Criticism and Social Integration of the Disciplines of Art

TOM ANDERSON

The Florida State University

The visual arts are a major component of that set of mores, values, understandings, social constructs, and institutions we call civilization (Broudy, 1987; Dewey, 1958; Langer, 1980). Culture, as the foundation of civilization, has carried humankind forward for thousands of years (Anderson, 1985; Brownowski, 1973). There is no civilization, however primitive, ever dug up by archeologists that did not exhibit some evidence of the existence of art. Art is intrinsic to civilization; it is an appetite of civilized life. It is a primary carrier of values (Dewey, 1958) and feelings (Langer, 1980).

It is desirable for all citizens to acquire a broad understanding of the visual arts in the context of their general education in order to be a part of the intellectual and expressive life of society. A primary tool for understanding art is art criticism. However, in curricula that have traditionally focused on art production as means to personal fulfillment, art criticism has been neglected.

Assumptions inherent in this attitude were articulated by the art critic, Clement Greenberg (1987), in a recent address when he asserted that children "don't see ... pictures as pictures[1]. They don't look *at* them. They look *into* them" (p.25A). His point was that children do not have what is called "aesthetic distance." He further asserted that "aesthetic distance in visual art cannot be taught" (pp.25A-26A). Later, in a response to a question about practicing art criticism with children, he said, "I say let them draw, let them paint. I wouldn't try to teach them to appreciate art before they are adolescent" (p.26A).

11

Ironically, the very next day, my own experience contradicted Greenberg's view. My three year old daughter, whom I consider more or less normal in her cognitive functions, was walking down the street with her mother. Watching her older sister ride away on a bicycle, she exclaimed, "Look, Mama! We're like painters because Carrie is so small in the distance." That recognition, requiring perceptual awareness as well as separation from the object of perception, certainly demanded the intellectual distancing that Greenberg feels children cannot acquire before adolescence. If one three year old child has aesthetic distance, is it outrageous to think there may be others?

It seems reasonable that perceiving art arises from the same urge as making art. We need to give meaning to our existence. We have a need to make some mark in the world before we die. It is inborn. It is human. It is irrepressible. In some of us it takes the form of being the mechanic who keeps Toyotas on the road. Others have progeny into which we pour our heart's energy. And some of us — poets, painters, cinematographers, and the like — spend our lives trying to describe the life in our minds, our feelings, or sensations. We try to make our mark translating the sound of the wind at the ocean's edge, transcribing personal triumph, social isolation, the rhythm of days or of a heartbeat.

There is no art without an impulse for expression. Yet the expressive impulse, while it is necessary, is not the sufficient condition for making art. A scream of pain is an unbridled, expressive impulse. *The Scream* by Munch is art. Art demands not only the impulse but the manipulation of concepts and materials which controls the impulse and gives it aesthetic form (Dewey, 1958).

Likewise the ability to interpret, to read environments, understand and manipulate Toyota engines, theorems, and works of art, while it arises from impulse, ultimately relies on cultural constructs for its mature definition (Berger, 1972; Ember and Ember, 1973). The continuation of art and culture depends on a coherent fabric of understanding, an order among marks, and an order in the process of their interpretation and understanding. So some of us must construct meaning by metaphorically making our marks in interpretation, semantics, scientific investigation, psychology, sociology, hermeneutics, and other sense-making occupations. Those who make sense of works of art and share their insights are called art critics.

The social construction of human reality (Berger and Luckman, 1967) requires that people communicate with each other. Many feel that art communicates insights unobtainable in any other way (Langer, 1980). The visual symbol, because of its nature, stimulates perceivers differently than language. Critics, whatever their system, can only use language as a verbal equivalent of the visual image, sensitizing the reader or listener to his/her own potential for aesthetic experience in the face of visual form. Criticism cannot and should not attempt to replace a painting or a sculpture. Instead, the critic's role is to lead the viewer up a path to a precipice looking over a vista where only a clear and heightened vision is found. The pedagogical critic and the teacher of pedagogical criticism has the task of leading students to this path so they can climb it at will.

Although there are many systems and methods of art criticism designed by aestheticians and metacritics, there is no one true way[2]. Is the objective to understand what the artist intended? to be aware of one's own responses to a given image? to chart cognitive/imaginative development? to develop increased sensitivity in recognizing formal relationships? to grasp thematic content explication? to place the symbols in historical context? Each of these emphases demands different critical systems. And they are all correct. The critical method follows from the reason for its use.

The function of pedagogical criticism is to teach students to see and understand individual works of art. The current trend toward discipline-based art education sees art as having a specific body of concepts and skills to be learned and mastered (Greer, 1985; Clark, Day, Greer, 1987). In this context art criticism not only explicates art content but stands as a process or tool for learning in its own right. It allows students who have mastered a method access to art content. The instructor who categorizes Van Gogh as expressionist, Mondrian as formalist, Corot as naturalist, totem art as primitive, or whatever, is no doubt less effective in instilling these constructs than the instructor who encourages direct student contact with images in the pursuit of such categorizations. Students who develop concepts of style, iconography, and thematic content in context and as a corollary to experiental discovery are more profoundly imbued with the concept than those who are handed it.

The development of concepts of style or types of compositional features may be better accomplished through criticism than any other art discipline since the use of mental constructs and the functioning of the sensory receptors are both essential in making sense of artworks (Carmichael, 1957). Perception "is the process by which sensations are organized and interpreted, forming an inner representation of the world" (Rathus, 1987, p.107). The power of perceptual constructs to alter vision is well documented in the study of perceptual constancies (Carmichael, 1957, McFee, 1972) in which the viewer sees not what s/he actually perceives, but what s/he knows about an image. Conversely, a lack of constructs impoverishes perception. Expectations, knowledge (Strauss, 1980), and the awareness of relations (Kohler, 1969) play a central role in productive seeing and thinking about what is seen.

Language facilitates this classification and concept formation in relation to art (Johnson, 1985). Koroscik and Blinn (1983) found that verbalization in relation to processing visual art information significantly increased processing and retention of the image. Artistically naive students are not likely to see formal qualities and compositional relationships such as focus, dominance, asymmetrical balance, and so on, simply because these culturally defined constructs have not yet become part of their mental set. Students see in terms of these basic design constructs when basic design has been linguistically defined for them. Language about art must develop concurrently with perception. It may be, in fact, that such constructs cannot exist in the mind without the concomitant language which defines them (Whorf, 1956).

Languages vary in their efficacy in defining certain concepts; some lend themselves to scientific thinking, others to mysticism, and so on (Whorf, 1956). It is postulated that within a given language — English in this case — there are at least two types of language which stress differing aspects of reality construction (Langer, 1980, Feinstein, 1982): the discursive and the presentationally affective. An example of discursive language follows, describing a forest:

> *Temperate rainforest ... differs from tropical rainforest in that it has comparatively few species and therefore large populations of one kind. The trees are somewhat shorter, with smaller evergreen leaves (especially the conifers, podocarps, and araucariods, which are frequently present). Large tree ferns are usually abundant ... The herb layer of the forest floor is frequently well developed. Sometimes a sheath of mosses invests the trunk of trees at a certain level. (Dansereau, 1987).*

The driving quality of this discursive/indicative language is its usefulness. It presents a construct in a utilitarian way. It tells you how to do it, how to act upon it, where it is found, how big it is, and so on. It is this literal functional language that is primarily used by students in art criticism in description and formal analysis (Mittler, 1980). The development of concepts established through discursive language use is not unique to art criticism or art education, however. In fact, such discursive development is the strong suit of education in general.

A second kind of language is the presentational (Langer, 1980) and affective, which presents images/sensations/feelings for their own sake rather than for an instrumental purpose beyond the presentation itself. An example of such language and thought constructs follows in a description of the same sort of forest:

> *Under the volcanoes, beside the snow-capped mountains, among the huge lakes, the fragrant, the silent, the tangled Chilean forest ... I pass through a forest of ferns much taller than I am: from their cold green eyes, sixty tears splash down on my face and, behind me, their fans go on quivering for a long time ... A decaying tree trunk: what a treasure! ... Black and blue mushrooms have given it ears, red parasite plants have covered it with rubies, other lazy plants have let it borrow their beards, and a snake springs out of its rotted body like a sudden breath, as if the spirit of the dead trunk were slipping away from it ... Farther along, each tree stands away from its fellows ...* (Neruda, 1976).

Presentational language taps the realm of feeling. Rich in metaphor and analogy, it is the language of feeling, of interpretive creativity which is found in poetry and poetic prose, and which is analogous in purpose to the other arts, including the visual. It is such language and thought construction which dominates the interpretive stage of art criticism. The artist as creator needs the viewer-critic as companion, as co-creator, to complete the cycle of artistic vision. Such creation on the part of the viewer demands the application of open ended, associative, interpretive cognition and language. It requires that the student free himself from literal perceptions and apprehend the significance of the form in a metaphorical and analogous sense, to make connections between the qualitative connotations and the forms that carry them (Eisner, 1985).

15

It is in the presentational realm, the realm of interpretive meaning, of applied analogy and metaphor, that art criticism may make its major contribution to education. Students are rarely asked to examine, develop, and talk about their feelings in an expressive mode and almost never in relation to the objective/observed world. Within the educational structure, students are predominantly required to stick to the facts: the provable, the measurable, the quantifiable, the memorized, the formulaic, the logically linear. However, in the arts students are allowed to venture into the depths of their psychic sensibilities, to examine those unique emotive impulses and responses that ultimately define their lives as human beings: lives like other human beings in many ways and yet unique and singular in many others. In creative and interpretive talk about art this form of conceptual development is not only tolerated but actually encouraged and sanctioned in our children's education.

I would argue that this development of a depth of sensibility in students is crucial to a continued civilized cultural heritage. Tools are useless without the sensibility to use them. Through giving students access to the feelings and fabric of art, we are not only giving them tools to see and understand art, but the greater vision to apply the resulting insights to their own lives.

As a tool for self development and understanding within a cultural framework, art criticism must be seen as functioning in a sociocultural context. It is in this need to provide a sociocultural context that art history and aesthetics inextricably tie in. Although Dewey (1958) obviously states a fundamental truth when he argues that the most integrated learning is experiential, it can be argued that personal experience, as motivating as it is, is also limited, especially with typical students. Succinctly put, the fewer years one has lived, the less experience there is to draw on. Redfern (1986), in discussing aesthetic education, argues that denying students first hand acquaintance with great art "leaves them imprisoned within the straitjacket of their own necessarily limited experience" (p. 94). The function of art history in this regard is to fund and inform art criticism, to give it a context, an awareness of the cultural continuum.

As social animals a major part of our individual psyches are socially constructed. It is the collective social identity which is our inheritance from the past that forms the foundation against which individual decisions are made and actions are taken. Campbell (1988) sees human culture as having many universal aspects — psychic qualities which are the same cross-cul-

16

turally — and many variations on those universals which he calls ethnic forms. The universals of human psychic energy may be understood somewhat through universal forms of archetypes (Jung, 1964) such as the mandala, the spiral, and the cross, but to understand ethnic forms, one must understand the culture of their origin.

For example, the concept held to this day in the West, that art reflects some metaphysical beyond-its-surface connotative reality, has deep cultural roots. The classic Greeks already had evolved the notion of art as representing the harmonies of a metaphysical universe. Thus the forms were tied to a conceptual reality which had seven planets (including the moon) after which were named the seven days of the week, the sounding tones of which form our diatonic scale, each associated with a then precious metal, and so on. The soul descending from heaven in medieval times passed through these planetary influences (and associated forms) and back through upon death, shedding the trappings of each to be judged (Campbell, 1972). Students may validly critique a kouros or a Byzantine mosaic in light of contemporary sensibilities only, and because there is a continuing collective subconscious, much of it may verify the image's intent. But how much greater will be the student's experience and resulting growth if criticism is funded by history? The richer the historical funding of criticism, the richer the experience for the individual.

Likewise, aesthetics serves as a source for art criticism and art criticism as a source for aesthetics. The perceptions of criticism nourish the questions that develop about art. Why does Duane Hanson make sculptures that look like people rather than sculptures? Is it art or a mannequin? And why do Hansen's and Bernini's (both realistic) works give us such different feelings? What then is the nature of naturalism? How does the cultural play a role? What about the artist's psychological inclinations? It is through looking at art that we get to the questions of aesthetics.

Like art history, aesthetics is tied to the culture of its origin in the formation of its constructs. Just looking at modern aesthetic theory should prove the point. Dominant aesthetic theories funding criticism in twentieth century Western cultures have included phenomenology, analytic, positivist, Marxist, romantic, pragmatic, structuralist, and deconstructionalist programs. Each of these presupposes a different set of assumptions. Each projects a unique conceptual reality based on certain philosophical premises held as true. What it boils down to is the presentation of life views held as truth and presented as foundational for structuring further inquiry into life through art. The values held in each case cannot help but be culturally determined, simply because they come out of a philosophical (cultural) tradition.

In this light, the question of whether Broudy's or Feldman's or Smith's or Hamblen's or Kaelin's method of art criticism is better is inappropriate. More to the point, what are the premises of a given method held as values within its structure, and is it adequate for the kind of question being asked? The point is that art criticism is funded by metacritical theory: aesthetics. Aesthetics as a philosophical venture examines the nature of art and the beautiful. This is a value-laden enterprise which is culturally embedded. One wants to be aware, therefore, what the bases are on which aesthetic judgements are made. It is extremely important in art criticism to understand, when one says a work is good or bad, according to whom, to what system, and based on what criteria. Students should be aware that aesthetic judgements are not absolutes and are based on culturally determined criteria.

The object of discipline-based art education is understanding the art object through developing skills and concepts related to the disciplines that attend to art. The ultimate goal is the development of students who have broad reflective powers (Broudy, 1987) and whose aesthetic depth of sensibility contributes to their whole being as an important aspect of their general education. To facilitate students' access to knowledge about art, the division of approaches into the disciplines of aesthetics, production, art history, and art criticism is very useful. It should be remembered, however, that this mode of knowing is also a cultural construct which frames the way knowledge is constructed about art and ultimately brackets the way we see things. Within a DBAE conception, then, it seems very important not to lose sight of how the connections between the disciplines also can and do inform knowing in art as significantly as the disciplines themselves. These connections, as modes of activity, reflect values, assumptions, and premises which are as much a part of the philosophical and cultural traditions as the structures of the disciplines. To be effectively taught, the disciplines of art must be integrated. Pedagogical criticism's ultimate goal of the development of intelligent perceivers and consumers of the art forms into which are woven insights intrinsic to civilized society, must be connective and culturally aware.

The development of students' depth of sensibility and their ability to apply associative and imaginative thinking to problems they encounter in life is one of the most significant goals of general education. Within this context, students who are taught a method of approaching and understanding artworks will gain access to understanding of their culture through the collective vision of the arts. Art, as a record of the past and an anticipation of the future reflects the collective cultural imagination. Students who develop ways to access this vision are in a position to actively engage the intellectual life of the culture. Rather than being acted upon by the events of their times, they will have the vision to be participants and shapers of cultural progress. This requires an integrated conception not only of the disciplines of art but of art as a way of recognizing life.

References

Anderson, T. (1985). Thought on social contextualism in art and art education. *Bulletin of the Caucus on Social Theory and Art Education, 5,* 51-60.
Berger, J. (1972). *Ways of seeing.* London: Penguin.
Berger, P.L. and Luckman, T. (1967). *The social construction of reality: A treatise on the sociology of knowledge.* Garden City, N.Y.: Anchor.
Bronowski, J. (1973). *The ascent of man.* Boston: Little, Brown.
Broudy, H.S. (1987). Art education: Proper claims and expectations of an exemplary program. *FAEA Forum,* Fall 1987, 13A-17A.
Campbell, J. and Moyers, B. (1988). *The power of myth.* Garden City, NY: Doubleday.
Campbell, J. (1972). *Myths to live by.* New York: Viking.
Carmichael, L. (1957). *Basic psychology: A study of the modern healthy mind.* New York: Random House.
Clark, G.A., Day, M.D. and Greer, W.D. (1987). Discipline-based art education: Becoming students of art. *Journal of Aesthetic Education, 21* (2), 129-193.
Dansereau, P. (1987). World vegetation zones. *McGraw-Hill encyclopedia of science and technology* (6th ed.) 19, 263-270. New York: McGraw-Hill.
Dewey, J. (1958). *Art as experience.* New York: Capricorn. (Original work published in 1934).
Eisner, E.W. (1985). *The educational imagination* (2nd ed.). New York: MacMillan.
Ember, C.R. and Ember, M. (1973). *Cultural anthropology.* Englewood Cliffs, N.J.: Prentice Hall.
Feinstein, H. (1982). Meaning and visual metaphor. *Studies in Art Education, 23* (4), 45-55.
Greenberg, C. (1987). The critic as educator. *FAEA Forum,* Fall 1987, 25A-27A.
Greer, W.D. (1984). Discipline-based art education: Approaching art as a subject of study. *Studies in Art Education, 25,*(4), 212-218.
Johnson, A. (1985). The role of discrimination and mediation in concept formation in art. *Visual Arts Research, 11* (2), 31-39.
Jung, C. (1964). *Man and his symbols.* Garden City, NY: Doubleday.
Kohler, W. (1969). *The task of gestalt psychology.* Princeton, N.J.: Princeton University.
Koroscik, J.S. and Blinn, L.M. (1983). The effect of verbalization in visual art processing and retention. *Studies in Art Education, 25* (1), 23-31.
Langer, S.K. (1980). *Philosophy in a new key: A study in the symbolism of reason, rite, and art* (3rd ed.). Cambridge, Mass.: Harvard. (Original work published in 1942).
McFee, J.K. (1970). *Preparation for art* (2nd ed.). Belmont, CA.: Wadsworth.
National Art Education Association. (1986). *Quality art education: Goals for schools.* Reston, VA.: NAEA.

Nuruda, P. (1976). *Memoirs* (L. St. Martin Trans.). New York: Farrar, Strauss, Giroux.

Nietzchse, F. (1976). Thus spoke Zarathustra. *The portable Nietzsche.* (W. Kaufman Ed./Trans.). London: Penguin.

Straus, E.W. (1980). *Phenomenological psychology.* New York: Garland.

Rathus, S.A. (1987). *Psychology* (3rd ed.). New York: Holt Reinhart, and Winston.

Redfem, H.B. (1986). *Questions in aesthetic education.* London: Allen and Unwin.

Whorf, B.L. (1956). *Language, thought, and reality.* New York: Wiley.

Notes

[2]Some of these methods are articulated in the following readings: Roucher, N. and Broudy, H.S. (1985). *A guide for teachers: Scanning works of art.* Decatur, IL Project Heart; Clements, R.D. (1979). The inductive method of teaching visual art criticism. *The Journal of Aesthetic Education, 13* (3), 67-78; Feldman, E.B. (1987). *Varieties of visual experience* (3rd ed.). Englewood Cliffs, NJ: Prentice Hall; Hamblen, K. A. (1984). An art criticism questioning strategy within the framework of Bloom's taxonomy.*Studies in Art Education, 26* (1), 41-50; Johnson, P. (1982). Teaching aesthetic discerning through dialog. *Studies in Art Education, 23* (2), 6-13; Kaelin, E.F. (1981). Between the innocent eye and the omniscient mind: Phenomenology as a method for aesthetic analysis. In D.W. Ecker (Ed.) *Qualitative evaluation in the arts.* New York: New York University; Langford, L. E. (1984). A phenomenological methodology for art criticism. *Studies in Art Education, 25* (3), 151-158; Mittler, G.A. (1980). Learning to look/looking to learn: A proposed approach to art appreciation at the secondary school level. *Art Education, 33* (4), 17-21.

[1]The papers referred to by Broudy and Greenberg were developed as a part of a Cultural Literacy Conference, April 5-7, 1987, sponsored by The Florida State University Department of Art Education and the Florida Endowment for the Humanities. The project director was Charles M. Dom. Reprints of the proceedings are available from the Department of Art Education, Florida State University, Tallahassee, Florida 32306-3014.

3

The Period of Transescence and Its Relevance for the Secondary Level Art Education Program

ANDRA N. JOHNSON

University of Georgia

The period of transescence, or the time of transition from childhood to adolescence, is an extremely critical period in the development of an individual. It is important to understand the unique characteristics and special needs of the student at this age level and to consider these factors when developing an art program for the intermediate and secondary school levels.

When planning and implementing an exemplary program in art education, the teacher needs to carefully consider the goals of the profession and the specific needs of the students at each grade level. The art curriculum at the secondary school level should provide students with direct experiences in art production and art history and a focus on possible future careers and interests in art. To ensure that the objectives of a strong art program are met, varied opportunities must be provided for the students to a) learn and use the language of art, b) explore a wide range of media, c) learn about the history of art and one's culture, and d) develop a foundation for the development of a lifelong appreciation for art. According to the National Art Education Association's position statement (NAEA, 1986) describing a quality art program, the art program should "increase the student's capacity to: 1) have intense involvement in and responses to personal visual experiences, 2) perceive and understand visual relationships in the environment, 3) think, feel and act creatively with visual art materials, 4) increase manipulative and organizational skills in art performance appropriate to his abilities, 5) acquire a knowledge of man's visual art heritage, 6) use art knowledge and skills in his personal and community life, and 7) understand the nature of art and the creative process" (pp. 2-3).

Curriculum Continuity and Interdependence

Optimally, the program at the high school level should be built upon the firm foundation of a carefully organized program at the middle school or junior high levels. It is important to develop a clear picture of the overall structure and continuity of the curriculum in terms of how it is being implemented at the elementary, intermediate, and secondary levels. While many art lessons at the elementary level can be characterized as experiential in nature, the art programs at the intermediate and high school grade levels should focus on abstract thinking and problem-solving processes, as well as the expressive/ affective nature of the lesson. Through careful integration of abstract reasoning skills, art history and art appreciation content, and advanced artistic and technical processes, opportunities can be provided for each student's growth in the program at all of the levels.

Art education provides the student with the opportunity to engage in the process of making and appreciating visual art. Visual art might be defined as "the expression of one's thoughts, emotions, and perceptions in an organized visual form" (Michael, 1964). Art education provides experiences for exploration of the creative process, and for organization and communication of ideas and self-expression through the use of tools, materials, and processes. Perceptual development is fostered as the student is engaged in activities which encourage one to become more perceptually aware of the visual world and to use the language of art.

The goals for quality art instruction, adopted by the National Art Education Association, call for a sequential program of instruction based on the study of aesthetics, art criticism, art history, and art production. Designing and implementing art programs which include art history, art criticism, and aesthetics, as well as production of artworks, has become a strong focus and goal of many educators in the field of art. The field of art education regards the concept of Discipline-Based Art Education (DBAE) as one of the possible models for implementing this goal. This model is not an entirely new one, but is, rather, one of the models based on a concept which is founded upon the strong belief that knowledge about art should include a language and content of art which exceeds the traditional focus of art programs in our schools. The four components of a program of discipline-based education in art include: 1) art history, 2) art criticism, 3) aesthetics,

22

and 4) production of artworks (Greer, 1987). This is only one of several possible approaches for enriching the content of the art curriculum, as well as the general curriculum. Many curriculum developers are using similar formats as the framework for the programs currently being designed for art (Ragans, 1988; Mittler, 1986). At present, many programs, both at district and state levels throughout the nation, have adopted this framework. In summary, the rationale underlying this approach is based on the belief that it is important for individuals to have a keenly developed sense of the aesthetic, knowledge of the history of art and of the methods and techniques used in art criticism, and an awareness of the ways that artists work, in order to foster a lifelong understanding of, and appreciation for art.

Another goal which has been described in the NAEA goal statement calls for the establishment, nationwide, of a requirement specifying one year of credit in one of the fine arts for high school graduation and for admission to a college or university (NAEA, 1986). It is important to consider the impact of this goal and the growth in secondary level programs which would occur if all students were *required* to complete one year of coursework in the fine arts in order to graduate. It is important, too, that strong sequential programs be offered at all grade levels. Without a strong sequential program as the basis, the art program at the high school will merely become a course in remedial art.

Another important focus upon which some art curricula are currently based is towards development of an understanding of the role of art in society. According to this orientation, the curriculum may be based on the uses of art in our society or "give students insights into the social purposes of art — art used to satisfy human needs and to glorify human ideals and values" (Michael, 1983, p. 93). Above all, it is important to reinforce and integrate the learning which is taking place in other areas of the school curriculum, for it is only through awareness of the interdependence of the disciplines that we can encourage development of the individual as a whole person.

Presently, programs offered at the middle grade levels may be the last formal art instruction many students receive. It is especially crucial that the art program include enrichment opportunities for students to explore their interests and introduce them to possible future careers. Such art courses at the intermediate levels are often exploratory in nature and allow for students to be involved in a broad range of media and art experiences. Courses at this level can also prepare students for art courses that they may later elect to take at the high school level. The art program which serves the student at this level also serves the secondary level programs by providing a necessary bridge between the elementary and secondary level art programs. The need for sequential programs which link the programs at all grade levels cannot be stressed strongly enough if we hope to optimize the learning potential of students in the area of art at the high school levels.

The Nature of the Learner

It is extremely important to understand the nature of the learner at the intermediate school level in order to fully integrate the goals and objectives of the program with the needs and interests of the students. *Transescents* are "pupils usually found in grades 6, 7, and 8 who are in the transitional phase of life between childhood and adolescence." (Eichhorn, 1984, p. 31) When measuring the impact of the art program on the learners at these grade levels, it is important to consider the nature of the students who are at the age where they are moving into an adult world and are making rapid strides in their social development as they are learning about themselves in relation to the world around them. Eichhorn (1966), a noted scholar on the nature of the learner at this level, identified *transescence* as:

> *The state of development which begins prior to the onset of puberty and extends throughout the early stages of adolescence. Since puberty does not occur for all precisely at the same chronological age in human development, the transescent designation is based on the many physical, social, emotional, and intellectual changes that appear prior to the time which the body gains a practical degree of stabilization over these complex pubescent changes.* (p. 3.)

It is important for the teacher to have a keen awareness of the process of maturation, or metamorphosis, which occurs at this age level.

Chapman wrote that "in the adolescent, emotional intensity, physical energy, and social awareness are delicately balanced against apathy, fatigue and personal loneliness" (1978, p. 203.). The transescents, or early adolescents, learn about themselves through their experiences and interactions with their world and the people who inhabit it. They develop and test their own set of values as they learn about the complex system of values and morals upon which the outside world is based (Chapman, 1978). Much of the interaction between the student and his world occurs in the school setting; therefore it is the responsibility of teachers and administrators to provide the proper environment for students to increase their social-emotional, as well as physical and cognitive capabilities. Students should also be encouraged to develop confidence in their abilities and to express their ideas through the use of art media.

Characteristics of the Learners

There is a wide range of needs and characteristics which are observed in students at this level. The teacher must consider these factors when planning the art program. The level of a student's involvement may be greatly affected by such physical characteristics as muscular development and coordination. Emotional characteristics such as emotional variation, interest span, powers of observation, the desire for peer approval, and interest in the opposite sex may affect the student's involvement in the art activity from one day to the next. Emotional fluctuations and self-consciousness are often exhibited in episodes of emotional outburst, extreme sensitivity to criticism, and self-critical behavior.

Physical changes also affect children at this level. The improved level of skills of muscle and eye-hand coordination at this age allows for the exploration of a wide variety of materials, while the broadening range of students' interests in subjects, themes, and current issues provides a rich storehouse of ideas and concepts for their artwork. At this age level, they are quite capable of using adult materials and of gaining some proficiency in difficult art processes.

Students at the transescent stage usually wish to create art which looks real and recognizable and to render space and objects as they appear in real life. This desire continues during their art experiences at the secondary level and is further heightened by an increased perceptual awareness of detail, proportion, and spatial relationships which occurs at this age level (Linderman & Herberholz, 1979). Students are also interested in learning to use color and line to create accurate representations of the world while working from both memory and direct observation. Most middle school students quickly develop their ability to understand and use the elements of design and the tools of perspective to create a more sophisticated and refined product than was possible at the elementary level. The program at the intermediate levels should provide an opportunity for students to learn to render objects in perspective space. It is important for the art teacher to combine his knowledge of cognitive and artistic development, with careful observations and assessment of each student's level of ability in order to blend assignments and consistant expectations with encouragement to help meet his fullest potential.

The Goals of the Overall School Program

The goals of the art program in the middle school years should be allied with the goals of the overall school program in an effort to best serve the learner at this level. These goals can be further predicated on the goals for education of the student in the preadolescent stages.

During the early stages of the development of middle school education, Alexander and Associates (1968) suggested a curriculum design that included an emphasis on personal growth, skill development, continual learning, and organized knowledge. These goals have continued to be supported by writers and researchers in the field of middle school education. Brown (1981) names twenty-one key ingredients for the making of a middle school. Among those mentioned are opportunities for exploration of many varied subjects through a strong elective program, for creative experiences as an outlet for student expression, for social development and development of social skills, and finally, for opportunities for values clarification, thus enabling students to identify appropriate values and clarify conflicting values. Learning processes, a knowledge component, and personal development comprise the model described by Eichhorn (1972).

A comparison of many of the curriculum models for this educational level (Eichhorn, 1980) illustrates that most authors agree on the need for acquisition of essential learning skills in a sequential and individual manner. The emphasis on structure and sequential learning is "in clear response to the diverse achievement levels, cognitive styles, and varied competencies that characterize learners at this stage." (Eichhorn, 1984, p. 35) There is added focus on the "interrelationships of knowledge" and added accommodation for the varied learning rates of individuals and the need for personal development (1984, p. 36).

The Art Curriculum and the Goals of the Program

There are many possible ways in which the art curriculum can serve the goals of the overall curriculum at this level and should, therefore, be considered as an effective means for meeting those needs. The art program can provide unique opportunities for the student's growth and development in the areas of a) creativity and self-expression, b) artistic skills, c) communications skills, and d) social and emotional development.

Creativity and Self-Expression

The middle grades curriculum should foster the development of the student's creative philosophy with an emphasis on self-expression. E. Paul Torrance (1963, p. 4) defined creativity as "the process of sensing problems or gaps in information, forming ideas or hypotheses, testing and modifying these hypotheses and communicating the results." Crowder (1984, p. 182) asserts that "creativity could be defined as the ability to tap one's experiences and come up with something new."

A successful program in the arts will allow students to develop confidence and gain satisfaction in art activities and will help them develop their creative potential. Creative growth can be evidenced by the student's increased ability to express himself in a wide variety of media, to continue to use art materials outside of the art classroom, to use materials in an unusual manner, and to explore the possibilities of the materials which are available. This growth may also be evidenced in the student's involvement in the art program at the secondary level and in continued activity in the arts during their lifetime.

Art experiences should enable the student to interpret and express his ideas in a unique and individual manner and to experiment and investigate a wide range of solutions to a set of problems. Through the study of artists and the methods of artistic inquiry, the student should learn about himself and grow in his ability to view himself and his ideas objectively, as well as view the work of classmates and peers with sensitivity and appreciation for the individuality of each person and his or her creative expression. Creative

27

activity can also encourage development of aesthetic awareness and sensitivity. Increased awareness of the shapes, colors, lines, values, patterns, and textures in the environment may instill a greater concern for the quality of design in the student's environment and in the aesthetic qualities of objects which surround the student in his everyday life.

The curriculum should be carefully sequenced to encourage the growth of life skills and confidence which are needed for students to experience success in the art classroom and further prepare them for a lifelong interest in creative activity. It is important for students to have experiences with materials which are relevant to their daily lives and which provide opportunities for involvement in those activities in which students focus on learning about themselves and their environment. Many successful art programs focus especially on those activities, (self-portraits, art projects relating to the school and the community, and the creation of products which youth can use in their own lives outside of the school) in an effort to make the art learning relevant to the development of the students at this level.

Artistic Development

While the elementary school curriculum introduces students to the terminology and processes of art, the middle school program demands the development of an extensive working vocabulary and competency in many of the techniques and processes which were only briefly introduced at the earlier levels. A strong middle school program introduces students to projects created with techniques that are used by artists themselves, including projects such as woodcuts, linoleum prints, monoprints, woodcarving, metal sculpture, batik, weaving, stitchery, copper repousse, clay sculpting, and many others. Technical skills using hand-tools and power equipment can be taught at this level. Students can also be introduced to more complex techniques of gesture and contour drawing, and to direct and indirect methods of painting. (Chapman, 1978).

The importance of a strong base of skills, taught at the elementary and intermediate school levels, is especially critical during this period. In programs where the elementary art program is minimal or virtually nonexistent, the program at the middle school level must also provide remedial instruction in the language, history, appreciation, and production of art. The need for, and importance of, a carefully structured sequential program as a basis for the high school program has already been stated, but it is extremely crucial factor in the development of the student's technical skills.

The content of the intermediate level art program is made up of areas of complex information of a similar nature to the disciplines of science and math. It is important for the students to be exposed to the scientific basis for the processes and techniques which they are using in the art room. At this level, art curriculum involves more than crayons and paint and can be related directly to the level of information and techniques which are presented at the secondary levels. Processes such as modeling in clay, printmaking, and photography are based on technical information. Students should be exposed to information concerning the chemical makeup and properties of clay and glazes, inks and photographic processes, as this content enhances the creative process and reinforces the relevant nature of the art content, while relating it to learning in other areas of the curriculum. Students can learn firsthand from the artists/teachers who are working with them. The teacher can help students to gain skills, knowledge, and an appreciation for art.

Communication Skills

The art teacher must be sensitive to the needs and concerns of the student at the transescent level and will find that there are many opportunities for expression and development of both visual and verbal communication skills. The middle school art teacher is often asked to act as counselor, confidant, and arbitrator. The very climate of the art classroom, with its emphasis on expressions of ideas, frequently provides the occasion for discussing problems and circumstances in the lives of the students.

Since the art curriculum provides opportunities for individual and group activities, for leadership, for interaction and cooperation with others, there are many chances for sharing ideas and for personal reflection, as the students learn ways of communicating their ideas and feelings. It is also possible for the teacher to relate the art work and assignments to the every day life of the students and to the larger community, in order to encourage development of a sensitivity toward the ideas and needs of others.

Social/Emotional Development

The art program can provide opportunities for increased self-actualization and development of a strong self-concept. An important goal of an effective art curriculum is the promotion of each student's personal development. Improved self-confidence and self-respect can be gained through activity in art. A sensitive teacher, whose focus includes the development of the whole child, can provide opportunities for growth in this area. The art curriculum at this level can support the set of purposes which have been identified for programs which focus on the students at this age level, including that of nurturing the emotional, social, and cognitive growth of students (Hudson, 1986) and can serve as a bridge to the program at the high school level.

The art curriculum also provides many opportunities for cooperative learning and for peer interaction. There are increased opportunities for students to learn about themselves and about ways to function in the larger society through the structure of the art classroom with its individualized and small group activities. Cooperation with classmates is developed while working together on a project or sharing tools and equipment. It is the belief of researchers in the field of education that students can develop affective skills through such opportunities, and will, as a result, consider the viewpoints of others more readily (Johnson, Johnson, Johnson, & Anderson, 1976).

Shared responsibility for learning is a goal which is important for the student at this level. Many art projects at the secondary level rely heavily on the student's ability to direct his own learning and to carry out art projects which often take more than a few days to complete. If the program at the middle grades level is to contribute towards the development of the student's ability to work independently, then the focus should be towards developing skills for continued learning and for assumption of the responsibility for the student's own learning.

The student can gain a greater perspective on his own experiences, as well as those of his peers and family, while studying how artists have expressed their own reactions to their world through their art. Lowenfeld described the important role which is performed by the art program in providing a means for the student to discover himself and to engage in the process of self-identification (Lowenfeld & Brittain, 1982). In today's world, students are constantly bombarded by television and by pressures from family and peer

30

groups, making the process of forming and understanding one's own set of values a difficult and confusing task. In the art program, the student is encouraged to make sense of a diverse range of ideas and options in order to respond to the world around him.

Art experiences also provide opportunities for the student to take risks in a protected environment. Students at this age are often unwilling to share their ideas, emotions, and feelings, since they are frequently worried about how they will be perceived by their peers. It is the nature and intention of the assignments in the art classroom to provide opportunities for experimentation and exploration of the student's ideas and feelings.

Arguments have also been made for the need for developing the cultural awareness of our students if we are to encourage their acceptance and appreciation of the many and varied backgrounds of the people of this nation. The study of artworks and of the cultural heritage of their own and other countries will, hopefully, provide the basis for the development of understanding and cooperation among future generations. The teacher's decisions concerning the design of the art curriculum can also encourage the development of an awareness of one's artistic heritage, through exposure to the ways in which artists have reflected the human condition and the natural world in their artwork. Besides learning about techniques and artists' use of a specific medium, students can also be taught to articulate their ideas about symbolic meanings. Dialogue about artworks can be used to teach students to "discuss levels of meaning as seen in subject matter, themes, interpretations, symbolism, and expressive content ... and non-objective and functional works in relation to the moods, feelings, and ideas they seem to invoke" (Chapman, 1978, p. 216). A strong program in art should also include discussion and dialogue about the meaning of art and its role in our cultural heritage. Transescent students are acutely aware of the social concerns which surround them in the society in which they live, and they seek opportunities to confront the economic, political, social, and ethical issues which they encounter in their daily lives. Through careful structuring of the art curriculum, art experiences can assist them in expressing their concerns about the realities of life which they encounter at home, within their peer groups, and through popular culture and the media.

Finally, art experiences and training can help students make better judgments and choices in their daily lives. Many projects may be relevant to future careers and interests in art. According to Glenn (1986), "Art offers choices of the teaching profession, commercial design, interior design, art history, industrial design, artist-craftsman, theatre-TV-stage design, and fashion, to name a few" (p.6). Many lessons which are learned in the art program can be applied to everyday situations. Art training and experiences can help to develop one's perception, and foster sensitivity for the arrangement of objects in the environment or for the designs of objects and projects used in everyday life. On a larger scope, this instruction encourages students to be concerned with the *quality* of their home, community, and the school environment.

Summary

The period of transescence, the period of transition between late childhood and the early stages of adolescence, occurs between the ages of ten and fourteen years. This is a period during which many physiological and emotional changes are occurring as the child attains physical maturity (Glenn, 1986). It is the very nature of the student at this age level which makes this period so critical in its affect on the student's adjustment to the demands and challenges of adolescense.

There are many ways that the art curriculum at this level can prepare the student to lead a richer and fuller life. Art experiences and training can help students to make better judgments and choices in their daily lives; what is learned in the art program can be applied to everyday situations; art learning and skills can be integrated with, and generalized to, other subject matter in the school curriculum. An exemplary art curriculum is designed to teach the specific language and vocabulary of art and should teach the concepts and skills which will enable the students to continue their own artwork and interests outside the classroom. The program should be consistent with the goals of the whole school program and focused towards the development of the student's fullest potential in the areas of artistic and communication skills, of creativity and self-expression, and of social/emotional development.

It is critical that the teacher have a well-developed understanding and knowledge of the sequence of learning and the physical and emotional changes which occur in the lives of the students before they enter the classroom at the secondary level. It is therefore necessary to build channels of communication with teachers at the elementary, intermediate, and secondary levels if we are to develop art programs which best serve the needs of the whole child as he develops and matures. The teacher at the secondary school level will be better able to build on the skills and the abilities of the students in the art classroom if open lines of communication are developed between teachers at all levels.

If art education is to contribute to the fullest development of each child's potential, it should strive to uphold the belief of Bruner (1966) that the aim of education should be the cultivation of excellence and the achievement of each individual's optimal intellectual development. It should provide opportunities for students to master specific skills and techniques while providing practice in tasks involving decision making, judgement, and the skills of inquiry.

References

Alexander, W. M., et al. (1968). *The emergent middle school*. New York: Holt, Rinehart and Winston.
Alexander, W. M. & George, P. S. (1981). *The exemplary middle school*. New York: Holt, Rinehart and Winston.
Brown, W. T. (1981). The makings of the middle school: 21 key ingredients, *Principal, 60* (3), 18-19.
Bruner, J. (1966). *Towards a theory of instruction*, Cambridge: Harvard University Press.
Chapman, L. H. (1978). *Approaches to art in education*. New York: Harcourt Brace Jovanovich, Inc.
Crowder, G. (1984). Creative experiences. In Georgiady, N., Heald, J. & Romano, L. (Eds). *A guide to an effective middle school*. New York: Irvington Publishers.
Eichhorn, D. H. (1980). The school. In M. Johnson (ed.) *Towards Adolescence*. Chicago: University of Chicago Press.
Eichhorn, D. H. (1984). The nature of transescents: In Loundsbury (ed.) *Perspectives: Middle School Education 1964-1984*. National Middle School Association.
Eisner, E. W. (1972). *Educating artistic vision*. New York: Macmillan Publishing Co., Inc.
Glenn, D. D. (1986, Sept). The middle school: Art, the transescent child, and the role of the teacher. *Art Education*, 4-7.
Greer, W. D. (1987). A structure of discipline-based concepts for DBAE. *Studies in Art Education, 28* (4), 227-233.
Hadley, J. H. & Asomi, E. J. (1972). *The Middle School*. The Bulletin: Alabama Association of Secondary School Principals, 8 (2), 21-24.
Hathaway, W. (1977) (Ed.) *Art education: Middle/junior high school*. Reston: National Art Education Association.
Henson, K. T. (1986). Middle schools: Paradoxes and promises. *Clearinghouse, 59* (4), 345-347.
Johnson, D., Johnson, R., Johnson, J., & Anderson, D. (1976). Effects of cooperative vs. individualized instruction on student prosocial behavior, attitudes towards learning, and achievement. *Journal of Educational Psychology, 68* (30), 446-452.
Linderman, E. W. (1980). *Teaching Secondary School Art*. Dubuque: Wm. C. Brown Publishing Co.
Loundsbury, J. H. & Vars, G. F. (1978). *A curriculum for the middle school years*. New York: Harper and Row.
Lowenfeld, V. & Brittain, W. L. (1982). *Creative and mental growth*. New York: Macmillan Publishing Co., Inc.

Michael, J. A. (1964). (Ed.) *Art education in the junior high school*. Reston: National Art Education Association.

Michael, J. A. (1983) *Art and adolescence: Teaching art at the secondary level*. New York: Teachers College Press.

Mittler, G. A. (1986). *Art in focus*. Peoria: Bennett & McKnight Publishing Co.

NAEA. (1986). *Purposes, principles and standards for school art programs*. Reston: National Art Education Association.

Pumerantz, P. & Galano, R. W. (1972). *Establishing interdisciplinary programs in the middle school*. West Nyack: Parker Publishing Co., Inc.

Ragans, R. (1988). *Arttalk*. Mission Hills, Ca: Glencoe Publishing Co.

Torrance, E. P. (1963). *Creativity*. Washington National Education Association.

4

Forms of Instruction Used by Art Teachers with Preadolescents

MARY STOKROCKI

Arizona State University

Research on teaching preadolescents concentrates on their needs, characteristics (Lowenfeld and Brittain, 1975), creative potential (Owen, 1962), and expressive interests (Burton, 1981). Some researchers have studied preadolescents in-depth (Churchill, 1970 and Folsom, 1976). Little focus, however, is spent on the instruction of preadolescents and their art teachers' perceptions of it. Outside of Degge's (1976) participant observation of a junior high art teacher's theory put into practice and Johnson's (1985) analysis of the acquisition of art knowledge in an eighth grade class, little exists. A few studies, however, include minority teachers' opinions about instruction at this level (Stokrocki 1988, and Stokrocki 1990). The purpose of this article is to discuss frequent forms of art instruction used at this level by six art teachers, which include three minority teachers and their perceptions about their art instructional practices as discovered through participant observation. This study also points out the role that this type of research plays in uncovering foreshadowed problems (Smith & Geoffrey, 1968) and how teachers cope with them. Insights on teaching at this level are thereby offered.

Methodology

Participant observation, the major method utilized, is a qualitative process of observing, analyzing, and interpreting data gathered from everyday situations to form insights which may be compared to other situations in generating theory and suggestions for better teaching. The method consists of two phases: data collection and content/comparative analyses. Data in this study was gathered via daily notes, informal interviews, and questionnaires. In order to understand the instructors' teaching better, instruction was analyzed via the quantitative method of time sampling, a method of timed note-taking with a stop watch (Barker, 1968), concentrating on three dominant instructional behaviors: substantive, managerial, and appraisal (Schmid, 1980, p. 18). (See Table 2). Instruction was timed in some cases, once a month; and in shorter schedules, every other week. A comparison of the time samples of all instructors is available upon request.

Substantial behavior is that which imparts the subject matter, in this case, studio, art appreciation, art criticism, and aesthetics. Managerial behavior is that which directs student discipline and class functioning. Appraisal behavior is that which judges change in student process or product.

Phase two involved content and comparative analyses (Glaser & Strauss, 1967). Content analysis is the examination of the data from one study into patterns of instructional behavior and meaning. For example, I discovered that in-process appraisal was the most frequent and informal way of evaluating preadolescents in one inner-city class. Then I used comparative analysis, the relating of my findings across situations, and found that in-process appraisal was frequently used by all the art teachers. Instructor clarification was used to confirm my findings at all levels of reporting.

Art Instructor Participants

An equal number (3) of male and female, Black and White, art teachers was chosen (See Table 1). Of the six art teachers observed, two were from the suburbs, one was from a rural area, and three were from the inner-city of a midwestern city. Since the preadolescent age span ranges from ages 9-13 (Churchill, 1970), and many schools offer art at either seventh or eighth grade, I chose two art teachers from each level (6, 7, and 8th). Length of program varied from one full year (sixth grade) to one-half year or nine weeks at the seventh and eighth grade level. Class time ranged from 80 minutes, 60 minutes, to 40 minutes twice a week. Two teachers in this study were identified as outstanding by their regional art education association, and three teachers were referred by their art supervisor, my student teachers, and their principals. One extreme and difficult case, that of Mr. D, is also included as a comparison with the more successful ones in order to verify results (Miles & Huberman, 1984).

Managerial Instruction

Managerial instruction, the control of student behavior and class functioning, generally occurred 29% of the time, although it dominated instruction in two cases (Mr. D's, 48% and Mrs. L's, 45%). Most art teachers of preadolescents can generally be regarded as benevolent directors. For example, Mrs. N, a Black, inner-city art teacher at the sixth grade level, used managerial instruction (17%) sparingly, but dictatorially. She commented, "My strength lies in my established rapport. I like my students to think of art as a place where they can be themselves." On the other hand, organization is extremely important in this setting, and she continued, "Order allows me to teach and my students to learn. Students should know clearly what is expected of them." She wrote requirements on the board and in their art booklets for parents to review. Positive student rapport is extremely important with preadolescents. Mrs. N added, "I empathize with my students' problems. They need attention and encouragement."

On the other hand, Mrs. L was a white, rural teacher, whose seventh grade class turned out to be one of those occasionally stressful types that we all experience. Discipline dominated her managerial instruction (45%). She stated, "Preadolescents are at the yoyo stage. One minute they are up, and the next, they are down. The adolescent crisis starts younger today." She realized that she needed a great deal of patience and that she had to be a good negotiator. She bargained with students, "I'll take your demerit away if you show me that you can control yourself." She also negotiated grades with them which affected their involvement in sports, which seemed to dominate school life. Negotiations even entered her relationship with the principal as she bargained for exchange of favors and scheduling.

Finally, Mrs. T, a Black teacher from a suburban school, discovered that her seventh graders' lack of concentration and confidence and their intense socialization were extremely annoying. Whenever she heard the complaint "I can't," she corrected, "I don't want to hear it. Use the expression, 'It's difficult,' and I will help you." She told them that the phrase "I can't" was an excuse for not thinking. She also found that they did not pay attention to directions and that she repeated herself constantly. To one student she remarked, "You are so busy 'flitting-around', you forgot what I told you." On the side, Mrs. T explained to me, "This is the third time that I told her what to do in the last five minutes." Furthermore, the girls constantly annoyed the boys, and vice versa. Mrs. T considered this tomfoolery irritating. On the next day, she mentioned to me, "I hate this class. They make me so mean." Managing discipline at the sixth grade level was less frequently a problem (17% to 11%) as compared to controlling the behavior of the seventh and eighth grade classes (48%, 45%). (See Table 2.)

Substantial Instruction

Substantial instruction, the formal instruction of subject matter, equalled the amount of managerial instruction (29%) used by art teachers at this level. For example, Mr. B, a Black, inner-city teacher, mostly used an academic approach (40%), since his students had only two years of previous art training. He started with the elements and principles of design in a six-week unit on lines in nature and in man-made things, which expanded into another unit on drawing Black portraits and ended with a unit on clay. He instructed, "The elements of art are like the ingredients in a cake, and the principles of art are like the cake directions" (Jan. 28, 1987). In his first lesson, he had students explore the expressiveness of lines through word association, and he asked them, "What kind of line does the word 'pain' bring to mind?" "Prickly, jagged," responded one girl. "Draw a painful line then," he directed his class. Later, he asked the class what the term 'overlapping' meant. "Criss-crossing," they answered in unison. Mr. B continued, "Good. Draw some overlapping lines. We will use these lines in our next project. Here, we start in a simple way." Mr. B's intention was to gradually build his students' confidence as well as their conceptual ability.

Students in all classes, except one where claywork was not offered, reported that it was their favorite project because they loved "to make things," "they never did it before," and "they could make what they wanted." Mr. B offered ceramics for the first time in years to his inner-city students by obtaining a small grant. This was possible because classes were smaller and the junior-high school was made into a middle school.

In contrast, Mr. D, a Black, inner-city teacher, had the worst situation and used the least substantial instruction (8%). His class started with 57 eighth grade students and, due to a computer mixup, ended up with all the school troublemakers. The administration believed that many students would be suspended, and therefore absent, and the class would get smaller. The class later consisted of 35 students (April 16, 1987). Towards the last days of school, his class dwindled down to 17. Needless-to-say, large class size, lack of administration support, and improper student behavior were his major problems, and this class became an extreme case. His formal instruction lasted about five minutes and consisted of the simplest skills, such as Gothic lettering (May 16, 1987). He could only teach through occasional individual instruction. However, during the last week of school, when his class was smaller and the troublemakers were absent, he taught an art appreciation unit on photography, which the remaining students appreciated. He had students read about the photography of Margaret Bourke-White, and he demonstrated how to use a camera effectively. However, printing and developing were done in camera club after school. His curriculum was primarily based on commercial art, because he believed his students valued art that was most useful to them. After reading my study, Mr. D honestly remarked, "This was the first time in my 22 year career that I felt I didn't have a handle on the class — bad combination of kids."

Half of the teachers in my sampling had a difficult time with art appreciation instruction, because students disliked it and hated to read and write. For instance, Mrs. L used art appreciation in small doses (10 minutes) with her suburban seventh graders. She commented, "I try to relate art appreciation in every lesson, but because my students get unruly and start fooling around, I give it in small portions." For example, she introduced a unit on environmental sculpture with the article, "Working with Everyday Objects" *(Art & Man,* 1982). She asked one student to begin reading for the class about "The World of Claes Oldenburg" (p. 3). She later informed the class that any large sculpture is environmental or public sculpture and that Oldenburg's was 34 stories high. Then she gave a synopsis of his clothespin ideas ("Monumental Objects," pp. 4-5). A heated discussion (3 min.) ensued with the typical response, "Anyone can do that!" Then she showed them a college student's architectural model with an abstract outdoor sculpture and instructed, "You need to make several sketches like Oldenburg did for his *Geometric Mouse.* We will use clay and other materials, when you come up with a good idea." This ten-minute art appreciation motivation was interspersed with nine student reprimands (Sept. 10, 1987). Her students complained about reading *Art & Man* (Informal interview, 10/12). One student exclaimed,"I hate it! I'd rather read about dirt bikes. I don't like art anyway. I'd rather build things." Mrs. L clarified, "I have been using *Art & Man* since they were in elementary school. They act the same way during a filmstrip."

Art and Man readings were also unpopular in Mr. B's class, but he found that guest artists were more successful. Every year he invited a local Black cowboy artist to demonstrate his art form — painting on cowhide. His inner-city students were amazed that the cowboy was Black and his drawing skills were so realistic. They loved to touch his textured collages as well.

Two of the sixth grade teachers from the inner-city, however, were successful with art appreciation in that they used role-playing techniques. For example, Mr. F, who had a degree in aesthetic education, had his students from an academic enrichment class work in teams and present reports on famous artists to the class in the form of a radio program, where one student interviewed another (5 min.). One student introduced the program and speaker, "Welcome to Channel 2 WKIP: Famous Artists of the World. Today we will talk to the art teacher of Jackson Pollock, who will tell us everything we always wanted to know about art." Although some of the reports were better than others and not all students finished, they enjoyed learning in this way — through an oral and kinesthetic format. Mr. F found that the more confident student helped the shyer one. Total time was five 20-minute sessions. He also had his students imitate the master artists' techniques. Again student reports were positive, although they found the assignment difficult. One student commented, "I'm doing Pollock, who made a drip design. He used ugly colors. I used a red to liven mine (painting) up." Another student chose to copy one of Renoir's dancers, "I had trouble drawing the figure, but mine is an impression like his." At times, one student assisted another as when one student demonstrated how to form the lips of Leonardo's *Madonna of the Lake*.

Appraisal Instruction

Appraisal instruction, through methods of informal evaluation, generally dominated class time by 36% (Table 2). In-process appraisal, the act of monitoring student performance and/or guiding further instruction (Sevigny, 1978), was consistently used by all art teachers. For example, appraisal instruction dominated Mrs. T's teaching (52%) and started at the beginning of the period (Feb. 18, 8 two-minute interactions, each with a different student). Most of her instruction occurred at her desk, from which she discussed student problems. She advised one student, "Get some detail in that shirt (drawing). It needs style. What kind of collar and sleeves does it have? Look at examples in this magazine." Later she noticed another student having trouble drawing the body and said, "Your neck is not drawn at an angle, it slopes down gradually." She therefore had him erase that part and start again and distributed anatomy guides to help the class. Students were also allowed to use a light box to trace figures at the initial stage in order to build confidence. She later tried to get one student to add hair to his model, but he insisted that the man was bald. She retorted to the class in general, "You always try to take the easy way out, but I won't let you. This was the first formal art class for these students, because no elementary art was offered.

None of the teachers used formal critiques. Mrs. L, for instance, believed that private appraisal protected each child's sensitivity due to peer pressure and competition at this age level. Her students would often criticize each other sarcastically during class. One student yelled out, "Oh, Kim. That is so beautiful!" Art teachers also used informal quizzes, questionnaires, and crossword puzzles as trial runs — to appraise student progress. In contrast, Mr. D, an extreme case, only graded on effort and work completed.

Only two inner-city teachers used art criticism/aesthetics, exploratory talk about art, in a small way with their sixth graders. On one occasion, Mr. F had students fill-out a self-evaluation questionnaire to criticize their action drawings in progress, which he regraded later. Based on Feldman's (1970) art criticism stages of description, analysis, interpretation, and judgment, he used open-ended questions to guide them. This technique is similar to aesthetic scanning — searching for artistic properties (Broudy, 1962). Students did well with descriptions and interpretations, but, when analyzing their drawings, needed more clues such as different viewpoints: back, rear, overlap, and bird's-eye view. On the other hand, Mrs. N surveyed her students' art preferences by asking them to write three sentences each about an artwork they liked and one that they didn't. Students favored realistic subjects and bright color. In both classes, responses were short, indicating a need for more alternative clues. Talking about preferences in art is also the beginning of aesthetic training.

Conclusions and Insights for Art Teaching

Results of this comparative study of the instruction of six art teachers of preadolescents indicate several insights for future teaching at this level. The dominant form of instruction at the preadolescent level seems to be informal appraisal. In-process appraisal, the guiding and encouraging of individual and small group work, is consistently used by teachers, and it is the only way to teach in an extreme situation. Students can be prompted to add details, to make corrections, and to use models. Individual performance can also be informally monitored via such devices as quizzes and open-ended questionnaires, which act as trial-runs. Open-ended self-evaluation questionnaires work well, but art teachers need to include more clues. Churchill (1970) also advocates the virtues of student self-appraisal and private student/teacher conferences. None of the teachers seem to use formal critiques at this stage, because they believe it would embarrass students. Thus, art teachers at this level should evaluate their students informally and privately.

The second most frequent form of instruction seems to be managerial instruction, the control of class functioning and behavior. Art teachers usually act as benevolent directors — firm and fair. Where discipline is occasionally stressful, negotiations dominate. Management also entails repeating directions, constant review, building student confidence, and controlling socializations. The older students (seventh and eight graders) seem to cause more management problems as compared to the younger ones as indicated through time sampling. Disagreement therefore is endemic at this age. Students crave attention and help, yet, when it is offered, they resent it. Conflict arises over teacher expectations and students' preferences. Churchill (1970) states, "These children truly love the teacher that can survive their treatment, and come back for more, [and] who does not humiliate them ..." (p. 112). Art teachers of preadolescents need to be patient and to assess their students' characteristics, needs, behaviors, and context, and to adjust their instruction accordingly.

Substantive instruction, that which deals with the subject matter, seems to be used the least. In schools where art training starts late, an art teacher of preadolescents can start by building student confidence and conceptual ability, beginning with simple expressive concepts such as mood and line variation. Commercial art activities, such as photography, seem to work best where discipline is a problem, as in my extreme case, because the activities are more practical and suitable to student interests. Some teachers find that tracing figures helps build confidence in the beginning. Students also report their preference for building things, especially for claywork.

Art appreciation can work in small doses and is often done only for 10 minutes in relation to a studio activity. This finding supports Galbraith and Spomer's claim (1986) that art history is neglected in today's secondary schools and is most often taught under the cover of creative art activities. In contrast to their findings that time and teacher preparation were problematic, I found that the greatest resistence came from students, especially about reading *Art & Man*. Teachers suggested that reading should be minimal, augmented by teacher synopsis, and related more to the interests of students, who prefer folk and popular art examples. Students also react better to an interactive approach to art appreciation, rather than a passive one. Art appreciation lessons that involve role-playing, oral responses, and cooperative group work seem to work well, Churchill (1970) states, "In this way, the autonomy of a gang or clique would be preserved and developed at will ..." (p. 10). Students also seem to appreciate the great art masters' work more, when they can imitate it in some way. Unconventional guest speakers and art projects, like photography, also inspire curiosity. Lewis (1981) found that his low-achieving male youths preferred and performed better with unconventional materials and art processes.

Situations where the administration supports the program and where classes are longer seem to be more successful. However, those art situations where school functioning is dominated by such things as computers or sports are extremely stressful. Art teachers in such circumstances need to know negotiation strategies for use with students as well as administrators.

In contrast to the more ideal art education prescriptions, the insights discovered via participant observation are descriptions of the realities of everyday art teaching — how art teachers instruct students and cope with difficult situations. These findings can be considered survival forms of instruction as compared to the more idealistic ones of discipline-based art education, since these teachers taught art appreciation sparingly, and art criticism/aesthetics even less, except in two cases. The study points out why certain approaches fail, such as using *Art & Man* to teach art appreciation, and it suggests a more interactive method. The importance of individual instruction and cooperative teamwork at this level cannot be emphasized enough. Finally, participant observation research unifies instructors' perceptions with findings of the researcher in collaborative research, so that both parties work toward improvements. The insights discovered in this study are limited and need to be compared with other regions.

*An expanded version of this study using eight cases is included in Stokrocki's (1990) article, "A cross-site analysis: Problems in teaching art to preadolescents." *Studies in Art Education, 31* (2), 106-117.

Table 1

Types of Teachers of Preadolescents, Their Contexts, and
Lengths of Programs

Teacher	Sex	Race	Context	Grade	Term	Class	PerWk.
Mrs. N	F	B	Inner-city	6th	1 yr.	60 min.	1 day
Mr. F	M	W	Inner-city	6th	1 yr.	80 min.	1 day
Mr. D	M	B	*Inner-city	8th	1/2 yr.	40 min.	2 days
Mr. B	M	W	Suburban	8th	1/2 yr.	60 min.	2 days
Mrs. T	F	B	Suburban	7th	9 wks.	40 min.	5 days
Mrs. L	F	W	Rural	7th	9 wks.	40 min.	5 days

*extreme case

Table 2

Time Sampling of Instructional Types at Preadolescent Level

Instructor	Managerial		Substantive		Appraisal		Nonf.		Total	
	Min.	%	Min.	%	Min.	%	Min.	%	Min.	%
Mrs. N (6th grade)	10	17%	23	38%	22	37%	5	8%	60	100%
Mr. F (6th grade)	9	11%	34	42%	30	38%	7	9%	80	100%
Mr. D (8th grade)	18	48%	3	8%	12	32%	4	10%	40	100%
Mr. B (8th grade)	9	22%	16	40%	13	33%	2	5%	40	100%
Mrs. T (7th grade)	11	28%	8	20%	21	52%	0	0%	40	100%
Mrs. L (7th grade)	18	45%	9	23%	9	23%	3	7%	40	100%
Average	13	29%	16	29%	18	36%	4	6%	50	100%

References

Art & Man, (1982, April/May). Mini-issue: Working with everyday objects, *12* (6), 4-15.

Barker, R. (1968). *Ecological psychology: Conceptual methods for studying the environment.* Stanford, CA: Stanford University Press.

Broudy, H. (1962). Enlightened cherishing: An essay on aesthetic education. Urbana: University of Illinois Press.

Burton, J. (1981, Jan.) Representing experiences: Ideas in search of forms. *School Arts, 80* (5), 58-64.

Churchill, A. (1970). *Art for preadolescents.* New York: McGraw-Hill.

Degge, R. (1976). A case study and theoretical analysis of teaching practices in one junior high art class. (Doctoral dissertation, University of Oregon, 1975). *Dissertation Abstracts International, 36,* 5750-A. (University Microfilms No. 76-5157).

Feldman, E. (1970). *Becoming human through art.* Englewood Cliffs, NJ: Prentice-Hall.

Folsom, S. (1976). The art educator in the preadolescent world: A phenomenological descriptive study of teacher and children. (Doctoral dissertation, The Pennsylvania State University, 1976) *Dissertation Abstracts International, 37* (11A), 6903. (University Microfilms No. 77-09765).

Galbraith, L. & Spomer, M. (1986). Does art history go to school? *Art Education, 39* (5), 10-13.

Glaser, B & Strauss, A. (1967). *The discovery of grounded theory.* Chicago: Aldine.

Johnson, N. (1985). Teaching and learning in art: The acquisition of art knowledge in an eighth grade class. Arts and Learning SIG *Proceedings,* American Educational Research Association Annual Meeting, Chicago, 4-32.

Lewis, W. (1981). The participation of low achieving male youths in art activities: A behavioral study of appropriate teacher strategies (Doctoral dissertation, University of Cincinnati, 1980). *Dissertation Abstracts International, 41* (07), 2891-A. (University Microfilms No. 8029676).

Lowenfeld, V. & Brittain, W.L. (1975). *Creative and mental growth,* sixth ed. New York: Macmillan.

Miles, M.B. & Huberman, A.M. (1984). *Qualitative data analysis.* Beverly Hills, CA: SAGE.

Owen, C. (1962). An investigation of creative potential at the junior high level. *Studies in Art Education, 3* (03), 6-33.

Schmid, H. (1980). Perceptual organization and its relationship to instructional arrangements in contributing to the effective instruction of a distinguished university teacher. (Doctoral dissertation, Ohio State University, 1979). *Dissertation Abstracts International, 32* (8), 4390-A. (University Microfilms No. DEM80-01824).

Smith, L. & Geoffrey, W. (1968). *The complexities of the urban classroom.* New York: Holt, Rinehart & Winston.

Sevigny, M. (1978). A descriptive study of instructional interaction and performance appraisal in a university studio art setting: A multiple perspective. (Dissertation, Ohio State University, 1977). *Dissertation Abstracts International, 38,* 6477-A. (University Microfilms No. 7806099).

Stokrocki, M. (1990). A portrait of a Black art teacher of preadolescents in the inner-city. In B. Young (Ed.) *Art and Minorities.* Reston, VA:The National Art Education Association.

Stokrocki, M. (1988). A study of a Black teacher's perspectives on teaching urban preadolescents. Journal of *Multi-cultural and Cross-cultural Research in Art Education, 5* (1), 83-97.

5

Are Art Teachers Prepared to Teach
The NAEA Essential Components?

ADELAIDE RUSCH

Cheat Lake Junior High School
Morgantown, West Virginia

WILLIAM J. THOMAS
West Virginia University

This paper addresses the question of whether or not the current population of art teachers is prepared to teach the NAEA essential components of aesthetics, art criticism, art history, and art production. We argue that, in fact, many teachers are prepared; the problem is how to make it apparent. This is accomplished by presenting a process that consists of ways in which art teachers can themselves address the NAEA essential components of aesthetics, art criticism, and art history through an examination of their own practice. The process focuses on these three of the four essential components since they are the most questionable in respect to the preparedness of art teachers.

The process itself is explained by first presenting a particular account of a junior high art teacher's own review and examination of her classroom activities. Specifically, this account exemplifies the linking of classroom activities to broader art issues. It also illustrates the way in which these issues provided the basis for identifying relations and degree of connection between their features and those of the NAEA essential components. Also, and perhaps most importantly, this account makes it clear that in order for this teacher to address these components, it was not necessary to abandon what were for her important characteristics of art in her junior high classroom. Characteristics such as enchantment, delight, rapture, musing,

47

and reverie, which might be associated with realms of romance and magic, were not found to be alien to matters of aesthetic perception. Since these characteristics are variable and relative with regard to different times and places, it was encouraging to find their story told so eloquently within art history. It was also found that relations between these characteristics and images were made understandable by critically constructing meaningful links between art and the lives of those encountering it.

Following this account of one teacher's use of this process of examination, features of the process itself are underscored, and suggestions are made regarding how to secure the relationships to aesthetics, art criticism, and art history that emerge by way of this self-examination of practice.

When we first began talking about matters of aesthetics, art history, and criticism in relation to their inclusion in the junior high curriculum, the considerations ranged from how to add these components to the curriculum to what form they should take. Fortunately though, the longer we discussed these items, the less strange and problematic they became. It simply became clear that the issue was not exclusively one of addition; but rather more a matter of excavation. Features of aesthetics, art history, and criticism are very likely embedded in many classroom activities. Instead of looking for ways and places to put something in the curriculum, it was decided that it might be a good idea to think about and examine what was already there. Also, why not take the position that current classroom practices (intentionally couched within the realm of romance and magic)were vital, full, and influential. They were designed and governed by a teacher who has been knowingly acting out of her own sense of wonder and commitment. In any event, these discussions were enough to provide a kind of signal, a call to step back and try to get one's bearings.

The following then is a general account of one teacher getting her bearings by engaging in a self-examination of her classroom activities. Five examples are discussed, and each has as its purpose the identification and establishment of relations between classroom practice and the components of aesthetics, art history, and criticism. The important consideration to keep in mind is that this was initiated within the context of what were valued characteristics of the existing art program. Characteristics such as enchantment, delight, rapture, musing, and reverie were, in effect, understood to be magical characteristics that were crucial and demanded to be sustained. Now, in this connection, and prior to an examination of particular classroom

48

activities, a broad idea emerged, one that addressed this teacher's overall intentions and goals. The idea was that these magical characteristics are meant to be such that they significantly influence the participants, namely the students as well as the teacher. At the same time, it may reasonably be claimed that art calls upon one's sensibilities, thoughts, and reactions in such a way that often in their application they undergo review, reappraisal, or confirmation.

In this respect, looking at and the making of images are intended to be influential, and therefore neither is well understood, nor are they effectively undertaken if they are confused with things that are merely fun or entertaining. Unlike entertainment, magic is not essentially an end in itself; it is meant to make things happen, and its participants are influenced to the extent that it significantly affects their approach to other things and ideas. Thus, the function of magic and the function of art are seen as somewhat similar; consequently, a broad idea about art is seen as complementary to a set of teacher intentions and overall goals.

This initial step toward getting one's bearings, while admittedly general and broad, nevertheless provided a useful approach to an examination of more specific classroom activities. The approach was to examine practices in order to link them to broad art issues and ideas which are also examined in connection with one's overall intentions and goals. In turn, this provided the basis or groundwork for identifying relations and degrees of connection with aesthetics, art history, and criticism. The following five examples provide an account of one teacher's examination of her classroom practices.

The Stump

On one occasion a rather large, rotted stump, which had rested in the woodland not far from the school, was brought into the classroom and placed on a table in the center of the room. Around and alongside its base were various kinds of growths ranging from moss to wildflowers; one section of the stump itself had eroded to form a dark cavity. During the next few weeks, and after it became evident that the stump was not there as something to draw or paint, the students progressively took into account various features of the stump. Observations were made about the continued growth of the moss, the strangeness of the projecting roots, and the activities of the spiders who had taken up residence in the cavity. Some observations

49

were aided by a magnifying glass, while others were enhanced by the students wondering and speculating about the character of the stump; it was even proposed that to return the stump to its prior setting would be to risk its destruction. All of this, of course, was meant to happen; the teacher knew that the stump could provoke this kind of activity. The students became fascinated and attracted by it to the extent that they were enchanted. They wondered about it, puzzled over it, and often wound up being absorbed in thought; they were musing about this evolving magical item from the woods.

Upon examination of this activity it was decided that what was basically taking place was the establishment of a certain kind of relationship, one that relied on a certain kind of seeing, thinking, and feeling, and, by extension, one that making and looking at art may also rely on. Consequently, the stump experience may be made to function as a model which could be referred to during subsequent classroom activities. These activities may involve such things as drawing and painting. But, in addition, this idea of building or establishing relationships by way of certain kinds of seeing, thinking, and feeling can also serve as the basis upon which relationships to aesthetics and art history can be established. In the first place, if the students were viewing the stump in respect to its variety and diversity of features, musing about this decayed but alive thing, charting its daily changes, and speculating about its connection with other things and ideas, then it may reasonably be granted that they were perceiving aesthetically. Also, further matters related to aesthetics could be engaged by simply entertaining the question of whether or not the stump could be considered a work of art.

Regarding the connection to be made between art history and the practice of establishing relationships by way of aesthetic perception, one can assume that human beings have done this kind of thing for a long time. Therefore art history has a story to tell about how others have done this at different times and under different as well as similar circumstances. In this case, the stump could be an interesting point of departure: what kind of magical relations have humans had with nature, and how have these been represented? French and English styles of gardens, for example, are very different, and each exemplifies a particular idea about nature. In which garden would the stump experience be more fitting?

The Time-Line

During a drawing activity one student was shown some examples of Leonardo da Vinci, and the question came up as to where to place him in time ... in his day did they have electricity, engines, or telephones? The student's response was: "I don't think so, probably not". This and other such instances indicated that the students in general had, at best, an incomplete sense of time and place. In response to this, it was decided that the construction of a "time-line" by way of an accordion fold would be appropriate. It would consist of small panels that could unfold across the tables in the art room. On various occasions it would be taken out, unfolded, and references, such as art reproductions, printed matter, etc., that related to a particular classroom activity, would be placed in "time". Thus, in effect, time or periods of time would be made visible. But, just as important, as things were placed in time, some spaces or holes in the time-line would naturally occur. These spaces would serve to provoke curiosity, puzzlement, and the activity necessary for filling in the gaps.

Upon review of this idea, other broad art issues were unveiled, particularly issues involving time itself and things associated with time such as memory, nostalgia, distance, the remote, and the ancient. Since these and other things associated with time have often been the subject matter of art works, it would make sense to trace some relevant examples and consider them in the context of their time and place. For instance, bodies of work by Joseph Cornell or Giorgio de Chirico, and kinds of work by the Cubists or American Luminists certainly did not emerge within a vacuum. They are related to specific historical and cultural contexts.

Portraits

Almost every year students had spent some time on portraiture, and the projects were set up in a fairly standard manner. That is, the class would look at some examples, discuss them, and then proceed to make some drawings of themselves or a classmate. However, on one occasion the teacher covered the classroom wall with a variety of examples. Following a lengthy discussion about the exhibited personalities, emotions, ages, time periods, and uniqueness of the presented individuals, the students were required to write about one of the examples that they found particularly appealing. Unexpectedly, this part of the project, which was to function as a preliminary to the drawing of portraits, turned out to be the most engaging. This preliminary brought into play much of what the students were familiar with or already knew. As far as the teacher was concerned, this was important because it seems that so much of the time students are not given credit for what they do know. Accordingly, during the writing the students were urged to think about their feelings in order to become knowledgeable of them. Overall a condition of reverie or of being lost in thought persisted throughout the class until the actual drawing of portraits got underway. In retrospect, what had happened was that these preliminaries were being rendered as just steps that would understandably fade as one got closer to their destination. In thinking this over, it became clear that the best features of the preliminaries had, in fact, nothing to do with their functioning as steps. If the looking, discussing, and writing brought into play what the students knew and came to know relative to the thoughts, feelings, and ideas that people can have, then an important art idea may be highlighted. The idea is simply that not only does art reflect and reveal important things and ideas, but, just as important, art often confirms our ideas and feelings. We therefore become more knowledgeable through the very act of confirmation. Of course this kind of response to art relies on aesthetic perception or, in other words, a reflective and sensitive reading of a work. Additionally, this kind of response is connected to art criticism, especially within the context of junior high school, in that it can be used to illustrate one basis upon which particular art works can be considered to be worthwhile and significant. If, through art, one can become more knowledgeable of his or her own feelings and ideas as well as those of others, then indeed, art takes on a social value.

Feathers

Another activity that upon examination yielded some very workable ideas involved a number of class periods devoted to the drawing of feathers. It was realized that what the activity had to offer was really a matter of how it was thought about or examined. The drawing activity itself required that the students observe closely, investigate, and make visible the feather's qualities and structure. Following what may be called a detailed drawing, other drawings were made, but with the addition of a variety of materials, some of which included color. As expected, the additional materials produced drawings that ranged from slight variations to radical differences in comparison to the initial detailed drawings. The allure of the materials was meant to encourage and provoke the students to become absorbed in the activity and muse over the emerging expressive effects. However, in a larger sense, it was determined that what could emerge was something fundamental to the making of images: namely, the perennial matter of changing a material into a medium. Producing and noticing aesthetic properties, getting expressive ideas along the way, proceeding from the familiar and literal to the new and expressive are integral parts of changing a material into a medium. In addition to the students' own works, this idea could be underscored by studying particular instances of artists doing the same thing. Also, and in keeping with the subject matter of feathers, it would be interesting to engage the art historical and critical issue of what constitutes appropriate subject matter. The common and the ordinary have not always been regarded as worthy or noble enough subject matter for art. For instance, Jim Dine's prints and drawings of tools would, at best, in certain times and places, be considered inappropriate and trivial. While, in other times and places, they would have very well been considered magical and suggestive personifications.

Guernica

Finally, the last classroom activity to be considered is one that was specifically directed toward cultivating the students' aesthetic perception. Picasso's *Guernica* was selected, and the students were taken through a critical review of the work. They were asked to notice and describe its features, point out how it was composed, and come to some conclusions about its content or message. As the students settled in, a slide of *Guernica* was projected large enough so as to fill the blank wall. It was intended that, initially, the students would be simply confronted with the work, and aside from a few comments regarding procedure, no other information was given. At about the midway point of the class period, more and more information about the work was provided, and, as intended, this information blended well with much of what the students were observing and commenting about. This served to increase the intensity and liveliness of the students' participation; they were being carried along by the work and their own activity. Their efforts were being confirmed and enlightened at the same time. Very frankly, this degree of rapture was the consequence of good teaching, but further reflection on the matter raised the question as to whether or not this magic could have taken place in conjunction with any work of art. What made this question even more pertinent was the fact that it was not expected

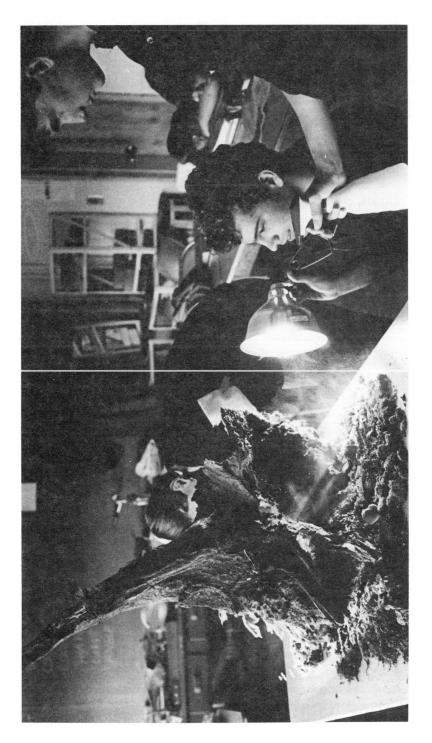

that this encounter with *Guernica* would absorb the whole class period. Consequently, an additional aesthetic as well as critical concern was identified in that the issue of appraisal was directly involved. It became questionable as to whether or not very many works would have had the power or magic to hold the students for a whole class period. Was it that the victims portrayed in *Guernica* were haunting, and that the brutality and harshness exemplified in the work allowed the students to see aspects of their own lives in terms of the work? These issues and questions could absorb yet another class period.

This account of the preceding five examples has addressed a teacher's review and examination of her own classroom practices. It focused on the linking of classroom activities to broad art issues which provided a basis for identifying relations and degrees of connection between aspects of these issues and the realms of aesthetics, art history, and criticism. By underscoring things that occurred within this account, constituent features of the examination process can now be identified.

Features of the Examination Process

1. First of all, it is necessary to keep in mind that before specific classroom activities were examined, thought was given to the overall character and goals of the existing art program. The result of this was the construction of a significant relationship between art and the valued characteristics of the program such as enchantment, delight, rapture, musing, and reverie. The relationship was based on a similarity of function: art and magical activities are meant to influence their participants' approach to things and ideas beyond the activities themselves. Therefore such broad thinking about classroom activities and art is an important initial feature of the examination process. It provides a context within which more specific classroom activities may be examined. Furthermore, the subsequent links to broad art issues and their relationship to aesthetics, art history, and art criticism are more likely to be consistent with one's overall intentions and goals.

2. The next phase of the process is the examination of specific classroom activities in order to link them to broader art issues. What must be done here is to take into account various aspects or parts of the activity and either generalize them or consider them in close detail. For example, a drawing activity that involved careful observation for the purpose of accurate

description, in the sense that the work should have the illusion of space and volume, may be generalized to encompass issues of resemblance, imitation, correctness, or accuracy. In turn, this may raise the question of what is to be resembled. If a student is dissatisfied with a picture of himself in the school yearbook, then is he upset about the resemblance, or actually what the photo resembles about him? In other words, is this a matter of what the photo has included or excluded? What makes a photo or drawing appropriate, successful, or acceptable, and how have standards and ideas about these changed over time?

If, on the other hand, an aspect of the drawing activity stresses the development of technique for example, the managing of tonal values in order to exhibit solidity or volume, then instead of generalizing, the matter of technique could be considered in more detail. For instance, values in a drawing may be managed so that they either slowly change or abruptly shift from lighter to darker in the process of depicting solidity or volume. If the drawing activity included the practicing of both techniques, then the question arises as to the basis upon which one technique would be selected over the other. Wanting to show solidity or volume will not provide the basis for choice, for in this instance the one technique is as good as the other. What then would provide the basis for choosing? The choice and development of technique is indeed a broad art issue; perhaps one approach would be to take into consideration various expressive purposes that could guide the choice of technique.

In the account of the classroom activity that involved the drawing of feathers this process of generalizing as well as focusing on a particular aspect of the activity was utilized. In regard to generalizing, the activity was thought of as essentially addressing the perennial problem of changing a material into a medium. Additionally, focusing on just the fact that feathers were being drawn served to raise a broad issue concerning what constitutes appropriate subject matter.

This second feature of the examination process is, therefore, generative. It involves taking into account aspects or parts of specific classroom activities and either generalizing them or focusing more tightly on them in order to link them to broad art issues.

3. The last feature of the examination process consists of identifying relations and degrees of connection between broad art issues and the areas

57

of aesthetics, art history, and art criticism. Broad art issues, which have emerged within one's overall intentions and goals, now provide the groundwork or basis upon which these connections can be effected. This is accomplished by taking into consideration what at this point in the process has already been achieved. The very matter of identifying broad art issues is actually an achievement that is the result of having critically examined classroom activities. Issues such as the function of technique, resemblance, subject matter, establishing relations with works, etc., represent an achievement in assigning potential meanings to classroom activities by connecting them with other things and ideas.

If this achievement of assigning meanings to classroom activities is thought of alongside the practice of responding to student art work (which is based not only on the teacher's knowledge of the subject but also on the teacher's own funded experience as a human being) then defensible connections between aesthetics and art criticism have been established. Identifying art issues and responding to student work require explaining and adding things to each. They involve seeing more in students' work then students do, seeing more in a classroom activity than meets the eye, and extending each work by connecting it with other things and ideas for the purpose of understanding its significance. Thus, assigning meaning to classroom activities and responding to student work are practices that can be consciously modeled by the teacher and, in appropriate ways, can be elicited from the students.

Tracing broad art issues and related ideas historically is one way of finding out how meanings are assigned to art and how art acquires meaning. Just as a broad art issue is linked to the classroom activity surrounding its emergence, so also may these issues be considered within their historical and cultural contexts. If the issue is relevant and consistent with one's overall intentions and goals, then its historical roots, origins, or setting may be worthwhile to address. Of course what makes this possible is that since the particular issue has been formed through an examination of one's own classroom activity; it may be reasonably expected that what is needed to accomplish this will be found simply because one knows what one is looking for.

Through an examination of their own practices art teachers can address the essential components of art history, aesthetics, and art criticism. We believe that there are at least two distinct advantages to this approach to the NAEA essential components. One advantage is that for teachers to start from within their present practice is to recognize and be able to draw upon its strength and authenticity, both of which are driven by commitment to their personal knowledge, intentions, and goals. To advocate and encourage this is to recognize the worth and professionalism of teachers. Another advantage is that this approach increases the likelihood of significant movement toward NAEA goals: namely, the improvement of the quality and status of visual arts education in the public schools. Common sense tells us that to ask teachers to examine what they already know and can do, instead of telling them what they do not know and are not capable of doing, is simply to extend a courtesy and call upon their best.

References

Arnheim, R. (1972). Toward a psychology of art, *Collected Essays*. Berkeley: University of California Press.
Blocker, H. (1979). *Philosophy of art*. New York: Charles Scribner's Sons.
Gombrich, E. H. (1970). *The story of art*. London: Phaidon.
Goodman, (1978). *Ways of world making*. Indianapolis, Indiana: Hackett Publishing Co.
Hobbs, J. A. (1975). *Art in context*. New York: Harcourt, Brace, Jovanovich.
Rader, M. (ed.) (1957). *A modern book of esthetics*. New York: Henry Holt & Company.
Russell, J. (1981). *The meanings of modern art*. New York: Harper & Row.
Selz, P. (1981). *Art in our times*. New York: Harcourt, Brace, Jovanovich.

6
Grading Student Artwork:
A Plan for Effective Assessment

CAROLE HENRY

University of Georgia

Evaluation and assessment are of major importance to administrators throughout the country. Teachers in all subject areas and at all grade levels are expected to account for student progress. Art is no exception. Art teachers tend to view evaluation and grading as two separate entities. Evaluation is universally viewed as a natural part of the educational process, while grading is often seen as something that must be done primarily to satisfy administrative requirements. Some art educators, particularly at the elementary level, do not recommend letter or numerical grades, although as Chapman (1985) cautions, grading must conform to school policy.

In the not too distant past, it was not uncommon to hear educators say that artwork was subjective and could not be graded objectively (Jefferson, 1969). This belief, carried to its logical extension, left the art teacher with no guidelines for grading except subjective response. According to Fearing, Mayton, and Brooks (1986), "A possible reason art has been considered suspect as a serious area of instruction is the impression that evaluation of instructional progress is based on the subjective assessment of artworks by the art teachers."

The assessment of artworks can appear to be primarily a subjective act complicated by the subjectivity of art itself. Granted, factual retention of art related information and historical fact can be measured in objectively designed tests, but other aspects of art, the making of an artwork, for instance, can be viewed primarily as a subjective experience. Art is based on the ideas and emotions of the individuals engaged in the artistic process.

Admittedly, subjectivity is an integral and desirable quality of art that

61

makes possible creative and divergent expression. Lansing and Richards (1981) argue that this subjective aspect of art can be addressed, however, in carefully formulated objectives. In other words, the subjectivity of art can be assessed objectively. Evaluation of student artwork is a process that ideally should involve the students and the art teacher working jointly to assess the students' work in terms of specified attainable objectives. It is quite logical then to formulate objectives which address such things as imagination and emotional content as well as levels of skill achieved or terminology learned. The art teacher who views artworks as totally subjective and evaluates the artworks based solely upon subjective response will encounter problems in student assessment.

Art teachers generally have no problem evaluating student artwork. These evaluations usually take the form of sensitive but succinct comments written on the back of the artwork. The comment may state something to the effect, "You've done a good job mixing colors. Try for more contrast next time." A letter grade is usually placed either preceeding or following the written comment. It is at this point that the art teacher begins to encounter some difficulty.

The assignment of a letter grade to a seemingly subjective work, no matter how carefully thought-out the grade, can appear to be arbitrary to some students. The letter grade will rarely seem arbitrary to those students whose artwork was returned to them with an "A" on it, but can frequently appear arbitrary to those students who receive a "B" or a "C" or less. In other words, students sometimes do not understand why a certain grade was assigned to them. It is an experienced and wise teacher who establishes a clear and logical system of evaluation and consistently follows this system.

Many systems are possible, and different circumstances will lead to different solutions. Generally, elementary art teachers evaluate student progress, but do not necessarily grade student artwork (Wachowiak, 1985). It is far more common for school administrators and students to expect middle and high school art teachers to grade individual art projects as well as to assess overall student achievement. Although letter grades are the norm, some districts may require numerical grades.

Numerical grades are the normal expectation on objective item tests, and it is quite logical to average the total of these grades and arrive at one numerical grade for reporting purposes. Assigning a numerical grade to artwork can be a way to clearly assess art achievement. Art educators generally agree that there are no clear-cut right or wrong artistic solutions, but there are varying degrees to which instructional objectives have or have not been met.

Understanding this basic fact is crucial to the development of an efficient grading system. Assignments must have clear, well-defined objectives which can be measured. One possible solution is to assign a certain number of points to each objective and to tally these points to reach a final score. Many other subject area teachers use variations of this theme in grading. For instance, a discussion question on a literature exam may count 20 points. The teacher may mentally break this down further: 1) content may be worth 10 points, 2) style may be worth 5 points, and 3) correct grammatical usage may be worth 5 points. The teacher may or may not reveal this point distribution to the students, but its existence provides the logic that underlies the grading system.

The same type of numerical system, of course, can be applied to grading artwork. Initially, a specific number of points can be earned for simply completing the assignment. Points can also be deducted from this numerical base for late or incomplete work. Additional points can then be assigned to each objective, and the number of points earned is then dependent upon the degree to which the objective has or has not been met. For instance, a teacher may decide that students will be given 70 points for conscientiously completing an assignment and that the remaining 30 points will be divided among the objectives specific to that assignment. It is suggested that some of these points be reserved for instances of original and creative experimentation.

Let's look at one particular assignment to see how this system might work. An eighth grade art class has participated in a sketching trip and drawn a farmhouse as a preliminary activity to a painting assignment. The class has been instructed to paint the drawing using shades and tints of only one color of tempera paint. As the students work, the teacher, of course, circulates and makes suggestions, encouraging the students to evaluate their own efforts in terms of the specified objectives.

Completed work is then evaluated by the teacher. First, if the artwork has been completed and submitted on time, the student earns 70 points. The student has already "passed" the assignment by simply completing it. Next,

A sketching trip to a farmhouse near the school provided many opportunities for student choice of subject matter.

Students worked hard to attain the prestated objectives of the assignment.

The students were instructed to paint the drawings using shades and tints of only one color of tempera paint. The degree to which this objective was met could then be reflected in the grading process.

Emphasis was placed on the composition and detail of the initial drawing and on the use of tints and shades in the finished painting. In this painting, these objectives were successfully achieved without sacrificing originality or personal style.

A simple road sign, across the road from the farmhouse, was fair
game for a problematic, at-risk adolescent boy. Painted according
to the objective criteria, the sign becomes part of a strong visual image
and can be graded as such. Objective-based grading made success
possible and helped to motivate the entire class.

the additional points must be allotted. Emphasis in this particular assignment was on the composition and detail of the initial drawing and on the use of tints and shades in the finished tempera painting. Therefore, these two objectives might be worth 10 points each, 5 points could be allotted for craftsmanship, and 5 points could be reserved for originality.

A simple form can be made out for each assignment providing the student with a clear explanation of the numerical grade earned. This form should include the assignment and the desired objectives. Actual points earned should also be included. The total number of points possible should be posted with the original objectives. This is an example of a similar evaluation form that was used successfully with middle school students:

TEMPERA PAINTING

Completion (on time)	70	
Detail and composition of drawing	10	
Use of tints and shades	8	
Craftsmanship	3	
Originality	+2	(extras added to farmhouse:
	93	cat in the window, clothes
		on the line, etc.)

Comments: Attention paid to detail makes this visually interesting. Sufficient use of tints and shades. Use a smaller brush to avoid losing details.

Examination of this grade form demonstrates that this student not only finished the assignment conscientiously and on time, but also planned a successful composition including rich visual detail. Further analysis reveals that the student mixed and used an adequate number of tints and shades. Craftsmanship could have improved with the use of a smaller brush. Additional points could have been earned by mixing more values of the individual color and by painting the detailed areas more carefully. The student added details (a cat in the window and a clothesline) that were not actually present thereby earning extra points for originality.

Sharing this or any other grading system and the rationale behind it with the students is crucial and will help avoid the appearance of personal bias on the part of the teacher. Students can look at the form and at the artwork and immediately understand the reasons for their individual grades. Efforts can then be directed toward areas of weakness, and improvement can be made in subsequent assignments.

References

Chapman, L. H. (1985). *Discover art*. Worchester, MA: Davis Publications.
Fearing, K., Mayton, E., and Brooks, R. (1986). *The way of art: Inner vision/outer expression (teacher's manual)* Austin, Texas: W.S. Benson and Company, Inc.
Jefferson, B. (1969). *Teaching art to children: Content and viewpoint*. Boston: Allyn and Bacon, Inc.
Lansing, K.M. and Richards, E.R. (1981). *The elementary teacher's art handbook*. New York: Holt, Rinehart, and Winston.
Wachowiak, F. (1985). *Emphasis art: A qualitative program for elementary and middle schools*. New York: Harper and Row, Publishers.

7

Environment of Middle and Secondary Art Classrooms: Becoming Aware of, Designing, and Implementing Changes in the Furniture, Facilities, and Spaces

ANTONIA ARACA

Euclid High School
Euclid, Ohio

One problem facing the contemporary art teacher is finding practical and effective ways to humanize the spaces and places where art education occurs. It is the purpose of this paper to provide strategies for analyzing, designing, and implementing plans and therefore to design the art environment most suited to the complex needs of today's art educators. One can choose from a variety of methods which can be used with the Index for Environmental Descriptors to evaluate and implement your design.

The framework of this paper emphasizes the art classroom. However, the environmental aggregate manifest aspects of the physical classroom: A) the people and B) the program or activities. A and B constitute the life-forces within the environment. Further, the environment is "the aggregate of social cultural conditions that influence the life of an individual or community" (Webster, p. 278). A good "fit" between the needs of one student population and a given classroom cannot always be generalized to another student population and classroom.

Historically, the enclosed space in a classroom along with its furniture and facilities was considered a minor aspect of the learning environment, since schools have established only minimum standards for size, accoustics, lighting, and heating (Weinstein, 1979). And Weinstein adds, once these minimal environmental standards were met, the child's learning depended solely upon pedagogical and social concerns.

"Buildings cannot by themselves create positive behavior results. Experience cautions us, however, that buildings which are apparently unsuitable for existing school programs may indeed yield negative outcomes" (Gump, 1980). This statement is made by an environmental psychologist as he makes his concluding assumptions about a highly controversial trend regarding open education and open space schools. The aforementioned concepts can be applied to traditional classrooms.

Who Is In Charge of the Art Classroom Environment?

A host of authors from various disciplines increasingly perceive the person, in this case an art instructor, as an authority regarding the environments he or she manages (e. g. Alexander, 1979, Broadbent, 1973: Ittelson, Proshansky et al, 1974). According to a sample study of twelve art classrooms examined (Araca, 1982), only about half of the art teachers interviewed were aware of the classroom. In varying degrees, these aware teachers designed and maintained their furniture and facilities according to the needs of the art activities and curriculum. Conversely, only about half of the teachers in the study were unable to take charge of given aspects of their classroom setting. Therefore, a need to educate teachers is recognized in this vital area.

Architects, planners, administrators, and custodians should not be the final authorities in making decisions about art classrooms. Although art teachers must attend to a multitude of other aspects within their teaching, it is essential that they become aware of and become actively involved in designing and managing the spaces and places in their art classroom environment. (Weinstein, 1979).

Five ideas have been identified as an emerging role for the classroom environment (Araca, 1983):

1. Classrooms should be humane and in tune with the community's cultural population mix.
2. Classrooms should be flexible, miniaturized, and mobile.
3. Classrooms should be minimally decorated (Weinstein, 1979).

4. Teachers should interpret their classroom setting in a holistic manner (NAEA, 1979).

5. Teachers should design the appropriate physical environment for various educational activities.

This paper will touch upon the above ideas.

The Index Method and Rationale Examined

The Index method has been used by many architects (e. g. Alexander, 1977; Ching, 1979; Wilson, 1977) and by educators (e. g. Bloom's taxonomy). It is a systematic way of developing clear observations and critical thinking. It furnishes a language with which we can begin to give special attention to every detail of a classroom. Alexander, an architect who assists individuals in designing their homes, claims "the source of life we create lies in the power of the language which you have." Ching concurs with Alexander. His book is used to teach architects (Architecture Form-Space and Order, 1979). He states that a vocabulary which contains depth and range will affect perception and shape a solution, because the solution is related to the way a problem is perceived, defined, and articulated. In other words, language has power. It is the vital tool with which we begin to open our thinking, pinpoint weaknesses and strengths, develop and implement solutions.

Therefore, this paper furnishes an Index for Environmental Descriptors, a grid on which you create floor plans and concepts for analysis. Finally, it provides methods, suggested plans for implementing the art environment suited to the complex needs of today's students and the curriculum.

The Content Within the Index

The Index for Environmental Descriptors (IED) has two parts: I) Inventory List for the Physical Factors; II) Inventory for the Space-time Form Factors. The IED is basically a checklist intended to arouse awareness of the physical classroom. It aids the teacher in selecting and arranging the furniture as it relates to the art activities. And also directs attention to the circulation paths within the furniture arrangements. Who uses them, when, and why?

71

The IED can further be used to examine the kinds of furniture and facilities which are present or absent. In our search, while observing, describing, analyzing, and designing our dynamic education environment, we need to distinguish good places from bad places. Ultimately, the physical setting must be examined to determine the "fit" between the physical environment and the program, and how the setting impacts on behavior.

Index, Part I: Physical Factors

The Index for Environmental Descriptors furnishes us with an essential language which will familiarize us — sequentially — with mobile and immobile furniture and facilities. For example, the facilities (room, floor, ceiling, and walls) are four individual descriptors. Subsumed under the descriptor *room* are factors such as size, shape, and number. The descriptors for *furniture* include various types of desks, cabinets, storage, etc. Under the descriptor *student storage* are listed the factors, tote tray cabinets, banks of drawers, and so on.

General Security (Table I, Part I) is one of the dramatic problems in the classroom which is dehumanizing our art rooms for both teachers and students. (Araca 1983, 1986; Sheldon Laboratory Systems, undated). Within the twelve art class classroom samples, it was found, in both urban and suburban art settings, that vandalism and theft was a pervasive problem. The absence of adequate or safe student storage was the number one problem.

At sites where students' lockers were a major problem, too many students were unable to work on their art projects. One instructor was frustrated about the aforementioned storage problem and the impact it had on students' level of achievement. In a wealthy suburban high school, new high density storage was provided for student use. Not every teacher will relate to this student storage solution or its high cost. However, commitment, analysis, and tenacity are essential to your solution. In another wealthy suburban site, the teacher did not have any student storage because he seemed to be unaware that any was needed. He stated that his administrators did not perceive his needs for furniture. Finally, one teacher had many unused tote trays in beautifully designed — yet unlocked — cabinets. He commented the trays were too long and too narrow for art supply. In addition, the

73

designers/architects did not bother to ask an art teacher for recommendations regarding furniture or facility design.

Problems regarding student storage often extend beyond the physical furniture. That is, some students or student populations lack the skills or values required for effective management of their supplies and tools. Here again, the Index serves a valuable purpose in humanizing the art environment. In order to bring life to the descriptors and factors, begin with the most ordinary observation such as locks on lockers.

The people and the program are the aspects manifested by the physical setting. They are the life-force within our places and spaces. To discover how the people, activities (space-time) "fit" the design of our physical settings is a dramatic and demanding activity. Alexander claims the "fit" between the environmental forces is as hard to achieve "as anything in theoretical physics." He attributes the difficulty to designers' inability to be precise. He urges us to describe the furniture and facilities as abstract spatial relations among well-defined spatial parts (Part II). The designer should use IED, Part II actively along with Part I. The major descriptor *organization of activities, space, and forms* will effectively aid in precision, abstract spatial relations, and so on.

Further, here is another precise description as it relates to space. High density modular student storage is manufactured in a compact fashion, thereby making storage units more mobile. This type of furniture stretches space. Further mobility is an important aspect of the next descriptor, *flexible.*

Flexible describes light furniture which is skiddable, stackable, has wheels, and is adaptable. It can be easily moved from space to space or from room to room. Flexible facilities and furniture are better for both long or short term needs. Flexibility is essential for arranging furniture for activities. Adaptability furnishes us with a more efficient and more effective learning setting. Indeed, in today's society — we are in future shock — the lag between the environmental change and the limited pace of human response is increasing. Toffler's concepts (1971) are still valid today. This is why flexible furniture and facilities enable us to meet the ever changing social realities.

In Part II of the Index, flexibility plays an important role in multipurpose rooms. When one room must accommodate many different kinds of media activities, different furniture arrangements are necessary. A few teachers interviewed still changed their furniture arrangements even though they had a number of specialized rooms (Araca, 1983).

Also, modular units (another factor) allow teachers to interchange or stack furniture, whereas, component furniture gives variety or units with multi-purpose function. Flexibility offers other amenities as well. The old type of built-in furniture keeps the floor space clear and open. Some furniture, usually anchored in place in a perimeter location (Part II, C of Index) in the room, may not offer opportunity for change or possible improvement over the long period. High density storage cabinets or student storage is a form of miniaturized furniture which stretches space (subsumed under *flexible*, in Part I of the IED). However, this type of furniture is expensive.

Index, Part II: Space-Time Form Factors

Part II of the Index is divided into three major descriptors: 1) *differentiating small to complex space-time;* 2) *organizing activity, space, and forms;* 3) *arranging classroom space, furniture, and facilities.* As you look at your room and consider the interrelationship among the spaces, events, activities, arrangements, circulation paths, cluster spaces, and furniture arrangements, such factors take on new meaning. Another way of looking at the overall design of the room depends on the furniture arrangement (configurations). It also depends on how you relate pieces to one another and to the over all space.

Part II of the Index helps us to realize the space-time activities contained in the greater physical setting.

To design or to reevaluate a cluster space for *special media activity centers,* consider the following: 1) teacher's efficiency managing students' spatial comfort, convenience with materials and productivity. 2) Free flowing paths between activities. 3) *Students' work surfaces* adequate to the number of students involved. 4) Sequenced stations according to process (e. g. inking, printing press/hand printing, drying).

In her extensive review of literature, Weinstein (1979) found that student achievement rose with design modification. The quality of physical space improved the availability and organization of materials, furniture, and equipment.

Rooms. In the 1930s, '40s and '50s, secondary schools had one all-purpose art room, whereas now a suite of art rooms is included (Araca, Sheldon Laboratory System). Even the ordinary room in the average household has become more complex. Today the home (or the classroom) encompasses complex needs (as *expressed in relationships between activities to space-time and forms)*, and functions equal to that of a spaceship (Venturi, 1979). Our task in attending to our classroom environment requires dedication and commitment.

Process and Dynamics of Change — Maintaining Our Classroom Environments

In the last decade many schools have undergone dynamic social, economic, and political changes. Consequently, the physical sites, including the classrooms, have often deteriorated and have become oppressive and inhumane. This would include safety precautions needed for students' and teachers' storage and materials. *National Education Today* (November, 1988) claims that research indicates that school districts which habitually postponed school maintenance are obviously inviting more serious main-tenance problems later on. What may not be so obvious, however, is that they may be cutting their students' achievement right now. The research goes on to indicate that schools which budget regular maintenance actually enhance student averages on standardized tests.

Methods For Solving/Exploring Classroom Design

The major method presented in this article is using the prescribed Index and floor plan method. However, additional methods are available as follows:
1. Templates (p. 89) are used with a floor plan for rearranging or exploring new furniture configurations without having to move heavy furniture.
2. Environmental design curriculum could be used to teach students interior design. Students are valuable users in your art classrooms. As such, students need the opportunity to create functional and aesthetic designs. Their ideas can furnish fresh essential solutions with a life-force. A three- or four-year plan could be used. This was my approach. The first year,

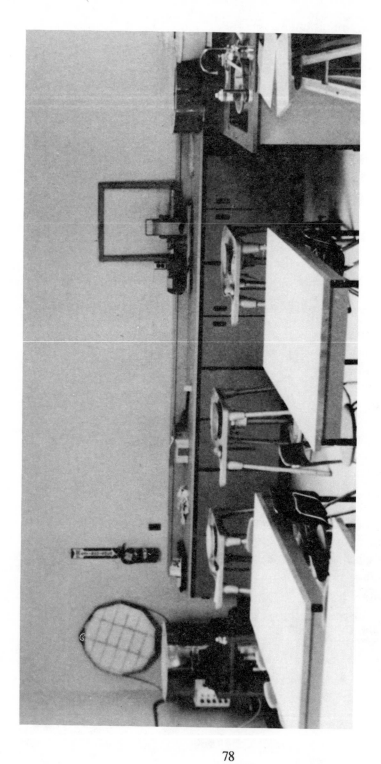

students are taught interior design skills as discussed previously. They also analyzed the pathways through the use of a floor plan and tracing paper.

Later the students were given an opportunity to examine their own classroom furniture arrangements. Their help and suggestions were innovative and functional. Students created three-dimensional cardboard furniture to scale for fact-finding information. Also the three-dimensional model approach gave students the opportunity to actually move miniature furniture around to places they had not imagined (Wilson, 1977). And it increased our range of choices.

Finally, the students established a color scheme. They threw out the institutional grey lockers and dark AV drapes. They made drapes and dyed them orange. They brought sunshine into their lives/room by painting the facilities and furniture with a harmonious color scheme. They became ecstatic.

3. Photograph the room from various angles and from different views.

4. Interview yourself and the students. What problems hinder the process of education, comfort, efficiency? Use partitions (see table 8) to create semi-private space.

5. Read the two issues of *Art Education* (April, 1978, March 1986) for greater scope and depth regarding the classroom environment. Kruz-Guilfoil offers techniques for evaluating behavior as it relates to the setting. Suzi deals with seating arrangements as they impact on student learning. Stokrocki defines the social aspects — teacher/student interaction — within learning environments. In the 1978 issue, philosophy and curriculum are examined.

6. Pore over ... become excited about, furniture in general education or specialized catalogs such as that published by Sheldon Laboratory Systems.

7. The teacher or the student can create his/her own cardboard furniture (Raskin 1975). Collect three-gallon ice cream tubs to create a modular storage unit. *Nomadic Furniture 1* and *2* (Hennessey & Papanek) tell you how to build lightweight furniture that folds, inflates, knocks down, stacks, or is disposable.

8. Have the custodian make furniture you have designed, or make it yourself.

Designing/Modifying The Art Classroom Environment

Take Inventory of the Furniture and Facilities

Take the index list and systematically check the physical objects present or absent in the classroom. Systematically measure the floor, desks, chairs, counter surfaces, storage furniture, and major equipment.

Are there any units of furniture you need? Do students have chairs rather than stools which support the back and give the student robustness while working? Do you have furniture which needs to be replaced? Any furniture or equipment which needs repair? Do you have furniture that should be thrown away? Can you find a needed unit within your own school building or school system which you can have but cannot afford to buy? Keep your ears open, and ask lots of questions.

Use the grid for the floor plan furnished in this article, placing a piece of tracing paper over it. On this graph paper (one square of 1/8 inch to the foot), draw the size of your room. Then sketch the furniture and equipment on the floor plan along with the related measurement for each unit of furniture.

Purpose and Use of the Furniture Templates:
Part II of the Index

Now you can examine the first floor plan you drew of your present physical setting. However, this time observe the furniture and activity arrangement.

Carefully read Part II of the Index to inventory and begin to differentiate the smallest access spaces, the circulation paths, and identifiable existing configuration of furniture and spaces. Continue throughout Part II until complete.

Jot down any problem areas and give yourself a pat on the back for all the well designed activity clusters. At this point you can create your second floor plan. What changes do you want to make? Small changes such as rearranging the furniture are important. Do you need barriers or partitions? In the twelve classroom sites I visited, *dividers/barriers* were used in the following ways: A) to give teachers greater control over their more precious art materials; B) to provide a somewhat semi-private space for herself/

himself; C) to furnish more private teachers' space; D) to create barriers which serve as work surfaces with media clusters; E) to divide or split a class arrangement in two parts in order to create central material and equipment center; and F) also to place a barrier between two groups, therefore, giving students within a given student population greater concentration power or time-on-task.

One need not buy expensive furniture to improve the artroom setting. In a school system where the art room has been neglected, that art teacher has a funding or advocacy project at hand rather than one of design. However, the above suggestions for solving furniture problems might be helpful.

To continue the planning procedure, take the graph paper and place a clean sheet of tracing paper over it. Block in the shape and size of the room. Show the wall 6" thick. Indicate windows and doors as well as the direction they swing. Include electrical outlets, radiators, built-in cabinets, partitions, etc. In order to see if new furniture will fit, rearrange the student desks and check the circulation paths. Then do the following:

1. Photocopy the furniture templates furnished in this article (a portion of Cullison's original templates have been adapted for art classrooms. Reprint permission has been granted). Cut out the templates closest to the size and shape of your own furniture. Don't be concerned if the cut-out differs a few inches from yours, unless you have very tight space problem. Furniture templates provided herein are in direct proportion to the graph.
2. Duplicate e.g. the number of student desks you will need, and duplicate all the varied furniture you need.
3. Move them around on the floor plan until you achieve the design of your choice.

The *New Decorating Book* is highly recommended as a general interior design book with a template kit.

The pathways should allow for flowing interconnections and ease in work areas, clean up, or storage places. As art teachers, we are aware of negative and positive spaces. We also can look at a floor plan as an interior designer's work of art. Does the floor plan indicate a balance between all cluster centers? For example, are there tight spaces in the student seating and too much space in another arrangement or configuration? Floor plan site nine, on page 91 is a good example of cramped working conditions. Conversely, the other side of the room has an unused enormous desk and space to spare.

The geometric space in which you and your students work one third of each week day is your slice of the universe. It is a delicate and precious place which you have designed and of which you are the caretaker. Effective design *could* impact directly on student achievement. Art educators must learn to thoughtfully design their classroom environment as effectively as they do other factors related to instruction.

Bibliography

Alexander, C. (1979). *The timeless way of building*. New York: Oxford University Press.
Alexander, C., et al. (1977). *A pattern language*. New York: Oxford University Press.
Araca A. (1983). (Doctoral Dissertation University of Oregon, 1982). Dissertation Abstracts International, *43*, 336-A (Order Number DA8301759).
National Art Education Association. (1986, March). *Art Education, 39* (2).
Broadbent, G. (1973). Design in architecture: *Architecture and the human sciences*. New York: John Wiley and Sons.
Ching, F. D. K. (1979). *Architecture: Form, space and order*. New York: (1984).
Cullison, P. (1984). *New decorating book*. Des Moines, Iowa: Better Homes and Gardens, (first edition, fourth printing).
Gump, P. (1980). The school as a social situation. *Annual Review of Psychology, 31*, 553-82.
Hennessey, J. & Papanek, V. (1973). *Normadic furniture 1*. New York: Pantheon Books.
(1974). *Normadic furniture 2*. New York: Pantheon Books.
Holcomb, J. R. Company. (1985-86). *Holcombs educational material*. Cleveland.
Ittelson, W. H., Proshansky, H. M., Riviln, L. G., & Winkel, G. H. (Eds.) (1974). *An introduction to environmental psychology*. New York: Holt, Rinehart and Winston, Inc.
National Art Education Association. (1979). Essentials of a quality school art program. (3rd ed.). Reston, VA.
National Art Education Association. (1979). *Report of NAEA commission on art education*. (2nd ed.). Reston, VA.
National Art Education Association. (1978, April). *Art Education., 31* (4) 4-7.
Pena, W. (1977). *Problem seeking: An architectural programming primer*. Cahners Books International.
Raskin, B. (1975, August-September). *Raise high the cardboard carpenters. Learning, 4*, (1), 102-10. (Eric Document Reproduction Service No. EJ 128 650)
Sheldon Laboratory Systems. (Undated). *Educationally correct art studios*. Jackson, MS: General Equipment Manufacturers, Manufacturing Facilities, P.O. Box 836, Kirk Street, Crystal Springs, Mississippi 39059.)
Toffler, (1971) *Future Shock*. (3rd ed.). New York: A Bantam Book/Random House, Inc.
Venturi, R. (1979). *Complexity and contradictions in architecture*. (3rd ed.) Boston: New York Graphic Society.
Webster's Seventh, New Collegiate Dictionary. (19th ed.) (1972). Springfield: G.E.C. Merriam Company.
Weinstein, C. A. (1979, Fall). Physical environment of the school. *A Review of Educational Research*, (1977), *49* (4), 577-610.
Wilson, F. (1977) *Graphic guide to interior design*. New York: Van Nostrand Reinhold Company.

Table 1: Final Index For Environmental Descriptors: Part I
Inventory List/Physical Factors

MOBILE/IMMOBILE FURNITURE
AND FACILITIES

Room
Size
Shape
Number of adjacent room/rooms
Door with locks

Floor
Wood
Linoleum
Cement

Ceiling
Accoustical tile

Walls/Vertical Surfaces
Windows — Treatment
   AV
Bulletin boards
   flat/folding
Chalkboards
Project screen

Dividers/Barriers
To and below ceiling
Furniture as barriers

Shelving
Display cases
Open shelving:
   metal/wooden
   open on all sides
   open on two sides
   closed on three sides

Storage Room
Long and short term:
   art materials
   shelving
With locks

Horizontal Surfaces
In addition to desks or tables
Special/multipurpose

Student Storage
Tote trays cabinets
Banks of drawers:
   metal wooden
Lockers
   metal
Vertical/horizontal barriers

Student Storage
Resource files
Bookcases
Drying racks
Drying cabinets/shelves

Students' Work Surfaces
Drafting desks/tables:
   folding
   wooden
   metal
   skiddable/light
Computer desk/unit
   multipurpose
   flex cart, wheels lockable
   skiddable/heavy with space for
      books

Easels
Drawing horses
Art benches

Students' Seating
Stools:
   with or without locks
   with or without wheels
   swivels
   high/low
Chairs:
   wooden

Storage Furniture
Low/medium/high
Floor cases
Smaller units
Built-in:
  cabinets
  double level
  base
Flat/regular drawers
Special storage:
  tool
  supply cart
  A. V. cabinets
  books/magazines cases
  file cabinets

FLEXIBLE: ROOM, STORAGE, FURNTIURE

Long and Short Term
Mobile furniture:
  large/small casters
  swivel/locking brakes
  carts/transports:
    tools
    A.V.
    supplies
  drying racks
  learning centers
  components
  chalkboards
  display units
  flat drawers
Modular units:
  interchangeable
  stackable
Components:
  variety of units
  multi-functional
Hi-density:
  shelves/display

metal
plastic
upholstered
swivel
with or without wheels
stackable
skiddable
folding
with spaces for books

Teacher's Furniture
Desk
Seat
Wardrobe
Personal/professional
  supplies/equipment

General Security
Storage furniture with secure locks

  drawers
Adjustability:
  furniture
  shelves
    bracket
  students'/teacher's
    seating
    work surfaces
Variety of sizes:
  cabinets
  drawers/doors/spaces
  height/width/depth
vertical/horizontal
12", 18", and 24" depths
Recycled:
  materials/furniture
Related to objects stored:
  frequency of use
  flat paper/boards
9" x 12", 36" x 24", to 45"
2-dimensional and
  3-dimensional art projects
3-dimensional items
wet art

Table 2: Final Index For Environmental Descriptors: Part II
Inventory/Space-Time Form Factors

<u>The Relationship Between Activities to Space-Time and Form</u>

A. DIFFERENTIATING SMALL TO COMPLEX SPACE-TIME
   1. <u>Access Spaces</u>
      a. <u>Access space defined:</u>
        Spaces to accommodate seeing, opening/closing or placing; and working, leaning, stretching, reaching, stooping, standing <u>human figures</u>; and the comfort of the human figure.
        Space to accommodate the opening/closing of <u>furniture</u> doors/drawers; <u>interior furniture spaces</u> to accommodate various sizes of art materials and equipment.
        Spaces to accommodate students'/teacher's <u>personal</u> work, and seating and personal belongings.
      b. <u>Access spaces in the classroom:</u>

Furniture:

doors	interior size, direction and
drawers	arrangement of spaces and shelves

Students'/Teacher's:

personal work spaces	bulletin boards
storage	clean up
resources	chalkboard
height of horizontal work surfaces	reachable height of furniture

   2. <u>Circulation Paths</u>
      a. <u>Circulation paths defined:</u>
        Space to accommodate the <u>movement and flow of human figures through space-time</u> as they pass through or intersect with other access spaces, paths, sequences, art activities, or large configurations; and as they enter or leave a room.
      b. <u>Circulation paths in the classroom:</u>

Students'/Teacher's:

storage	bulletin boards
resources	clean-up
wet/dry	chalkboards

B. ORGANIZATION OF ACTIVITY, SPACE, AND FORMS
   1. <u>Configuration of Furniture and Spaces</u>
      Students' seating arrangements: These arrangements are infinite; however, some examples are:

grid	square	circle
half circle	horseshoe	modular
cluster	linear	random

   2. <u>Cluster Spaces</u>
      a. <u>Cluster spaces defined:</u>
        Cluster spaces in a classroom can have similar or dissimilar

furniture, facilities, and equipment as well as similar or dissimilar functions and activities. But they are related to one another by function, proximity, or circulation paths.

3. <u>Students'/Teacher's Private Semi-Private Spaces:</u>
Students':
        private   small groups
        semi-private/isolated
        from the group
Teacher's:
        private   in the classroom
        semi-private

4. <u>Special Media Activity Centers</u>

Painting/drawing	Printmaking
General crafts:	Photography
ceramics	Art appreciation:
metal crafts	resources
enamel	Art evaluation:
fiber	art products
wood	Exhibits
sculpture	Research centers:
	students'/teacher's

5. <u>Activity/Instruction Arrangement for Students' Furniture</u>
Large/Small Group
  a. <u>Large group:</u>

lectures	discussion
instruction	demonstrations
audio-visual	activity centers
written	other

  b. <u>Small group:</u>
      work   discussion
  c. <u>Students' tables/desks:</u>
      groups of 2, 3, 4, or more

C. CLASSROOM SPACE, FURNITURE, AND FACILITY ARRANGEMENTS
Multipurose room
Specialized room/rooms
Adjacent rooms

Arrangements:	Split arrangements:
central arrangements	central and perimeter
perimeter arrangements	variations

Table 3: FLOOR PLAN GRAPH
Scale 1/8" = 1'
Room: size, shapes, furniture, spaces, large equipment
measurements and arrangements.

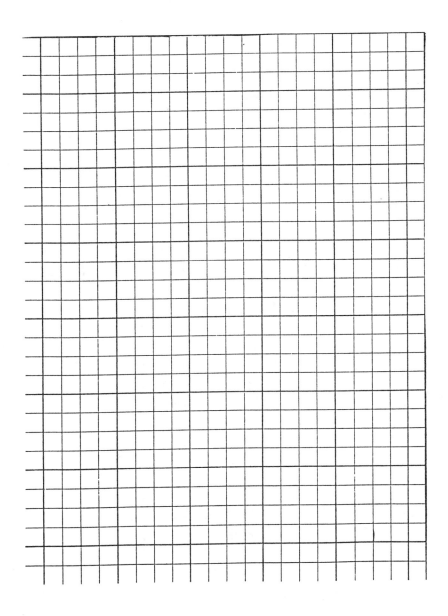

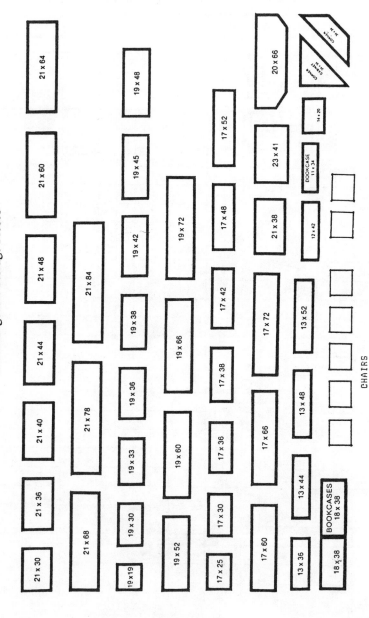

Table 4:
TEMPLATES PART I
Interchangeable Storage Pieces

88

Table 5:
TEMPLATES PART II
Tables and Special Pieces

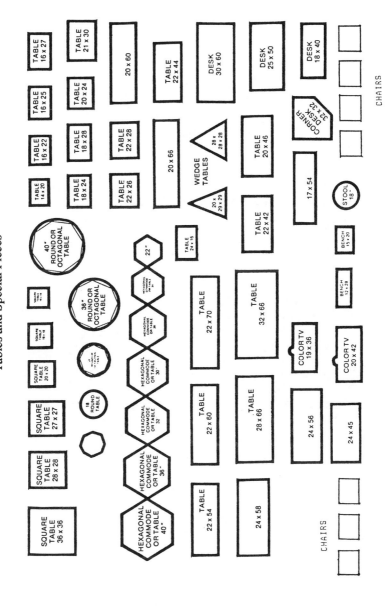

89

Table 6:
Floor Plan List for Furniture, Facilities, and Equipment

1. Dividers
2. Display shelves
3. Open shelves
4. Built-in cupboards
5. High storage
6. Low storage
7. Special storage
8. Student storage
9. Student desks/tables
10. Horizontal work surfaces
11. Work bench
12. Drawing horse
13. Teacher's desk
    Filing cabinet

14. Flat drawer
    file/storage
15. Drying cabinets
16. Potter's wheels
17. Ceramic kilns
18. Loom
19. Grinding/buffing
    wheels
20. Spray booth/
    ventilation system
21. Enlarger/drawing or
    photography
22. Enamel kiln

Table 7:

SITE 9. Multipurpose room: The cluster of student seating is overcrowded. The pathways within it are cramped. The student storage and chairs are unsafe or broken. The access space to doors is limited. The opposite end of the room, conversely, is too spacious and contains a large used drafting table. Therefore, the overall arrangement of the furniture is unbalanced. The teacher's budget was extremely low, and this site was in the inner city.

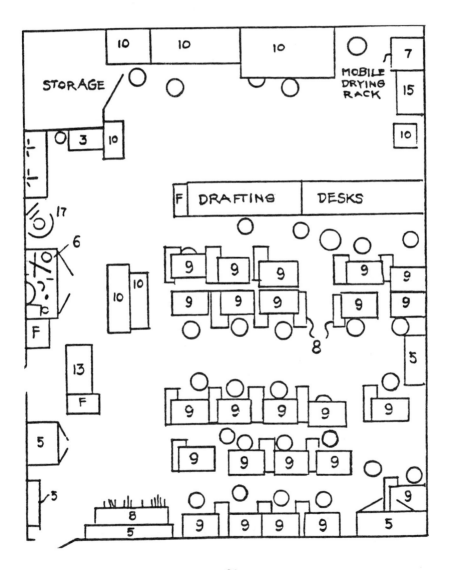

Table 8:

SITE 11. Multipurpose room: The overall design of this setting is well balanced in the following areas: all spaces are open and free flowing; media areas are sequenced; art supply areas are protected by furniture, barriers or partitions; there is a private space for teacher; high density student storage, and other ammenities. The teacher was paid for his custom-designed, hand built furniture. The site was in a middle to high socio-economic area.

Therefore, the student populations between sites 9 and site 11 were distinctively different.

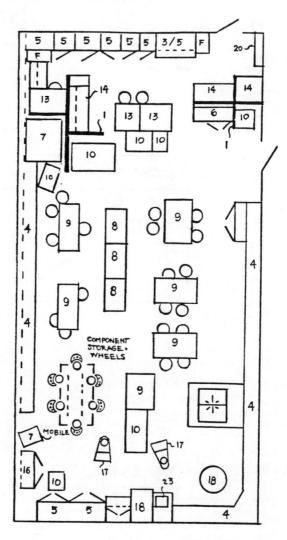

8
The Art Classroom as a Behavior Setting

FRANK D. SUSI

Kent State University

To many art teachers, controlling discipline problems in the classroom is the biggest challenge they face on a daily basis. Today's multicultural classroom often includes students from diverse ethnic and cultural groups who confront teachers with a variety of conflicting needs and divergent values.

While many of the factors associated with managing student conduct are complex and difficult for teachers to control, the physical setting is an often overlooked resource that affects behavior. As an aspect of the instructional process, the room environment is readily accessible for manipulation and can be part of an overall approach to teaching that emphasizes the prevention of problems and the development of responsible student behavior.

Many of the concepts related to the development of supportive room environments are common sense. In fact, most experienced art teachers have a tacit sense of what is involved in preparing suitable learning environments. To be best understood and used as a tool of art instruction however, physical space variables must reflect an awareness of how environment and behavior co-function in all aspects of the art program. This paper will discuss a series of concepts and ideas that can be helpful in developing, implementing, and evaluating art room settings that reflect the nature of art activities while emphasizing the prevention of behavior problems.

Because classrooms are so familiar in schools, they tend to be taken for granted, and their potential impact on student behavior and instructional processes is often overlooked. However, the education reform movement of recent years has focused attention on the physical setting and the role it can play in effective teaching. Accordingly, art educators have begun to consider ways to create settings that are geared to specific aspects of art curricula.

Art programs of today feature both traditional instructional techniques found in typical classrooms and the diverse laboratory activities associated with specialized study in art. Students working in studio areas need an art room that will permit them to safely and comfortably explore the expressive potential of various media.

For response activities such as the study of art history, aesthetics, and art criticism, physical arrangements that function in accord with those areas must be designed. To be most effective, environments prepared for both expressive and response dimensions of art should be made with consideration for the range of interpersonal and work-oriented behaviors that are expected to occur.

Art classrooms tend to be dynamic environments that shift and change to accommodate many social and instructional components. For example, a single art lesson may include a presentation that features examples of works of art by famous artists, the preparation of a printing plate and the pulling of an edition of prints, and a critique of finished work by class members. To be most effective, each activity should be conducted in a context designed to encourage the specific learning activities. For example, what works well as a physical setting for conducting discussions may be awkward or impractical for work making prints. In general, the room space layout should be visualized as it will be perceived, used, and responded to by its inhabitants. In most cases, an ideal arrangement suitable for all instructional need is not likely to be found.

The Art and Science of Teaching Art

To best understand how room environments and student behavior are related, it may be helpful to think of the teaching process as a blend of science and art. The scientific aspects are based on research into effective practice in such areas as discipline, teaching methods, and the factors that relate to effective spatial organization. Scholars in such disciplines as environmental psychology, communications theory, architecture, and sociology have developed a sizable body of information that can be useful in guiding environmental decisions.

Artistry in instruction is an outcome that results from the combination of the specialized knowledge held by the teacher combined with that individual's unique personality characteristics and educational background. When designing classrooms, many concepts are drawn together to reflect each teacher's preferences and priorities. In effect, good teaching results from an elegant blend of science and art that serves to enhance the potential for student learning (Kindsvatter & McLaughlin, 1986).

Much like the creation of a work of art, the layout of a classroom for a given instructional function will most likely result from a process of experimentation that involves an awareness of the environmental variables involved, the behavior patterns of the students, the physical resources available, and the nature of the activity taking place. While the physical characteristics of any classroom clearly play a secondary role to the academic program, the ultimate authority and responsibility for fitting all of the pieces together rests with the teacher (Brophy, 1983).

When planning room environments, decisions about specific arrangements should be made with an awareness that every person has different needs and preferences for his or her work environment. For example, some students like to spread materials out on a large counter or table; others prefer to work in a neat, orderly setting with everything at their finger tips. While some students are not bothered by having to work in tight or confined spaces, those same conditions would make many of their classmates uncomfortable. Providing opportunities for students to select different types of work spaces, when possible, can be an asset to the instructional environment.

Every teacher develops a personal style for arranging and using the classroom space available. Most display a tendency to concentrate their time in the front-center zone, an area which affords quick access to the chalkboard (whether used or not) and to the entrance to the room. Students respond to these patterns of teacher behavior by seating themselves around the teacher zone, some in-close, others in more distant areas. This results in a sometimes uneven use of the available space (Rivlin & Rothenberg, 1976).

Static and Dynamic Features

The physical environment of an art room is defined in terms of its interior

Students engaged in studio activity need work areas that will permit them to safely and comfortably explore the expressive potentials of media.

space and includes the furnishings and props that are part of the venue where teaching takes place. The fixed or static elements in the setting include installed furnishings such as display panels mounted on walls, large cabinets, and counter areas that cannot be easily moved. Fixed features define the basic architectural shell of the room.

Items such as desks, tables, and file cabinets that can be moved with relative ease are the non-fixed or dynamic features. Since students are mobile and can be assigned to specific locations, they should also be considered as dynamic aspects of the environment.

Well planned classroom spaces tend to be dynamic, fluid environments that move and change in patterns that reflect the characteristics of a lesson. Designing room layouts that are tailored to a given lesson can be best accomplished by starting with a basic room arrangement. As the activity or instructional nature of the lesson changes, the locations of dynamic elements can be shifted into pre-planned sub-environments that have been designed to support those behaviors.

Effective Teachers

Various researchers have studied teachers who were deemed to be especially effective (Arlin, 1979; Evertson, C. & Emmer, E., 1982). They reported that the classrooms of those individuals shared several common qualities that reflect an awareness of the link between environment and behavior including:

1. The room layout is organized into distinct areas or zones arranged according to the activities or functions expected to take place. Lessons are planned with particular attention paid to the amount of space needed by students to work efficiently. When the lesson required clean-up, the proximity of students to sinks was carefully considered.

2. Specialized tools and equipment that have to be stored each day are easily obtained and replaced. In art rooms, the materials required for creating batiks, making relief prints, or carving into blocks of plaster can be kept close to student work stations. Carefully mapped out procedures expedite clean-up. The practice of clustering storage and work areas together limits unnecessary travel around the room by students, a potential source of

distraction and misbehavior. This practice also enables art teachers to monitor different activities that are occurring simultaneously in different parts of the room. For example, while plaster carvers work in one area, students across the room can be drawing a still life. One goal of effective spatial planning is the creation of the least restrictive setting for the activity taking place.

3. In the classrooms of effective teachers, the basic floor plan, including storage areas and traffic flow patterns, are organized before the start of the school year. In the weeks that follow the opening of school, routine procedures are reviewed frequently, and expectations for work-related behaviors are discussed.

4. The configuration of desks or tables allows all students to sit in places where they can be easily visited by the teacher. Blocked or restricted aisles discourage monitoring visits by the teacher.

5. The classrooms of effective teachers tend to be arranged to facilitate easy movement of students within the room while preventing congestion around sinks, doorways, or other potentially busy areas.

The instructional practices of effective teachers share many environmental features that affect interpersonal conduct including:

~ An emphasis on order, predictability, and purposefulness. When those factors are present, good discipline tends to result naturally from a combination of sound instructional practice and absorbing learning activities (Stedman, 1987).

~ At all times, students know where they are supposed to be, what they should be doing, and what materials are needed. Unnecessary journeys around the room by students are kept to a minimum. Careful implementation of these practices can serve to minimize distractions while encouraging an orderly and purposeful work environment.

~ The amount of time students spend on-task, engaged in productive academic/artistic activity, is maximized during every class meeting, especially during the first days of the school year.

Effective teachers can be described as resourceful in preventing problems

For short presentations, such as critiques, students can be guided into positions around the teacher. In some cases, this arrangement is well suited for question and discussion sessions.

rather than dependent on tricks or gimmicks for dealing with them once they occur. These colleagues plan environments which limit the opportunites for inappropriate behavior.

Examining Classroom Quality

While the social architecture is assumed to be the dominant factor in most classrooms, the physical context serves to reenforce or subvert the efficiency of that interpersonal system. In art classrooms, many subtle factors can block the effectiveness of sound instructional approaches. Consider this situation:

> A middle school art teacher is introducing a unit on line quality to a class of seventh graders. To illustrate some of the key points, the teacher has prepared a series of overhead transparencies showing examples of work done by several artists. The classroom is comprised of twenty-four students who are seated at desks clustered into six groups of four. Twelve students are seated facing the screen, while the others have their backs at least partially turned toward the teacher.
>
> As the presentation proceeds, the latter group shows little inclination to turn and look toward the screen. From time-to-time during the 20-minute presentation, some students crane their necks to glance toward the screen, but mostly they just sit, fidgeting in their seats, looking at one another and giggling or staring at the sides or back of the room.

An examination of this situation indicates that the teacher's approach to presenting the content seems sound, but the room arrangement and the part it plays in the presentation have been overlooked. Half of the students can easily see the screen and the teacher, while the others have been unintentionally excluded from the presentation.

Another problem in the example relates to poor eye contact between the teacher and students. Eye contact is a vital link in the process of communication because it provides visual information that helps both speaker and listener understand each other. For example, during verbal exchanges, people tend to look at each other in the eyes through a series of quick glances. Speakers watch the eyes of listeners to obtain clues that will help them judge the impact of what they have just said. This visual feedback instantaneously tells the speaker to keep going, slow down, or back-up. Teachers who can watch the eyes of their students can quickly make adjustments when furrowed brows or glazed-over stares are spotted.

Listeners (students in this case) watch the speaker's eyes and facial expressions to get a more clear understanding of what has been said. Students who can clearly see the teacher are able to complete the eye contact connection; those who are turned away are less able to maintain the visual link. In the example, eye contact between the teacher and class members is confined to the students facing the screen.

Another important factor to consider in the example centers on the modular arrangement of the students' desks. Researchers have reported that clustering student work areas appears to be a design poorly suited for control of student behaviors, and many perceived it to be an uncomfortable layout for teaching. They found that in the modular plan, students tend to have more interactions with one another and are likely to be wasteful of time. Such conditions tend to set the stage for behavior problems. The modular layout seems best suited for small group activities where students work cooperatively with one another on a single project such as a mural (Feitler, Weiner & Blumberg, 1970).

Distance is another concern in the example. Teachers who are physically close to their students during instructional transactions are perceived more positively than those who regularly sit or stand behind their desk. Greater distance between the teacher and pupils lowers feelings of warmth and friendliness (Hessler, 1972).

To create a more suitable physical setting for the presentation described in the example, the art teacher could devise a plan based on several alternatives. For example, before beginning the presentation, the room layout could be changed so that all students are facing in the same direction. In many classrooms, moving only chairs or stools will suffice; the location of desks or heavy tables will not have to be changed. The row and column (sometimes called gridiron) room arrangement is well suited for media presentations because it places students in a configuration much like the audience seated in a movie theater. They can see clearly, and the teacher is in a good position to observe responses and monitor behaviors. Adjustments can be made if students begin to show the early warning signs of boredom or confusion. The gridiron plan also enables the teacher to see the hands of students when questions arise.

When the presentation is concluded, students can be directed to return chairs to their original desk or table locations. At first, such moves of furniture may be a bit noisy, but once students become used to making changes, rearranging the room space will become part of the regular classroom routine. To facilitate the process of making floor plan changes, a designated "homebase" location for rows or tables can be marked on the floor with tape or paint for quick reference (Musgrave, 1975).

Another option the teacher could consider for making the presentation on line more effective for all class members involves gathering students at the front of the room much as if they would be grouped around a demonstration table. For short presentations, most students will be comfortable standing. In these cases, they can be guided into positions around the teacher, much like a choir director arranges singers for a performance. Care should be taken to locate all students where they can be easily seen. If students take positions behind the teacher, eye contact with those individuals is severely limited. When the presentation is concluded, the students are directed to return to their homebase seat locations. In some cases, the close-in arrangement may also be effective for a question and discussion session.

Decisions about environmental arrangements should be based on a reasonable strategy and a systematic plan for how it can be implemented and used. Since the layout of a classroom is part of the overall instructional situation, it should be designed to address specific goals. Just as the selection of a given media is made to fulfill specific learning objectives, the room layout used at any particular time should be planned to coincide with the nature of the content being featured.

Environments and how they are arranged send a myriad of nonverbal signals to their inhabitants. In the example, the teacher may be unconsciously indicating disinterest in whether or not the students understand what is being presented. A carefully arranged setting may show that the teacher cares about the students and what they are learning.

The nonverbal aspects of setting may also be used to help students understand what behaviors are expected. When settings to which students have become accustomed during one aspect of a lesson are changed, the occupants are alerted to expect a shift in their behaviors. For example, when students enter a classroom that has been shifted from a series of work stations to feature a display of pots on a central table with seating gathered

For their work setting, each person has different spatial preferences. Some spread tools and materials out on their desk or table; others like a neat and orderly work area.

around that focal point, expectations become geared to sitting and discussing the works of art. Art teachers can use this concept to help students adjust behaviors to suit a particular lesson or activity.

Conclusion

While many aspects of the physical environment of classrooms are based on common sense, quick fixes and simple, broadly applicable formulas do not exist. Art teachers are challenged to become experts in the best use of the physical features of their classroom. The goal of achieving an acceptable congruence among instructional objectives, teaching techniques, and social behaviors is achievable.

Many of the issues related to the role of the environment in art education await thoughtful and systematic examination. For example, we do not know much about the impact of aesthetic improvements on student performance or how specific physical space factors interact with student behaviors.

Planning environments ultimately involves making decisions about social and instructional factors that have a bearing on the behaviors of students during art lessons. When implemented by industrious and inventive art teachers, environmental interventions can be a handy means to promote positive behaviors and the creation of a setting that supports art learning.

References

Arlin, M. (1979). Teacher transactions can disrupt time flow in classrooms. *Journal of Educational Psychology. 16*, 1. 42-56.
Brophy, J. (1983). Classroom organization and management. *Elementary School Journal. 83*, 4. 265-285.
Everston, C. & Emmer, E. (1982). Effective management at the beginning of the year in junior high classes. *Journal of Educational Psychology. 74*, 4. 485-498.
Feitler, F. Weiner, W., and Blumberg, A. (1970). The relationship between interpersonal relations orientations and preferred classroom physical settings. Paper presented at the American Educational Research Association Convention, Minneapolis, MN. (ERIC Document Reproduction Service. No. ED039 173).
Hessler, M. (1972). An investigation of instructor use of space. *Dissertation Abstracts International. 33*. 3055A.
Kindsvatter, R. and McLaughlin, M. (1986). The dimensions of discipline. In Kindsvatter, R. and McClain, S. (Ed.). *Teaching About Discipline in Teacher Education*. Ohio Association of Teacher Educators Monograph Series No. 11. 1-12.
Musgrave, G. (1975). *Individualized instruction: Teaching strategies focusing on the learner*. Boston: Allyn and Bacon.

Rivlin, L.G. & Rothenberg, M. (1976). The use of space in open classrooms. In H.M. Proshansky, W. H. Ittleson, & L. G. Rivlin (Eds.), *Environmental psychology: People and their physical settings* (2nd ed.). New York: Holt, Rinehart & Winston.

Stedman, L. (1987). It's time we changed the effective schools formula. *Phi Delta Kappan, 68,* 5. 215-224.

9
Sketchbooks

ROBERTA W. RICE

University of North Carolina, Greensboro

SUE ELLEN MCNEIL

Humanities Consultant
Winston-Salem, North Carolina

Sketchbooks: A Place of Discovery and Cognition

When a student makes art or views art, it is important to have a way to save what is thought, felt, discovered, or learned in the process. It is equally important to have an activity that allows students to observe how their minds work and encourages that knowing, that editing of sensation into meaningful experience, as they deal with their contacts with art curriculum and the world.

An extended sketchbook or visual diary offers just such a place to capture this kind of immediate and unfolding creative search and form seeking.[1] It is a place of discovery where sensations are recorded. Also it is a place that nurtures "critical incidents" that come from art study; study in terms of art history, art criticism, aesthetics, and production.[2] In other words, in this meeting between person and discipline, historical awareness is brought into the present, attitudes needed for aesthetic openness are reshaped, and increasing mastery in studio media is demonstrated. Therefore, plans for inclusion of sketchbook activity in the classroom, as places of idea generation and critical inquiry, are enormously important for instruction and are personally relevant for the individual.[3]

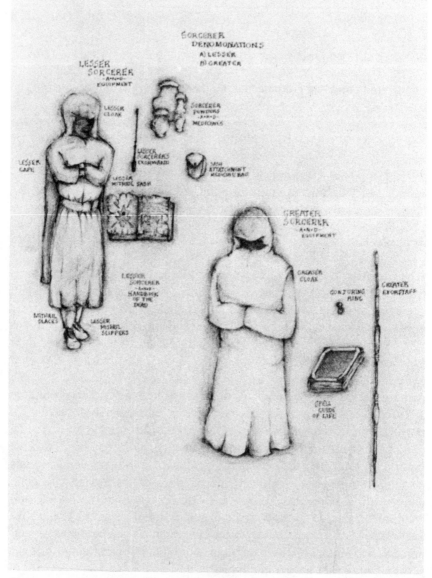

Sorcerers — independent drawing in sketchbook.

Recording Evidence: Sketchbooks and the Personal Realm

Initially, sketchbooks provide a personal entry into knowledge. Shelia Tobias reminds us that the reason a student fails or has trouble learning is because the student is still a newcomer, not an expert, who is" ... standing outside of the conventions, rituals, and expectations of discourse in that field — all of which are second nature to the specialist ..."[4] Serving as a portable studio, a private place to work, a sketchbook of images and words captures impressions, thoughts, unconscious connections, and allows the student to arrange them into a cohesive form that may be recalled, edited, regenerated, and later connected to the existing world of ideas. The sketchbook becomes an arena " ... in which [a person] explores the meanings that are latent in his concerns." "Art is what you do about something that interests, worries, or pleases you." says Edmund Feldman [1970]. He continues, "[A person] may have to read, to question his friends, to collect pictures, to write down strings of words, to explore his neighborhood looking for images [or words] to tell the story, to make some drawings."[5] A student may draw as a way of recording facts or may act as a way of rehearsing what happens. The student's writing is a way of recording and remembering the action, the idea, the information. Because it has been recorded, then it will later be available for the student to analyze, manipulate, and mold into a reasonable creative effort. What is important here is that the student's urge to save, to hold, has initiated the actions that make this a world confronted; the individual has personally connected with the environment.

A byproduct of this ownership is that sketchbooks give power. Just as handwriting is the individual's alone, so too are the arrangements and selections in a sketchbook. "It is a sanctuary where all the disparate elements of life — feelings, thoughts, dreams, hopes, fears, fantasies, particularities, worries, facts, and intuitions ... can merge to give you a sense of wholeness and coherence."[6] Because it is the individual's book alone, thoughts depend upon trusting one's self. With sketchbooks, one has the power to construct, and may use that power to define for oneself who one is and what art is all about.

Preconceptions do exist, however. For most of us, our first introduction to the process of keeping a sketchbook or journal is an assignment in school. For some students, this activity is a delight; there is curiosity about one's own process. Reflectiveness becomes valuable. For others, it is a chore, best done quickly. Learning to pay attention to our own process and to save evidence of our work requires conscious effort and technique. Building data for reflection may seem meaningless at first. Diversion creeps in. Ideas and observations seem tangential. Progress is erratic, and students lack the patience to await what scientists call the "critical mass," where efforts suddenly merge into new domains of knowledge, as connections are made between ideas that were once disconnected.

Similarly, students have concerns over rules about what is proper and not proper to put into the sketchbook. They think that the format is a given, that it is a public document that will be viewed on demand by others, or that it is an assignment that will be graded. Students are right: as an assignment, the sketchbook may well be graded.

Further, there is a worry about neatness and documenting mistakes. Students may even think that it is busy work. And in many ways it *is work* and it *is busy*. Learning to be patient with our own process and to save evidence of our work does require conscious effort and technique. The end result, however, is not only that the students have a new set of ideas to deal with, but also reflection becomes a skill as well as a habit.

Finally, sketchbook activity produces hypertext: a nonsequential record, an explorable, informalized whole with anecdotes, jokes, cartoons, enrichment material, and anything else that seems important. If the student is comfortable and familiar with the content of the discipline, he or she may take a playful approach, adding after-thoughts, questions, facts, dimensions, notes on material, all of which are added layer upon layer. Such playfulness adds sticking power for facts in the student's memory. Often the play will lead to an understanding, since humor results in both higher order thinking skills of synthesis as well as a sufficient mastery of content materials.

Usually there is a battle for the student between expression and technique; the sketchbook offers the first, protected place for this struggle to occur. The student seeks to rearrange thoughts, to master expression, and to prioritize the material. It is in the task of focusing and polishing the idea that the student comes to an understanding of art.

Yet, what students often do not know is that this is a typical way of working for creative thinkers. It is a place to practice, to dream, to let off steam, and to hold on to the quick and fragile seeds of ideas. It allows the student to

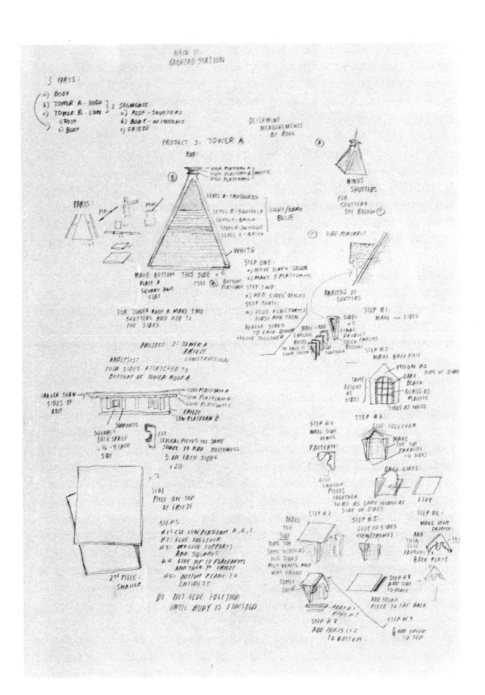

Directions for making a model railroad station.

monitor progress, to watch how feelings, excitements, and frustrations about the work go up and down as work gets done. In this personal mode of working, the student generates new ideas, thinks on paper, collects and saves bits and pieces. The end result is a private and internal, as well as a public and traditional, form of research methodology for creative and intellectual persons.

Analysis and Manipulation: Sketchbooks and the Cognitive Domain

In addition to providing a place for personal connections, sketchbooks foster cognitive and intellectual growth. They are the seed bed as well as the fruits of ideas. "Creative people in many fields have traditionally kept journals because the form encourages the creative process. The journal provides a place to deposit the first flush of creative inspiration or impression. It allows you to capture the essence of the moment while it is still vivid and fresh in your mind."[7] It also allows one to store this thought so that it may sit, grow, and ruminate over a period of time, fragile, undeveloped, and yet" held in the diary like eggs in a nest, until you have time to nurture them to completion."[8] The mind may shift and sort without fear of outside interruption or distraction.

Sketchbooks give an arena for imaginative musings; the work becomes a motivational prompt. The sketchbook not only encapsulates the lived experience through images and words, it also offers it up for examination. While artists or writers are recording, they are also interacting, judging, eliminating, or adding to data which they have saved. Because the material is enclosed, ordered, reproduced, students may intelligently relate these sensations to present and future writings or drawings. The students' choices are more than a simple technical linkage, because they are dealing with a history, a lived experience, not with disembodied facts. This wealth of source material acts as triggers for new works. These new works may be creative expressions, or they may be critical or aesthetic responses to historical or contemporary works of art. This wealth of source material contains memory in vivid ways.

This practice in active problem solving tells students what they have learned. Because it documents their unfolding process, the students may read back over it, dredging it for content and coherence. The process of drafting, revising, and compiling slows one down; students may see what has been done. They may also see what has not been done and make note

112

of it. It saves what we *pay attention to* as well as what we *ignore* in our work, or our thinking lives.[9]

What is important then in sketchbook activity is that we provide part of the material and let students work with it. We encourage students to collect and arrange their own materials as well. We respect their choices and give worth to their efforts when students share. As Piaget pointed out, "Each time we teach a child something, we keep him from inventing it himself. On the other hand, what we allow him to discover himself will remain with him."[10] In doing the drawing or writing, we invent and save our knowing; we do it ourselves so that it will stay with us.

This is not to say that sketchbook activity must be free from all teacher intervention. The sketchbook allows the teacher and student to carry on a dialogue about the ongoing work, to touch the personal dimensions of the learning act, as well as to share the content of the discipliine and to monitor the levels of mastery in the student's efforts. The teacher may help the student to see and value the strength of the student's response in some passages while helping the student to reconsider the weakness of others. New directions or ideas may emerge from the dialogue and sharing of the work accomplished. However, one caution in inviting personal responses from students must be followed. We must allow students the choice of sealing pages that, upon their reflection, they deem too sensitive for public sharing.[11]

Descriptive Imagey: Teacher Directed Student Activities

Exercises may be assigned for the students to include in their sketchbook. For example, students may be asked to visit an exhibit, choose an art work to confront and to respond to in a variety of ways. Suggestions might include: after an initial glance, the student should pull out one idea or word that the art work suggests, or make a verbal translation by writing something about what is going on in the work or what the student would care to say to the work. The student might be asked to make a pictorial translation by drawing something that connects in some way to the image viewed or an idea that comes from the image viewed. The student may also be given a formal critical procedure to follow in viewing and responding to the work.

As another exercise, we might give students a small selection of writings

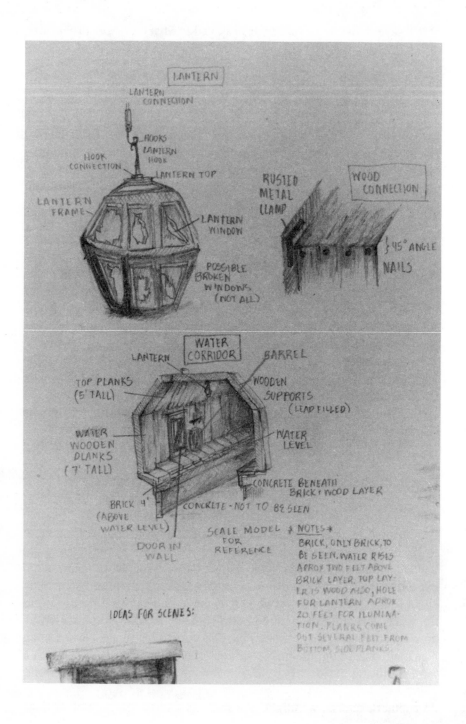

LANTERN

LANTERN
CONNECTION

HOOKS
LANTERN
HOOK

HOOK
CONNECTION

LANTERN TOP

LANTERN
FRAME

LANTERN
WINDOW

RUSTED
METAL
CLAMP

**WOOD
CONNECTION**

45° ANGLE

NAILS

POSSIBLE
BROKEN
WINDOWS
(NOT ALL)

**WATER
CORRIDOR**

LANTERN

BARREL

TOP PLANKS
(5' TALL)

WOODEN
SUPPORTS
(LEAD FILLED)

WATER
WOODEN
PLANKS
(7' TALL)

WATER
LEVEL

CONCRETE BENEATH
BRICK + WOOD LAYER

BRICK 4'
(ABOVE
WATER LEVEL)

CONCRETE - NOT TO BE SEEN

DOOR IN
WALL

SCALE MODEL
FOR
REFERENCE

NOTES

BRICK, ONLY BRICK, TO
BE SEEN. WATER RISES
APROX TWO FEET ABOVE
BRICK LAYER. TOP LAY-
ER IS WOOD ALSO, HOLE
FOR LANTERN APROX
20 FEET FOR ILUMINA-
TION. PLANKS COME
OUT SEVERAL FEET FROM
BOTTOM SIDE PLANKS.

IDEAS FOR SCENES:

and ask that they find images to go with, to explain, to illustrate, or to extend some idea that connects all the parts. We might also encourage students to pursue themes of their own selection. Students might produce drawings or writings of their own as a part of the response, as well. In this way each student generates work built upon the knowledge and ideas of the previous work. The taking apart and the rearrangement of elements is what enables students to understand the underlying form and meaning. The workings, taken together, constitute a sketchbook, a map of the individual confronting the world and oneself in that world. This map tells students what they thought about the journey, the place, the meeting.

We might also ask students to record in their sketchbooks what they think are the best or worst aspects about other studio work they are doing. We might ask that they list what was discovered in working with a new media, to comment on any surprises that the work produced. While the action of the work is still fresh in mind, we invite students to react, reflect, and retrace the involvement of the work by documenting it. In this sense, the work is personal, reflective, and based on recorded first-hand information.

Quality Time: Expected Student Benefits

Cognitively, the student has gained from sketchbook activity because the sketchbooks give a focus for thought: the ability to fix ideas makes a qualitative difference in terms of thinking. "At first there is a saturation. We find out as much as possible about the problem. Then, we sift, absorb, arrange, and rearrange incoming new information along with previously known 'old' information without ever drawing conclusion. One works on this process for long periods, deeply immersed in seeing, without a sense of time passing. This quality of timelessness permeates all intellectual activity."[12] Then, quite suddenly, the ideas cohere, and the image as a whole resonates, a clear singular idea encompassing all its parts. We become insiders, sharers of the information of the discipline, privy to the special ways of working that characterize an expert rather than an outsider trying to decode what is going on. "As students become observers of their own learning, they become not only more interested and tolerant of their own errors but also better analysts of them. When they write their questions down, they take them more seriously, they try to answer them and make them a part of how they go about solving them."[13]

Furthermore, sketchbooks, through frequent activity, increase time-on-task and add to the quality of that time. Students are often quick to discard their first efforts or to make judgments on the work before there is sufficient work to judge. How often do students wad the paper and toss it, after a few lines in a drawing or after writing or rewriting just a sentence or two? With the sketchbook, students are encouraged to save these initial efforts, which become documentation. One can always add a page or turn to a new page: these provide us with a history to record. Too often we think nothing happens, and yet, each minute is fluid with events. It is, rather, our attention to events that doesn't happen. The sketchbook prompts that attention.

Klauser [1986] has best described this. "Somehow," she says, "an energy comes from keeping such a record, even if you do not go back and pull the information all together and make connections ... just keeping track of what was happening to me and my writing generated energy."[14] The same is true with drawing. With the first marking, drawn from a personal store of images, the material and skills of our lives become the basis for learning as they bolster and nourish our natural desire for curiosity and competence. This was shown so eloquently in Eliot Wigginton's Foxfire experiment recorded in *Sometimes a Shining Moment: The Foxfire Experience* where high school students used the rural communities of Georgia as sources for writing. Those experiences sustain us as we stretch to understand the new ideas and information in our explorations of the discipline.

Because the sketchbook gives us permission, we are free to write or draw. In fact, we are invited to write and draw. Word and image are equally valid tools for clarification. And this combining of the writing and drawing gives further assistance to our ways of thinking. The mix and match of word and image provide us with a store of metaphors from different disciplines, each capable of unlocking or reaffirming the problem under consideration. When we work from the strengths of what we know towards those parts of the discipline base that we don't know, our personal fund of knowledge and ownership is increased.

Both emotionally and cognitively then, sketchbooks fulfill the need to be introspective or reflective. *The New Diary* sites Carl Jung, Marion Milner, Ira Progoff, and Anais Nin as diarists, saying that, "All of them recognize a need in the modern world to reflect calmly upon knowledge that comes from within."[15] Jung drew mandalas, circular geometric patterns, in his notebooks, observing that the patterns changed from day to day in correspondence with his moods and his needs. Milner, in *On Not Being Able to Paint,* stated that free association in drawing was a valid technique for her achieving self-understanding.[16] Through the sketchbook, one is able to examine the singular, one's own actions and motivations, and translate that into future thought. If for no other reason than this, sketchbooks qualify as a valid school activity.

Logistics: Questions to Consider in Assigning Sketchbook Activities

If emotive and cognitive growth are a result of sketchbook or journal activity, the question becomes how might we best utilize sketchbooks in the classroom, and what form will this activity take? There are many questions connected with such an enterprise concerning the use of instructional time. How often should students engage in this activity? What will be the motivating force: need, urgency, or special projects? To what extent do we push to move beyond the personal vignette? When does sketchbook work become a habit of frequent activity? What kinds of personal choices are needed? What kinds of instructional suggestions are needed? For whom and why is this activity to be undertaken? What happens if self-acceptance is stifled, or when anxiety stifles? Finally, can and should this private domain be required to be shared? Many of these questions can be answered only in terms of the importance of this kind of activity as compared to other curricular priorities.

A place to address these issues is in the discussion of form, that is, the nature of the sketchbook. Many factors may influence: factors of time, portability, or use of materials. If we want the activity to be manageable and free from preconceived fears, then we must choose a form in which work may be produced at any time and any place and which is different from or more simple than other classroom materials. For our exercises, we have chosen a specific but often used structure, that of image and word intermingled on blank sheets of paper. Singular blank pages are chosen because of their similarity to self: a continuous, non-divided structure whose sum total is composed of any parts one picks up. The idea that there are no dates or sections within self, that time and task is thus subjectively long or short, fast or slow, come from *The New Diary*.[17] There is also a linear time manifest in our work, as continuity and the unfolding process are the intents of the sketchbook activity. The end result is a concrete structure: a sketchbook that is sustained over a period of time.

117

The Importance of Connecting Image With Word: An Answer

The idea that image and word should be combined has many sources. First, there is the belief that creativity and intellectual engagement needs a rich variety of data from many sources in order to fund the imaginative store. Wilson, Hurwitz, and Wilson [1987] suggest that creative endeavors are not so much inborn as they are achieved by a mix and match of the existing elements of the world which reaffirm the importance of discipline-based art learning.[18] Image and word, both in historical models and in the student's emerging works, are two sources for this data of the world.

Historically, voice and vision, word and image, text and graphic have been brought together to share a whole idea; some form of book has been the most frequent container. Most formal meaning comes from encounters between the two. Each information form contributes to the knowledge and understanding we have of the world, and each has its own contribution to make to the vocabulary and mental resources of the individual.

Images display a rich fabric for words to operate in because they are retained by the mind's eye longer than mere verbal descriptions. Images serve as illustrations; they are works in their own right. Images give a richness to language and a power by involving our senses in the experience. They allow us to judge the message based upon its arrangement in the composition.[19] Words, on the other hand, focus attention on elements that are essential. They eliminate clutter. They add to the strength of an image, and occasionally present a picture more rapidly and in smaller space than pictorial elements would have. In talking or writing about a drawing, the artist is able to show ideas, identify problems, and even display joy in the work in a form that everyone can understand.

Making and reading images, then, is not just a series of technical exercises. Both have intellectual activity as their foundation. To translate gestures, sounds, and configurations into a spatial or symbolic system, to make a drawing from a host of idiosyncratic information embedded in memory is to respond cognitively.

Combined, we see that word and image are different threads of the same fabric: punctuation and composition are ways of spacing thought; spelling is a way of looking at a word; sentences and thumbnail sketches are

118

IDEAS FOR SCENES:

DOOR

SUPPORT BARS

SLIGHTLY AJAR

collections of images that retell; images form compositional narratives and give us a sense of the whole before we can name it.

In a sense, an architectural structure is shared by images and words. Point of view is revealed through an examination of voice or tone, cultural embellishments, focus and attention. Just as the artist crops his picture, so does the writer as he creates characters or stories so big they will not be confined to the page. Often a character will dominate to the extent that events of his life are told as footnote.

Both word and image rely on a culturally specific symbolic vocabulary. Yet, each has its own signature: predictable regularities in context or style. As Betty Edwards [1986] has pointed out, drawing is not syntactical, not like the orderly, grammatical rules of language; but just as language has a certain way for words, phrases, and clauses to be put together, so too paintings require rules of color, harmony, or design.[20]

Finally, both depend upon re-combinations for their final form. For example, Picasso regenerates elements of African art, and Andrew Lloyd Webber revives T. S. Elliots' obscure cat poems as a musical play. Both create new images and invite us to again examine forms previously neglected. Thematic ideas are revisited as well as reinvented. They guide us to a new way of seeing ideas. A combination of the two produces a further desirable outcome; both word and image are made stronger by one being placed alongside the other. This placement causes preconceptions to diminish. It can be used to imagine one's self in another's predicament, physical location, or using a style of drawing. This interchange of modality between writing and drawing was noted by Gauguin, who began his intimate journal with the phrase "this is not a book." According to the *New Diary*, he repeated the line frequently throughout the journal to remind himself that writing a diary was not like writing a book or any other form of literature. He wanted to write his diary as he painted his pictures: dabbing a few experimental colors at first, adding more as his intuition told him to follow his fancy, "following the mood," discovering the pattern from what had occurred by chance.[21] It is from this cross-over that we are able to acknowledge the value of each element. M. C. Richards [1966] says," ... the writer may acknowledge the material aspect of his craft and the craftsman may acknowledge the soul-force emanating from his objects. The writer then takes into himself the craftsman's feeling of 'forming,' and the hand craftsman takes into himself the writer's feeling of 'uttering'.[22]

Thought in one word or image, triggers thought in the other. When image and word are interconnected, a pull is created in which words compete with images for clarity. Non-conscious juxtapositions sometimes produce startling combinations. This tension calls for resolution and demands a thinking through of the original premise stated by both. A Wallace Stevens poem read in conjunction with a Robert Mangold abstract painting requires closure. Does the abstract become imbued with the familiar, or does the poem change significantly to become vignettes? The question confronts us when both are viewed together. The question invites action in the sketchbook.

Conclusions: Why We Need Sketchbooks

In conclusion, is there then a place for sketchbook activity in discipline-based art education? It would seem so, with the unique contribution of this activity being that of uniting the personal dimension of discovery and reflection with specific cognitive exercises in which students attend to and expand the disciplines of art. Sketchbook activity encourages respect for the students' own unfolding process, causing them to have a personal interest in meaning making. It also creates a context that holds on to emerging thought and understanding and uses existing disciplines as a reflective mirror against which individual thought is played. Students are able to find both an expanded mode of perception and an affirmation for their way of thinking and working. They find models of these ways of coming to know art in the historical, critical, and creative performances recorded in the various art disciplines. Both their idiosyncratic answers and the shared understanding of critical and historical knowledge become valid. The resultant writing and image making embrace and expand the culture we share.

The sketchbook is distinct from any other form of art work, bridging drawing and writing, bridging thought and experimentation in media, and bridging the personal and the discipline sources. It is not so much that we teach the subject, but we teach a student to find the subject, the valid subject being that which has connection to the content of the discipline: that body of knowledge, objects, writings, images, and techniques that we deem culturally significant. What we as educators generate in the classroom setting is a culturally appropriate time and place in which students are best able to pursue knowledge of their own invention, flair, and appropriateness. It is their right and responsibility to conceive of their own solutions.

Notes

[1] A sketchbook in the extended form that we are advocating has elements to it that may be characteristic of a diary, a journal, a scrapbook, a sketchbook, a notebook, or a calendar. Some artists have referred to this extended form as daybook

[2] Taylor R., *Educating for art*. London: Longman Group UK Limited, p. 46. Taylor calls a critical event an "Illuminating Experience."

[3] Polanyi, M. (1958) *Personal knowledge,* Chicago: University of Chicago Press. We agree with Polanyi who "... regard[s] knowing as an active comprehension of the things known, an action that requires skill. Skillful knowing and doing is performed by subordinating a set of particulars, as clues or tools to the shaping of a skillful achievement, whether practical or theoretical."

[4] Tobias, S. (Winter 1988): Insiders and outsiders, *Academic Connections,* 1.

[5] Feldman, E. (1970). *Becoming human through art* (Englewood Cliffs, New Jersey: Prentice Hall), p. 196.

[6] Rainer, F. *The new diary*. Los Angeles: Jeremy P. Tarcher, Inc., p. 18

[7] *Ibid.*, p. 292.

[8] *Ibid.*

[9] Mallon, p. 15. [An example, that Mallon points out, is what the 18th century British Parson Woodford's diaries revealed that the war between France and Britain touches his life but little. References to the war were practically non-existent or lost in a piling up of "dinner today of boiled chicken and a pig's face and some beef steaks.]

[10] Wigginton, E. (1985). *Sometimes a shining moment: The foxfire experience,* (Garden City, New York: Anchor Press), p. 209.

[11] We appreciate this suggestion from Susan Farmer, Assistant Professor, University of Wisconsin-Madison.

[12] Edwards, B. (1986). *Drawing on the artist within,* New York, Simon and Schuster, p. 36, 40, 134.

[13] Tobias, p. 5.

[14] Klauser, H. A. (1986). *Writing on both sides of the brain,* (Boston: Shambhala), p. 22.

[15] Rainer, p. 21.

[16] *Ibid,* pp. 22-23.

[17] *Ibid,* p. 31.

[18] Wilson, B., Hurwitz, A., Wilson, M. (1987). *Teaching drawing from art*. Worchester, Massachusetts: Davis Publications, Inc., p. 12.

[19] *Ibid.*, p. 160.

[20] Edwards, p. 43.

[21] Rainer, p. 28.

[22] Richards, M. C. (1966). *The crossing point*. Middletown CT: Wesleyan University Press, p. 16. [M. C. Richards often includes poems, music, change of colors of ink in the printing of the text, and photographs to expand and enrich the meanings of her writings.]

Bibliography

Berger, J. (1973). *Ways of seeing*. London: the British Broadcasting Company and Penguin Books.

Edwards, B. (1986). *Drawing on the artist within*. New York: Simon and Schuster.

Elbow, P. (1973). *Writing without teachers*. London: Oxford University Press.

Feldman, E. (1970). *Becoming human through art*. Englewood Cliffs, New Jersey: Prentice Hall.

Fink, M. (1981) *Drawing with words: A studio concept of composition*. Landham, Md.: University Press of America.

Goldberg, N. (1986). *Writing down the bones*. Boston: Shambhala.

Klauser, H. (1986). *Writing on both sides of the brain*. San Francisco: Harper and Row.

Mallon, T. (1986). *A book of one's own: People and their diaries*. New York, New York: Penguin Books.

Polanyi, (1958). *Personal knowledge*. Chicago: University of Chicago Press.

Rainer, T. (1978). *The new diary*. Los Angeles: Jeremy P. Tarcher, Inc.

Richards, M. C. (1966). *The crossing point*. Middletown, Connecticut: Wesleyan University Press.

Rico, G. L. (1983). *Writing the natural way*. Los Angeles: J. P. Tarcher, Inc.

Taylor, R. (1986). *Educating for art, critical response and development*. London: Longman Group UK Limited.

Tobias, S. (1988, Winter). Insiders and outsiders. *Academic Connections*, 1-5.

Wigginton, E. (1985). *Sometimes a shining moment: The foxfire experience*. Garden City, New York: Anchor Press, Doubleday.

Wilson, B., Hurwitz, A., and Wilson, M. (1987). *Teaching drawing from art*. Worcester, Massachusetts: Davis Publications, Inc.

10

Computers in Art Education

DEBORAH GREH

St. John's University
Jamaica, N.Y.

For some ten years computers have been in our schools. Although art educators are quick to adjust and adapt to innovation and change, computers have yet to gain wide acceptance or usage in art education. There are as many reasons for our hesitency to explore this new medium as there are students in our classrooms. Some may be apprehensive of the technology itself; machines are foreign to them. Others may agree with Ken Knowlton (1987) who notes that works on computers" ... are not beyond the gee-whiz stage of cuteness and stunts and novelty for its own sake." There are, however, a great number of art educators who are anxious to try computers in their classroom, but are not quite sure what it is computers can do, and how they might be used within the art curriculum.

What computers may do is present artist, art teacher, and student artist with the possibility of expanding artistic vision, of watching ideas grow, and of playing with and integrating images. Computers provide many students with a non-threatening environment in which to play with images ... risk free. In that respect, they prompt some of the very essential elements of creativity, play, and experimentation.

What Computers Can Do: A Rationale

The Computer as Medium

Works created on computers are being increasingly recognized as an art form; they can be seen in galleries and museums throughout the country. Art education strives to give students a breadth of experience in a variety of

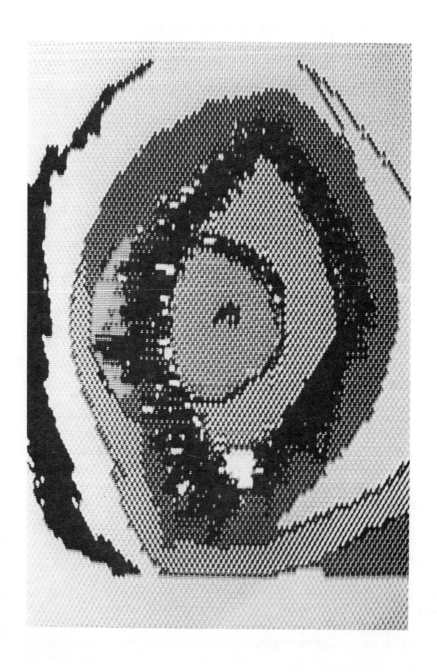

media, as well as depth in one or more. On this argument alone, computers can be established as a medium for study. The argument certainly cannot stop there. Students confront computer imagery daily. The use of computers in the creation of various visual effects in film and video warrants that students explore computers images and become critical evaluators of them. These visual forms require critical appraisal; the new medium must be explored. Further, these images might best be explored from the perspective of creation as well as criticism.

Some would suggest that with computers anyone can become an artist. This is a dangerous statement and far from true. Although a variety of software packages have made some artistic skills more accessible (for example, the formation of a line, circle, rectangle), ease of production does not guarantee artistic creation. However, the availability of various graphics libraries allows computer users to incorporate many more graphic representations of ideas or concepts than may have been previously possible. These libraries are available in software application programs, spanning data bases, animation, sign making and drawing or paint programs.

What these developments may suggest is that there is an ever growing need for students to explore the imaging potentials of computers, and become evaluators of the resulting images. Computers do not create art, nor do they ensure artistic creation. Rather, they may have made the images of the artist more accessible. The implications seem to be that computers should be used in art classrooms as a medium, and the resulting images, whether created through programming, paint programs, or graphics libraries, should become a subject for critical discussion and analysis.

The Computer as Playground

Play is an important part of freeing creativity. Computers may encourage playing with ideas and images, and for that reason are of value in art education. Powerful commands, like "fill and undo", make it possible for students to quickly and easily create components of larger images. They also allow students to combine and recombine shapes, lines, colors, and forms in a variety of ways. Students can play with visual relationships knowing that if the introduction of some part of an image is unsuccessful, whether it be a simple line or major color fill, they may "undo" it. Thus, students will play with images more freely, encouraging a fuller exploration of their imaging abilities and imagination.

127

When presented with paper and pencil, students often fall into two categories. First, there are those who do not think before they draw or sketch, but rather commit immediately to paper, saving judgment until the work is near completion. Second, there are those students who visualize many alternatives before they will commit to paper. Computers allow for both types. With the commercial software presently available, students can save their drawings and/or designs in stages of development. If a particular section of a work is not successful, or if an addition to a picture is not what a student hoped for, it may be deleted entirely or in part without altering the original idea or image. The student who settles for the first rendition of a drawing can return to the original and make adjustments. The student who must visualize before committing to paper will feel freer to use computers because it will allow him/her to save the work in process. Being able to make changes without endangering the image is a powerful stimulus to experimentation.

Creating on the computer does not seem to impose the feeling of permanence and finality to the degree that paper, pencil, or brush do. This is not to suggest that students view works on the computer as disposable; they do not. However, they do approach the computer as one would a sketch pad, where ideas can be tested and explored. If students are encouraged to save even their most playful images, they can be referred to and used in the development of finished works.

Risk Taking

Computers encourage risk taking because with computers many of the hazards involved in working with traditional media are removed. The ability to take risks is closely associated with the concept of play, yet there are different attributes. Playing with ideas is how great ideas begin. However, once an idea is more concretely formulated, students approach the creation or completion of an image with more determination and precision. For many, this determined approach negates the introduction of a variant or new idea, for fear of endangering or destroying the original concept.

With computers, students may save their images in various stages of completion. If a new idea or element is suggested, it can be introduced to the

128

screen without fear of endangering the original image. Experimentation with color, line, and form takes on a new "risk free" dimension, allowing students to explore a variety of alternatives before bringing a work to conclusion.

Repetitive Tasks

There are a number of traditional concepts in art education which are best accomplished if they are explored via a single drawing or design. One can best see the effects of color on an image if one explores variations in color on the same image. However, students tire quickly of drawing and redrawing the same image a number of times. Computers can ease some of the drudgery of this repetitive task by allowing students to save an initial image and recall it to the screen an infinite number of times. Thus, students can experiment with a number of color studies without the drudgery of redrawing an image for each study. Designs or segments of designs can be saved to allow the student-artist to push or rework a design or drawing in a number of alternative ways without losing the original sketch or idea. In like fashion, thicknesses of line can be tested; positive and negative space can be explored.

The Process of Creating

In the development of technical skills as well as critical and analytical skills, art educators often find that they are forced to deal with a student's final product, rather than the development, or process of an image through various stages of development.

Computers allow students to save their work in steps or stages, providing teachers and students opportunities to explore, not only the final product, but the process and decisions that the student/artist has made in reaching that final image. Images can be discussed, analyzed, and even experimented with. Criticism then, is not only reserved for the final product, when students are reluctant to make changes, but may be made on the way to that final product ... all the "what ifs" can be answered.

Class size often limits the amount of time an art teacher can spend with individual students. Assignments are often finished before the teacher has

130

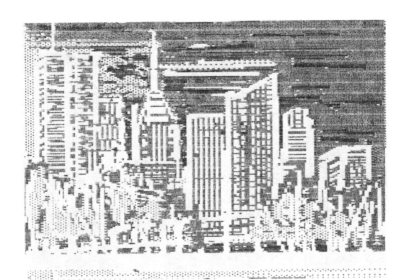

had an opportunity to offer suggestions and present alternative solutions to the visual representation. Rarely does the teacher ever see the full process of an idea unfold. If students are encouraged to save their computer images in stages, and if they become accustomed to doing so, one can literally see an image unfold such as where and when decisions to use a line, or color, or other element were made. Teacher and student are afforded the opportunity to observe an idea in process.

Redefining Artistic Talent

For most students, artistic talent is defined by a person's ability to render objects with traditional realism. Many avoid art courses because they assume that since they cannot "draw", they are not artists. When using computers, students seem to come to an understanding that there is much more to artistic talent than the ability to render objects realistically; traditional representation is only one aspect of creativity and artistic skill. Computers allow students to explore design, composition, and color freely. They seem to learn quickly that careful placement of images is important, that there are other media that also define artistic talent, and that artistic sensibilities go beyond work with pencil and brush. Computers, with commands that allow students to draw "perfect ovals" and "straight lines without a ruler," may open the world of art to a number of students who assumed they had no artistic talent and, therefore, no business being in an art course.

Working With Abstraction

Young children seem to have a wonderful sense of play, and often appreciate abstraction. Clearly, this is a subjective emotional response, but one that children lose as they approach their teens As stated earlier, most students see traditional realism as the only "true art," having little respect for design and abstraction. The limitations of computers (such as low-resolution, limited color, and cumbersome input devices) seem to force students into an exploration of design and abstraction they might normally avoid in traditional courses. Objects cannot be rendered accurately; color is limited; shading difficult. Students tend toward design work, using broad areas of color, and geometrically based images. They seem to attend to the more abstract properties, such as the form, composition, force, and tension

132

found in images. Discussions are centered around the nonrepresentational qualities of images, rather than the accuracy of detail and skill of rendering. They neither attempt realism in their creation of images, nor try to find representational objects in finished works. Further, this appreciation for abstraction seems to carry over to works done in traditional media.

Teacher as Student

Many teachers who have begun an exploration of the computer as an artistic tool note that as they become learners again, they become better teachers as well. Most art teachers using computers are self-taught. With limited resources and educational opportunities, they have consulted popular computing journals or drawn from the interest of a family member, colleague, or student. Aware that they do NOT have all the answers, teachers are learning WITH their students. For many, there has been a rekindled love of teaching; there is an energy and excitement one cannot discount.

Computers in the Art Curriculum.

It seems clear that many art teachers, though operating in isolated pockets throughout the country, are attempting to explore the possibilities of computers within the curriculum. However, with no guidelines available, they are drawing from instinct based on experience. This is not to discount the validity of curriculum development based on experience; it may well be the best source for realistic goals. In fact, many of us revise and develop our curriculum as needs change. Certainly, however, a foundation based on principles of art education is needed.

Art educators are facing serious decisions that may determine the future role of computers within art education. Successfully incorporating the computer within the art curriculum demands a clear understanding of the goals and objectives of the department. It is also necessary that art teachers understand what computers are capable of and how to use computers to their fullest capabilities.

McCulloch (1984) has observed" ... the introduction of computers in the art program should not replace current methodologies, but should be an extension of the creative process employed in any valid art instruction" (p. 46). Jeffers (1986) has reinforced McCulloch's views noting that art teachers, like all teachers, need to ask certain questions when planning lessons and determining appropriate uses for the wonders of technology. Can objectives be attained without technology? What is it that only electronic machinery can do for a lesson, as opposed to other teaching tools? Ettinger (1988), has noted that computers "can not simply be plugged into existing programs." (p. 60) While I agree with these authors, and share their concerns, it seems clear that although computers may change what we teach and how we teach, teachers will and probably should begin by incorporating computers into an existing curriculum. Once one begins to explore the capabilities of the new technology, new approaches and new curriculum will evolve.

Personal Observations and Student Response

All this being said, what exactly have students done on computers? What does their work look like? What have they learned? Is there a difference? The following observations are based on six years of working with high school students using computers in the art room.

Form and Content of Students' Work

The majority of works done by my students on computers are based on geometric designs. As noted earlier, limitations of computers inhibit traditional attempts at realism or renderings of objects. However, the menu commands available, such as line, frame, and oval, provide students with quick and easy placement of the basic elements of design, promoting easy design experimentation.

When students go beyond design work to create more traditional works, the content of these images are not significantly different from those done with traditional media. For example, students' works often include landscapes, butterflies, dragons, cars, and so forth. More often works are cartoon images and outlined forms filled with color. They are simple images with minimal detail and little attempt to suggest depth. Only the more creative students explore depth and detail, and work with the textures and brush strokes available. Clearly, computers do not replace artistic talent.

In general, one might conclude that although the content of students' works is not significantly different, students do seem to develop a sensitivity and appreciation for nonrepresentational design, particularly geometric design works.

Student Response to the Computer as Medium

The majority of student response to using computers is favorable. When students were asked to explain why they enjoy using computers, they noted they work faster and play more when using computers; their work is risk free so they experiment more with ideas and images; and computers are ideal for people who can't draw but are creative. As one senior noted: " ... the computer is great for people who can't draw but are creative ... granted, art is not a game, but that's where it starts sometimes."

Many students have commented that they had been hesitant to take an art course because they felt they lacked the necessary drawing and technical skills needed to create art. They enrolled in a computer art course because they assumed that the computer was going to somehow create art images for them. I am reminded of similar experiences with students in photography. The shared element is that both computer art and photography are machine mediated. In other words, students do not have the same hesitation at using computers or cameras that they might have when using pencil or brush. They can attribute unsuccessful results to the camera, the film, or the paper. When using computers, unsuccessful images are attributed to computer limitations. For teenagers in particular, machine mediated studio experiences seem to provide a shelter for apparent deficiencies in skill, training, and aesthetic sensibilities. Further, students gain confidence in themselves and in their artistic abilities.

Computers seem to provide students with an environment that promotes the development of creativity. Students who enjoy playing with computers are really playing with ideas and imagery. If they do not have technical drawing skills, they can use menu commands such as frame, oval, or line, or stored shapes to create their works. Further, students with no art background have created many dynamic images with the use of these commands and dramatic color and textures.

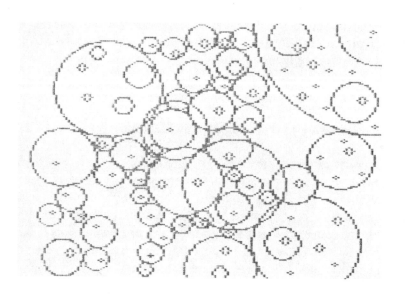

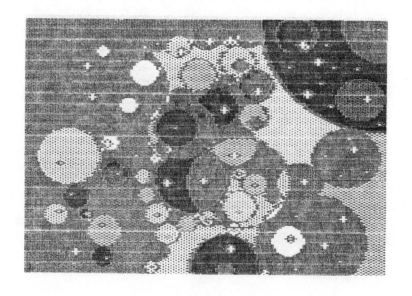

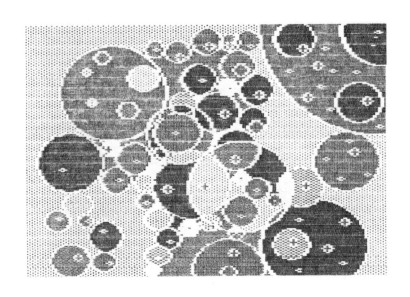

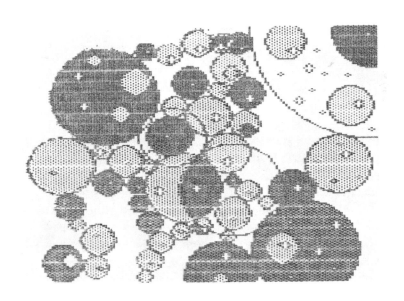

137

It is interesting, but perhaps not surprising, to note that students with an extensive art background sometimes look disparagingly at computers, while students with little or no background are usually quite enthusiastic about their accomplishments. I suspect that the limitations described earlier are a source of frustration to more experienced students who have gained some level of mastery in one or more media.

Observations of Students Working with Computers

Many students who elect to work with computers are initially enchanted by the mystique of the machine; they have based their ideas of computer images on those seen in arcade games or in video. These students are quickly frustrated by the size of the screen, manipulative abilities of input devices, screen resolution, and color capabilities. Once these limitations are recognized, most students are quick to adapt, and regain any lost enthusiasm.

Many students have the misconception that the only mark of artistic talent is the ability to render objects skillfully with pencil or paint. They do not realize that there are a variety of facets to creativity which do not require technical drawing skills. Computers offer the advantage of menu commands and graphic libraries which place previously defined shapes and images on the screen. Using stored images provides students who have limited drawing skills with opportunities to experiment with the placement of images and words, or to create a completed work based on these images; with some encouragement, most eventually design and create original works. Students who had never taken a studio art course often find that they have creative abilities.

With a limited visual vocabulary to refer to, students must visually experiment with elements of a work to have a real understanding of the effects of one element upon another. As noted earlier, with traditional media this can be a long and tedious task that may alter the intended effect of an image. Computers allow for easy manipulation of many design elements at little or no risk. I have seen students using computers approach their work with a daring and freedom not seen with more traditional media; they explore more, testing a variety of options before making final decisions. Computers seem to provide students with an environment where they can experiment and play with ideas and relationships of design elements. Further, they seem to respect the necessity of play and experimentation more than students in traditional art clases. Students spend more time on preliminary experimentation with ideas than those working in traditional media. Although these comments are based on observation alone and have not been measured, it seems that students may also use different, perhaps more analytic thinking skills in the creation of computer images, particularly when they attempt animation. They learn the necessity of planning and predicting movement and motion because their works must unfold in time and space.

The boldness and vitality of student images tempts me to say that they exceed the quality of imagery produced by most first year design students in any medium. One might suggest these works are exceptions. However, looking at the larger body of works created by students on computers in the last five years, and comparing those images to those done in traditional media, I am convinced that more students seem to push their ideas farther and with a boldness I have not seen before. Moreover, when working on design projects, students produce more works by using computers than by using traditional media. Certainly, more does not mean better; however, because there is more experimentation and playing with images, students seem to develop stronger compositional skills and carry these skills over to traditional media.

As previously stated, when students save images in stages of development, teacher and student can explore the development of works as they unfold on screen. Criticism does not have to be reserved for the final product alone, but can follow the decisions students make on arriving at that final product. This allows for an exploration of artistic decisions, and experimentation with alternative solutions. Critical discussion is not restricted to teacher and student; in fact, a sense of teamwork often develops. Students often gather around a student's monitor to offer help or suggestions, and these suggestions can be tested quickly and easily. From my observation, the computer promotes a sense of teamwork and cooperation that often does not exist in other media.

Looking to the Future

While present day computers have serious limitations (the screen is too small; the resolution is too low for smooth lines and well defined images; the color variation is limited on most monitors, and the variations of color between monitors can be significant), these shortcomings will gradually be overcome as the higher technology workstations and computers now available to industry migrate into education. The following developments seem probable.

- The cost of computers will continue to fall, and the memory of computers and graphics capabilities will increase; more color and color mixing will be available in computers schools can afford.

- There will be an increased ability to record the process of creation, and a capacity for merging and expanding images with other communication technologies.

- Monitors with greater resolution on significantly larger screens will be available. This will provide better use of computers for artists' works and for demonstration, and it will also allow for larger image and larger and larger movement of line and arrangement of shape and form in space.

- Printers will be able to produce exact copies of the images on screen.

- Software will continue to be developed that will not only be user friendly, but will include the development of input devices which can be manipulated like more artists' tools.

- Optical disk technologies, including videodisc and CDs, with their vast storage capabilities of visual images will provide teachers with access to literally thousands of reproductions of art works.

- Hypermedia will provide a new way to create and access information, allowing the user to access and link information.

- The development of optical technologies and software which can "read" the visual images will allow for the interactivity of students with computer images and/or the works of artists stored on disk. The computer could also be used as a catalyst for student works, introducting selected or random design elements from which students might alter shape and form to bring it to some aesthetic conclusions. Other applications might include computer assisted instruction and teacher demonstrations.

- The continual development of optical disk technologies and hypermedia will change the concept of interactivity, and alter the very process of

140

creating and playing with images. At the very least they will challenge educators to alter the way we approach teaching.

Final Thoughts

Although computers may promote some artistic activities, they are not a substitute for artistic talent; as Nam June Paik noted (Gardner, 1984) "Art is what artists do." Talented students who have worked on computers usually create interesting images. However, computers may offer the possibility of developing creative talents in students who do not perceive themselves as possessing the technical skills associated with artistic endeavors. Computers seem to provide an environment in which students may explore their ideas freely and push them to a variety of conclusions.

The limitations of personal computers used in schools at the present time may inhibit their use in the creation of finished art works. However, even with the current limitations, computers seem to be particularly useful in exploring design principles and in promoting a sensitivity and appreciation for abstract geometric design. At the very least then, computers and optical disk technologies offer an alternative medium for students to explore and with which to learn. Moreover, their greater advantage may lie in areas just beginning to be explored; in opening the world of art to students who otherwise may not have entered, in promoting a variety of artistic sensibilities that often are left untapped, and in allowing teacher and student together to follow the process and development of a work through to completion.

Bibliography

For More Information on Computers and Related Technologies:

Anderson, F. (1985). Electronic media, videodisc technology, and the visual arts. *Studies in Art Education, 26*(4), 224-231.
Bernstein, S. & McGarry, L. (1986). *Making art on your computer.* New York: Watson Guptill Publications.
Brouch, G. (1986). Microcomputer survey report. *NAEA News, 28*(6), 8-10.
Clements, R. (1985). Adolescents' computer art. *Art Education, 38*(2), 6-9.
D'Angelo, J. (1989). Computers for art teachers. *Art Education, 41*950, 41-44.
Deken, J. (1983). *Computer images: State of the art.* New York: Stewart, Tabori & Chang Publishers, Inc.

Ettinger L. & Roland C. (1986). Using microcomputers in the art curriculum. *Art Education, 39*(1), 48-51.

Ettinger, L. (1988). Art education and computing: Building a perspective. *Studies in Art Education, 30*(1), 53-62.

Gardner, P. (1984, April 22). Think of Leonardo wielding a pixel and a mouse. The New York Times, pp. 1, 13.

Gregory, D. (1989). Hypermedia: Laser video-audio technology and art education. *Art Education, 42*(1), 66-69.

Greh, D. (1986). Technology and art. *Electronic Learning, 5*(4), 29-37.

Greh, D. (1990). Computers in the artroom. Worcester, MA: Davis Publications.

Greh, D. (1986). Using computers in secondary art education. *Art Education, 39*(6), 4-9.

Hubbard, G. & Linehan, T. (1983). Arcade games, mindstorms, and art education. *Art Education, 36*(3), 18-20.

Hubbard, G. (1985). Computer literacy and the art program. *Art Education, 38*(2), 15-18.

Hubbard, G. (1989). Hypermedia: Cause for optimism in art curriculum design. *Art Education, 42*(1), 58-64.

Jeffers, C. (1986). The electronic revolution. *School Arts, 85*(7), 38-39.

Knowlton, K. (1987). Why it isn't art yet. *Computer Graphics, 21*(1), 11.

Leavitt, R. (1976). *Artist and computer.* New York: Harmony Books.

Madeja, S. (1983). Computer graphics: The new subject matter for the art curriculum. *Art Education, 36*(3), 15-18.

McCulloch, D. (1984). A change of image: Computers in the art room. *Art Education, 37*(4) 44-46.

Pauler-Stovall, D. (1985). A computer art station in the artroom. *School Arts, 85*(6), 19-22.

Phelan, A. (1984). The impact of technology and post modern art on studio art education. *Art Education, 37*(2), 30-36.

Phillipo, J. (1988). An educators' guide to interactive videodisc programs. *Electronic Learning 8*(1), pp. 70-75.

Prueitt, M. (1984). *Art and the computer.* New York: McGraw Hill.

St. Lawrence, J. (1984) The interactive videodisc here at last. *Electronic Learning, 3*(7), 49-54.

Truckenbrod, J. (1986, August). [Computer graphics opens artistic options: Interview with Joan Truckenbrod]. *Computer Graphics Today,* pp. 4, 23.

White, D. (1983). Advanced technology, art, and art education: Reaching toward the third millennium. *Art Education, 36*(3), 8-10.

White, D. (1985). Creating microcomputer graphics with the koala pad. *Art Education, 38(2), 10-14.*

11
Health Hazards in Secondary Art Education

SALLY HAGAMAN

Purdue University

There are many potential health hazards in middle school, junior, and senior high school art classes. The art teacher is at particular risk, not only from hazardous materials and procedures themselves, but also from the possibility of being sued by an injured student. Hence, it is imperative that every art teacher at the secondary level become aware of potential health risks and means for minimizing them in the art classroom.

How Hazardous Materials Enter the Body

There are three major routes by which hazardous or toxic materials enter the body:

1. **Inhalation** of toxic fumes, dusts, vapors, spray mists, and smoke is hazardous. Some materials, such as sulfur dioxide gas given off by kilns or glacial acetic acid (photographic stop bath), can cause immediate damage to the lining of the airways and lungs. Other materials, like clay dusts, can cause chronic damage which builds slowly over a number of exposures. Generally, the finer the inhaled particle, the more damaging it is. Larger particles are trapped by the mucous membrane of the upper body, but very fine particles travel deep into the lungs. Some inhaled materials, such as turpentine vapors, go beyond the lungs and are carried throughout the body via the bloodstream.

2. **Skin contact** with hazardous materials is a common route of entry to the body. Although the skin is designed to protect the body from injury, its protective ability is greatly or completely destroyed by contact with

substances such as acids, bleaches, and organic solvents. Such substances "de-fat" the outer skin, leaving the skin layers underneath vulnerable to damage. Certain chemicals, such as turpentine, toluene, and methyl alcohol, actually go deeper, entering the bloodstream and thus traveling through the entire body.

3. **Ingestion** of toxic materials may be direct or indirect through mouth contact with hands, pencils, food, or cigarettes which have come into contact with such materials. Adolescents, like younger children or adults for that matter, may be apt to chew on a fingernail or point a paintbrush with their lips, thus allowing ingestion of hazardous material.

Risk Factors

There are several factors which help determine how damaging contact with toxic materials may be. Quantity is important: How much of such a material are you exposed to? For how long? How often? Limited exposure to hazardous materials is less likely to cause injury than repeated exposure. Here we see the enhanced risk for the art teacher in a classroom contaminated with toxic substances. Students come and go throughout the day, but the teacher suffers repeated exposure to such substances. There are many reported cases of severe bronchitis and chemically induced pneumonia among art teachers in daily contact with clay dusts and/or toxic vapors.

"Total body burden" is another risk factor. If one is using ceramic glazes with lead, the total exposure from that lead source must be added to all other environmental exposures to lead, as from car exhaust or water carried through lead pipes. This cumulative amount of lead is the total body burden for that substance, and it may leave little room for additional exposure without severe effects.

Combinations of different chemical substances can cause increased harm. For instance, the inhalation of toxic vapors by someone who smokes creates a much greater risk of injury than for a non-smoker. Likewise, contact with a volatile solvent by someone who also ingests alcohol is more dangerous than for the non-drinker. Whether we care to admit it, we know that at least a portion of secondary students do smoke, drink, and ingest drugs. There is also an increased risk for students who are under prescribed medication for the occurence of combined or synergistic effects with toxic substances.

Finally, certain groups are at greater personal risk than others. At the typical secondary level, those high risk groups include people with allergies, smokers, drinkers, pregnant girls or women, people with chronic heart, lung, or liver problems, and mainstreamed students with various learning disabilities, emotional problems, or other handicaps. Actually, all children and adolescents fit within the high risk category for two major reasons. First, their bodies tend to be smaller and lighter than those of adults, making them more susceptible to hazardous materials. They are still growing and have faster metabolisms than adults, so any toxic substance enters and travels through their body more quickly, with greater potential for serious harm from even a relatively small exposure. Second, children and adolescents may be less able to understand fully and follow correct procedures with potentially hazardous materials or processes. Certainly a fetus carried by a pregnant secondary student is subject to enormous harm through the mother's contact with toxic substances, especially in the first trimester of pregnancy when, unfortunately, the teacher may have no knowledge of the condition. All of these risk factors make it very important for secondary art teachers to eliminate as many health hazards as possible from the art classroom.

Common Toxic Materials and Processes

Many art materials and techniques that teachers learned to use during their own education are surprisingly dangerous. We do tend to teach as we have been taught, so some of these dangerous processes are transferred intact into the secondary art class.

It is becoming easier, however, for art teachers to determine which art materials are safe for use with students. Those materials which bear the AP or CP seals of approval (from the Arts and Crafts Materials Institute) are toxicologist certified safe for use with children (and no other art materials should be used with children under the age of 12, in the view of this writer). Other art materials may state that they are "non-toxic" on their labels, however, this claim does not necessarily mean that they have been tested for chronic, long-term effects. The CL seal of the Arts and Crafts Materials Institute means that these products have their potential acute (immediate) and chronic (long-term) hazards listed on the label. Such products are often suitable for secondary use, if correct precautions are taken. Art teachers should be wary of materials purchased in bulk and re-packaged for sale by a "middle man." Such repackaging rarely includes needed safety or ingredient information.

Such a restriction to AP or CP approved products is fine for the elementary level, but most junior and senior high art teachers want to offer more exciting and challenging media and techniques to their students. It is important to realize the potential risks in such offerings and minimize them as in the following examples:

1. **Ceramics** poses several health hazards. The clay itself can be toxic, especially if it contains large amounts of crystalline-free silica (SiO_2). Prolonged inhalation of silica dust or Kaolin dust can lead to silicosis. The talc traditionally found in low-fire clays has often been contaminated with asbestos, a cancer causing substance. Many companies now offer talc-free clay and asbestos-free talcs.

Clay dusts inhalation is most severe when mixing clays, so it is best to order pre-mixed clay. If one does mix clay from powder, use of local exhaust systems and/or toxic dust respirators is advised. The clay dust covered studio is also a problem. Always wet mop or vacuum with a HEPA-type vacuum cleaner. Never sweep in such a situation.

Glazes can be quite toxic, especially if one mixes them. They often contain silica, flint, talc, feldspar and the like, and, in addition, potentially hazardous metals like lead, barium, and lithium. (Lead frits reduce but do not eliminate the hazards of lead poisoning). Some glazes contain colorants which may cause cancer, like chromium, nickel compounds, zinc chromate, iron chromate, manganese, cadmium, and vanadium. Toxic dust respirators should be worn when mixing glazes; spraying of glazes should only be done in a spray booth exhausted to the outside; and students should be instructed to keep glazes off hands and skin (especially where small cuts increase toxic entry).

Firing ceramic kilns releases toxic fumes and gases. All kilns *must* be well ventilated. Canopy hood systems are the best ventilation solution.

One should not look unprotected into the peephole of a kiln. Such action over a number of years may cause cataracts, due to the infrared radiation produced when objects within the kiln reach very high temperatures.

Infrared goggles should be used to protect the eyes.

2. **Painting** may pose health problems depending upon the types of pigments and vehicles used. Some inorganic pigments in common use, such as the chromate and cadmium pigments, may be carcinogenic (cancer-causing). Lamp black has been found to cause skin cancer, and the dangers of lead pigments are well documented.

Acrylic emulsions contain small amounts of ammonia and formaldehyde which may cause lung and throat irritations without use of proper ventilation, and may cause allergic reactions in some people.

Turpentine and especially solvents for varnishes (methyl alcohol and ethanol) and lacquers (toulene and perhaps glycol ethers) are very toxic and should only be used with extreme caution and proper ventilation. The least toxic solvents are acetone, denatured alcohol, isopropyl alcohol, and mineral spirits.

3. **Printmaking** involves a range of risks, depending upon the method employed. The use of solvents in silk screen printing affords multiple, prolonged exposure. Local exhaust ventilation is required to prevent a dangerous accumulation of toxic vapors. It is highly preferable to use water-based inks for all silk screening (and other printmaking as well).

The major dangers in intaglio and lithography are in the acids and etches. Acids may cause severe burns. Etching copper or zinc gives off highly toxic gases that may, in large exposures, cause chemical pneumonia or, in repeated, smaller exposures, cause bronchitis or emphysema. Always remember to add acid to water, never the opposite. Students should never mix acid baths. Rubber gloves, aprons, and face protectors should be worn while working with acid. No use of acids should be included in the art program without ventilation hoods in place over the acid baths.

4. **Jewelry** techniques and materials can be quite hazardous. Local ventilation must be provided over welding and soldering areas. Brazing silver can be especially hazardous because the lowest-melting silver solders contain high proportions of cadmium, which may cause chemical pneumonia from a single exposure. One should use cadmium-free silver solders instead. Also, borax fluxes should be used rather than the flouride fluxes commonly used with silver solders. Sparex solutions should be used for cleaning

metals rather than sulfuric acid solutions. Both are toxic due to their acidity but the Sparex solution is less corrosive.

Many copper enamels are lead-based, so teachers should be certain to purchase only the lead-free enamels now available. Heated enamels give off infrared radiation, so infrared goggles should be worn to protect the eyes from injury (as with ceramic kiln usage).

5. **Photography** requires proper ventilation in the processing components, because many of the chemicals required are potentially toxic. The biggest danger is in mixing stock solutions and during this procedure, it is important to wear protective gloves and goggles, as well as maintain adequate ventilation. During processing itself, tongs should always be used so that hands are never put into developer, stop-bath, or fixer.

Kodak recommends at least ten changes of room air per hour for black and white processing. Toning, mixing, and color processing require local exhaust ventilation.

6. **General art materials** often used in drawing or commercial layout may be hazardous. The most obvious of these is rubber cement (and rubber cement thinner) which contains large amounts of highly toxic hexane, a chemical which causes dermatitis, narcosis from inhalation, and possible inflammation/paralysis of the arms and legs from chronic inhalation. Use wax for layouts and substitute other adhesives for other purposes if possible.

Spray fixatives and adhesives are toxic from the inhalation of solvents including toluene, petroleum distillates, and chlorinated hydrocarbons. Spraying should be done outside or in a spray booth ventilated to the outside.

Wax heated for batik or encaustic may be very dangerous. When over-heated, wax decomposes to release formaldehyde and acrolein fumes (this occurs when melting wax and when ironing it out of fabric). Heat wax to the lowest effective temperature. Using a hot plate on a high setting or using an open flame to heat wax may result in flash fires or explosions.

7. **Equipment** used in various art techniques must be carefully maintained and appropriately used. Students should be instructed in the proper use of items such as potters' wheels, papercutters, printing presses, buffers and

grinders, and airbrushes. It is advisable to require that students pass (perhaps at 100%) tests over correct procedures before allowing them to use such equipment. Be certain that all potentially dangerous equipment is labelled as such and cordoned off (if possible) from the general student population.

Hazards to Teachers

As explained earlier, the risks of health hazards in art class are twofold for teachers: they risk damaging their own health, and they risk legal action on behalf of the student injured while under their supervision. A careful evaluation of potential hazards can reduce both kinds of risks. One may be using materials unsafely if any of the following symptoms develop: dizziness, blurred vision, loss of appetite, breathing difficulties, or repeated bouts with sore throats or coughs. If such symptoms persist, one should see a physician, making sure to inform him or her of any potentially toxic materials used.

Legal liability may be reduced by minimizing the introduction of potentially toxic materials or processes into the art class and by testing students on correct procedures. If a student is injured, not only the supervising teacher, but also the school system may be sued. The National Art Education Association offers liability insurance to member art teachers. Some school systems cover teachers under their blanket policies. Every art teacher should find out what his or her coverage actually is. Many states hold teachers in "loco parentis" to their students, meaning they must do *more* than the typically reasonable person in preventing injuries to students. To find out more about the risks of certain art materials and processes, what is and is not proper ventilation, and answers to other questions about health hazards in secondary school art education, contact "The Center for Safety in the Arts" (CSA), 5 Beekman Street, New York, NY 10038, (212) 277-6220, and/or see the sources referenced below. Clear knowledge about potential risks is the best ally in designing and implementing a safe secondary art program.

References

Clark, N. , Cutter, T. & Mc-Grane, J. (1984). *Ventilation: A practical guide*. New York: COH.

McCann, M. (1985). *Health hazards for artists,* 3rd Edition. New York: Nick Lyons Books.

Qualley, C. (1986). *Safety in the art room.* Worcester, MA: Davis Publications.

Rossol, M. & Peltz, P. (1985). *Children's art supplies can be hazardous.* New York: COH.

Rossol, M. (1982). *Teaching art to high risk groups.* New York: COH.

Shaw, S. (1983). *Overexposure: Health hazards in photography.* Los Angeles, CA: Friends of Photography.

12
Recurring Themes: A Program for Interdisciplinary Learning

ARNOLD AMSTER

Clarkstown South High School
West Nyack, New York

How can the arts become central to the school and the community? How can we engage the imagination and interest of high school seniors? Would they elect to take a more vigorous course of study if it were offered? Could seemingly diverse and disparate ideas and concepts of the arts be presented in a cogent and stimulating manner?

Now in its tenth year of operation, the *Recurring Themes* program at Clarkstown South High School, a comprehensive high school in West Nyack, New York, has provided affirmative answers to these questions. Students have shown a willingness to elect the course and to diligently tackle the burden of diverse and scholarly reading and research assignments. The district and school administrators and departments of art, english, and social studies have managed to overcome the multitude of staffing, curriculum, preparation, and scheduling problems such a course presents. As a result, *Recurring Themes: An Interdisciplinary Honors Program* is flourishing.

The idea for the program orginiated in the early 1970's when a group of teachers and department chairs met informally to discuss problems in presenting content and subject matter to students without the fracture of thought associated with compartmentalized learning.

Several integrated programs were conceived. Clearly, *Recurring Themes* sounded wonderful. Now the problem: how can we sell the merits of interdisciplinary learning, scheduling, budget considerations, and the absolutely vital ingredient — faculty cooperation — to central office staff and building level administration?

Our faculty *ad hoc* committee decided the first need was to find three teachers willing to cooperate in a new venture, to engage in a dialogue without ownership of past curricula, and to open themselves to risk.

With these persons in place, we selected three advanced placement courses — offered at South High School — as the core for our program and prepared a prefatory statement:

The *Recurring Themes* program consists of three discrete courses integrated into an overall program of study. The courses are: an honors European history course, which provides a survey of European history and prepares the student for the European History Advanced Placement Examination; an honors World Literature and Composition course, which provides a survey of European and American literature, as well as an intensive composition course, and prepares the student for the Literature and Composition Advanced Placement Examination; and an honors art history course, which provides a survey of visual, plastic, and aesthetic forms and prepares the student for the Art History Advanced Placement Examination.

The essential difference and innovation in the program lies in the attempt to integrate the three segments into a unified whole through the coordination of subject matter, poetic form, and pedagogical approach. The educational assumptions of the course include a belief that there is an intrinsic value to teaching the major works of the various disciplines; a belief that there is an interrelationship between the disciplines that include not only an overlap of content but intellectual and philosophical conceptions as well; and a belief that there is potential for increased learning when the disciplines are effectively integrated in an academic program.

After developing this rationale and an introductory statement, we then studied the master schedule of the school and proposed several ways through which the three courses could be scheduled back-to-back.

Additional monies for 35 mm. slides, textbooks, and related visual materials were funded through existing departmental budgets.

For the first few years of the program, student selection required the development of prerequisites, teachers' recommendations, and recruiting.

152

In essence, students selected should have a strong background in reading and expository writing. Students must have the recommendation of their current teachers and department chairs of art, English, and social studies. Successful completion of honors level social studies and English courses in the 11th grade is advisable.

In the past two years, we have presented the *Recurring Themes* program to Art teachers and English teachers in New York State. At these conferences and in the *Teachers Guide to Advanced Placement Courses in History of Art* (Lerch, 1987, pages 61-71) the following course organization and attendant examples were offered:

SUGGESTED ORGANIZATION OF UNITS — BY THEME AND TOPIC

The ten suggested unit topics have been identified utilizing the literature in the field as a guide. *Historical Perspective,* one of the central topics that moves through a time-line structure, was used as an example.

Introduction

    Topic: An Overview of the Arts in Contemporary Society
    Topic: The Nature of Art
    Topic: The Nature of Literature
    Topic: The Nature of History

Unit 1. Man's attempt to deal rationally with his condition
    Topic: Classical Greece and Rome
    Topic: Age of Enlightenment
    Topic: Age of Science

Unit 2. Man's search for individual identity
    Topic: Classical Greece and Rome
    Topic: The Gothic Age
    Topic: Renaissance
    Topic: Twentieth Century

Unit 3. Forces seeking an intense loyalty of man

Topic: Growth of Christianity
Topic: The Middle Ages
Topic: Age of Rationalism
Topic: Rise of Fascism
Topic: Rise of Communism

Unit 4. The impact of change on the human condition
Topic: The Baroque
Topic: Industrial Revolution
Topic: The Twentieth Century
Topic: Atomic Age

Unit 5. Man's protest against his condition
Topic: The Reformation
Topic: The American Revolution
Topic: The French Revolution
Topic: The Russian Revolution

Unit 6. Man's complacency with his condition
Topic: Feudalism
Topic: Victorian England
Topic: Czarist Russia

Unit 7. Man's search for symbols
Topic: Religion
Topic: Early Christian and Byzantine Era
Topic: Nationalism

Unit 8. Man's need to understand the unknowable
Topic: Religion
Topic: Philosophy

Unit 9. Man's need to control his environment
Topic: Age of Science
Topic: The Modern World
Topic: Industrial Revolution
Topic: Twentieth Century

Unit 10. Man's search for the perfect society
Topic: Ancient Greece and Rome

Topic: Christianity
Topic: Nineteenth Century
Topic: Twentieth Century

Conclusion
Topic: Contemporary and Present Day Expression
Topic: Recurring Themes

UNIT TITLE: INTRODUCTION — TOPICS 2, 3 & 4

A. The Nature of Art
    1. What is art?
    2. What constitutes a work of art?
    3. What is an artist?
B. The Nature of Literature
    1. What is literature?
    2. What constitutes a work of literature?
    3. What is a writer or poet?
C. The Nature of History
    1. What is history?
    2. What constitutes an historical work?
    3. What is a historian?

UNIT TITLE: THE NATURE OF ART

Enabling Objectives:

The student will identify qualities common to selected art works produced
    from the classical period to the present. The student will develop a
    definition for the following:
    What constitutes a work of art?
    What is a work of art?
    What is not a work of art?
    What do all works of art have in common?
    What is expression?
    What qualities are endemic to distinctive forms of expression?
    What is an aritst?

Learning Activities/Materials:

The teacher will select slides, reproductions, and readings from historical periods that exemplify diversity in style, medium, and approach in the creation of visual and poetic expressive form.
For example:
Leonardo da Vinci
Claude Monet
Michelangelo
Donatello
Kandinsky
Mondrian
Picasso
Manet
Velazquez
Duchamp
Christo
Albers
Kienholz
Lichtenstein

The teacher and the students will develop, through question/answer/discussion, possible responses and definitions to the questions stated above. Finally, a working definition will be formed.

For example:
"Art," for our use in this course, "will refer to a formal, man-made product conceived and developed with expressive intent."

Enrichment Activity:

Utilizing the definitions developed in the previous class discussion, lecture, and seminar, the student will identify creative performers within his or her individual experience. The list should be kept current throughout the school year.

Evaluation:

Utilizing the definitions developed as a guide, the student will select two works of art from the list compiled that best satisfy or exemplify the concept of an artist. The student will discuss the works selected for careful examination in a three-page paper.

UNIT TITLE: THE NATURE OF LITERATURE

Enabling Objectives:

The student will identify qualities common to works of literature produced from the classical period to the present. The student will develop a definition for the following:
What constitutes a work of literature?
What are the various genres of literature?
What is a work of literature?
What do all works of literature have in common?
What is a writer?
What is a poet?
What is a dramatist?

Learning Activities/Materials:

The teacher will select works of literature or significant sections of works from historical periods that exemplify diversity in style, genre, and approach in the creation of literary and poetic expressive form.

For example:
Homer
Aristophanes
Dante
Geoffrey Chaucer
Raymond Carver
Alice Walker

The teacher and the student will develop, through question/answer/discussion, possible responses and definitions to the questions stated above. Finally, working definitions will be formed.

UNIT TITLE: THE NATURE OF HISTORY

Enabling Objectives:

The student will be able to arrive at an understanding of historical inquiry through an examination of excerpts in which historians explain the nature of their work.

The student will be able to discuss the following questions:
What is history?
What constitutes a work of history?
What is an historian?

The student will be able to formulate definitions related to the above stated questions.

The student will be able to outline the steps involved in the historical method of inquiry.

Evaluation:

The student will be able to write a three-page paper in which he or she describes how to investigate a problem using the historical method of inquiry.

UNIT TITLE: MAN'S SEARCH FOR INDIVIDUAL IDENTITY (UNIT 2) — TWENTIETH CENTURY (topic 3)

Man's Search For Individual Identity — Twentieth Century

"We used to represent things visible on earth ... Now we reveal the reality of visible things, and thereby express the belief that visible reality is merely an isolated phenomenon latently outnumbered by other realities."
(Paul Klee, as quoted by Helen Gardner, 1980, page 807).

In conjunction with the study of the fragmenting and problematic nature of various aspects of the arts, the recurring themes student will develop an understanding of the sense of individualism and uniqueness in the twentieth century artist's view of individual identity, the loss of common vision and public metaphor, and the movement towards a vision of alienation and private metaphor.

SELECTED READINGS:

William Butler Yeats:	"Easter 1916"
	"The Second Coming"
	"Sailing to Byzantium"
	"The Tower"
	"Lapis Lazuli"
T. S. Eliot:	"The Love Song of J. Alfred Prucrock"
	"The Hollow Men"
	"The Waste Land"
	"Little Gidding"
Wallace Stevens:	"Sunday Morning"
	"Anecdote of the Jar"
	"The Snow Man"
	"The Emperor of Ice-Cream"
	"Of Mere Being"
James Joyce:	"A Portrait of the Artist as a Young Man"
	"The Dead"
Franz Kafka:	"The Metamorphosis"
Wilfred Oweg:	"Dulce Et Doerum Est"
Sigmund Freud:	"Civilization and its Discountents"
Jose Ortega Gasset:	"The Revolt of the Masses"
Franz Alexander:	"Our Ages of Unrest"
Jean-Paul Sartre:	"The Wall"
Albert Camus:	"The Myth of Sisphius"
Joan Dedion:	"The White Album"
Philip Toynbee:	"The Fearful Choice"
David Bell:	"The End of Ideology"

SELECTED VISUAL WORKS:

Gustav Klimt:	"Death and Life"
Oscar Kokoschka:	"The Bride of the Wind"
Max Beckmann:	"Departure"
Pablo Picasso:	"Guernica"
Vasily Kandinsky:	"Composition IX, No. 626"

Giorgio de Chirico:	"The Delights of a Poet"
Henri Matisse:	"Dance"
David Siquerios:	"Echo of a Scream"
Ben Shahn:	"Handball"
Edward Hopper:	"The Night Hawks"
Piet Mondrian:	"Composition with Red, Yellow, Blue"
Albert Giacometti:	"City Square"
Francis Bacon:	"Number VII"
Hans Hofmann:	"The Gate"
Willem de Kooning:	"Woman I"
Edward Kienholz:	"The Beanery"
George Segal:	"The Diner"

Clearly, the interdisciplinary study of literature, history, and art requires the development and understanding of thematic topics that transcend general historical divisons. The outline, developed for Unit 2, Topic 3, represents, in our view, a substantial theme necessary in understanding the twentieth century.

Other aspects, found engaging by the instructors or identified by the literature in the varied disciplines, may be developed in a like manner.

The units and topics within a selected area of study in the *Recurring Themes* program may be offered in a broad chronological approach with the topics presented as they emerge in each period. However, the topics may also be presented thematically if the instructors so desire.

The units and the topics are not especially unique, brilliant, or particularly original. The key to the program is the development of an understanding of the interconnectedness of the literary arts to the plastic arts. That is, an integration of knowledge, critical understanding, and discernment beyond that of the parts of the program itself. As John Russell has stated,"... the history of art is the history of everything ..." (Russell, 1981, page 3) Our results in the past ten years underlie our faith and belief in this approach.

For example: in the 1986-1987 and the 1987-1988 school years, between 90% and 100% of students enrolled in *Recurring Themes* (the average class size was 23) received a grade of 3 or better in the Art History, English Literature and Composition, and European History Advanced Placement

160

examinations. On a national basis, between 70% and 75% of the students sitting for these examinations received a grade of 3 or better. (Source: Clarkstown South High School, "AP Exam Comparison [Report]," dated 22 August 1988.)

Clearly, the continued success of interdisciplinary learning must be judged by the value the course and content have for our students now and in the future. Comments from *Recurring Themes* graduates report a sense of ease and confidence in understanding literature, art, poetry, philosophy, and, of course, ideas, as a unity, in college and graduate school.

The selections read and the art works discussed are intended to present a view of the topic and are not intended to be seen as providing a definitive understanding of the particular artist. The works presented in each topic, as with the entire program, are intended to provoke interest and curiosity in the material, to whet the appetite for further study at other junctures in life — be it undergraduate, graduate school, or continuing education in later years. Thus, the breadth and depth of the material covered is not as important as the quality of the works selected.

On a daily basis, we do what all teachers do: we engage students in a dialogue. Often we meet in a common area and spend three full periods, 125 minutes, in philosophic discussion concerning symbols and objects that explore time and period, ideas and concept — poetic developments that recur in history, art, and literature.

In essence, the courses become one, enriching each element through the recurrence of central theme and idea, providing insights into the richness of human thought and the grandeur of the search of knowledge.

By discussing with interested, motivated students the complexity of the human quest for answers, the *Recurring Themes* program hopes to provide the desire and the humility to be well-prepared and to accept future academic challenges.

References

Klee, Paul as quoted by Helen Gardner (Horst de la Croix and Richard Tansey revision (1980). *Art through the ages*. New York: Harcourt Brace Jovanovich, Inc.

Lerch, R. J. (1987). *Teacher's Guide to advanced placement courses in history of art*. New York: The College Board.

Russell, J. (1981). *The meaning of modern art*. New York Harper & Row, Inc.

Author's Note

I want to thank my colleagues — the other two members of the *Recurring Themes* team — Raymond Roswell, chair of the English department, and James Nash, member of the Social Studies department — for their contributions, editorial suggestions, scholarship, and friendship.

13
Teaching Exceptional Students in the Regular High School Art Classroom

ROBERT D. CLEMENTS AND CLAIRE B. CLEMENTS

University of Georgia

Most high school art teachers face the situation in their regular art classes of helping mentally challenged and disabled children who are at very different stages of development to learn along with non-disabled peers. A regular high school art class might contain students with a variety of disabling conditions, for example, a hearing impaired student, a student in a wheelchair, three mildly mentally challenged students, two moderately mentally challenged students, and three students with behavior disorders. Herein, each disabling condition is discussed in regard to how individuals with that handicap can learn and participate in an art program side-by-side with non-disabled children, and ways their non-disabled classmates can assist in the student's normalization are discussed. Suggestions are provided to assist the art teacher in meeting these special students' special needs. Art classes are where students of varying abilities and problems can be grouped along with non-disabled peers in order for the beneficial effects of main-streaming to occur: creative and intellectual challenge, progress in speech, social growth, and learning better ways of handling day-to-day life situations. The order of this article is to discuss first the more physically obvious disabilities of visual impairment, hearing impairment, and orthopedic and neurological disabilities, then mild, moderate, and severe mental challenge, then giftedness, then hyperactivity, and lastly, behavior disorder.

Youths with Visual Impairment

"Judy is the kind of student that an art teacher dreams about having in the classroom. She is bright, cute, persevering, honest, talented, friendly, and lovable. She is also blind. She lost her sight when she was in the third grade and has retained many child-like impressions of the world in her mind since that time. In talking with Judy to determine what media she felt would work the best, we decided that black glue drawings (with a squeeze bottle of white glue to which black paint had been added) on a white ground would, for her, be a most helpful tactile aid. She chose to use crayons as her media because of the wax they leave on the paper. As she draws, she can refer to the crayon marks on her paper in order to keep her place. We would discuss the subjects on which she would like to improve, and then I'd make her a glue drawing about that subject, for example, a tree. Judy used her tactile sense to explore the glue drawing and then would draw the tree by herself. After she finished a drawing, we would discuss her work both visually and tactily and talk about ways it could be improved. Often her drawings were much nicer than my original because they would have a sense of movement and change about them, in contrast to mine, which were rigid and structured. Another nice thing about Judy's work was that she never stopped with her daily assignment. After she learned to draw one tree, she would draw an entire forest complete with hills and a sky. All I had to do was give her a beginning place, and she'd take it from there."

Like Judy, some students must feel and touch to supplement their seeing ability. Most visually impaired students have some vision; only one out of ten legally blind persons is totally blind. For such a partially sighted individual's two-dimensional work, media which leave a slightly raised line with a different feel than that of the paper, such as glue line, grease pencils, crayons, or oil pastels, are recommended. Other media leave a recessed line indentation; these media include using a stylus or dull pencil on styrofoam meat trays, used X-ray film, or heavy aluminum foil, inscribed on a padded surface. For those who can see sufficiently so that they do not require tactile assistance, bold marking instruments are suggested; wide-tip felt marking pens give bold contrast lines.

Don't be embarrassed to talk about something a blind student cannot see. The student wants to be a part of the world, and your art talk about colors and light help to increase ability in aesthetic visualization. Talk with your sight-impaired students about colors, light, shapes, and textures. Use metaphorical language to create vivid mental images, e. g. "blue like the water in the swimming pool," "a soft dim light like at 8:30 on a summer evening." Visually impaired persons don't want to be treated differently. Use the same language as would you with sighted persons.

Promote the visually impaired student's pride in the activities the student does well; many blind students enjoy folk dancing, marching, rollerskating, swimming, dancing, and wrestling. Making pipe cleaner figures or wire figures of these activities can reinforce, in one's mind, one's sense of self-satisfaction with his or her body. Have the student model his or her face and head, expressing different emotional states. Through your choice of topics you can facilitate emotional growth. Topics like "What I Can Do Well" can help the student overcome self-pity and negative self-regard. Topics like "Being Left Alone," "Falling," and "Being Lost," help one to express negative feelings. Since the student's art work will not be as realistic as that of sighted peers, tell your class that art can be abstract, that artwork need not always look like something recognizable, and that what is important is the expression of feeling. To become aware of the tactile three-dimensional awareness of sculpture that their non-sighted peers have, sighted students, blindfolded, can also create, feel, and describe each other's sculptures.

Not only three-dimensional media but also sensory stimulation materials are recommended for the totally blind students. The exciting squeal and smell of the marking pens were enjoyed by one student who painted pretending that the brush strokes represented cars careening down roads and around curves. Fragrant smell-coded colored marking pens are available; red is cherry, purple is grape, yellow is lemon, etc.

Let the student know of your approach when you come up to an individual who is blind; clear your throat or softly say the student's name so you don't startle the student unexpectedly. If you meet the student away from the art classroom, let the student know who you are. Because the student is deprived of so much peer feedback on visual appearance, clothing, and grooming, your responses are especially appreciated — all the more so because you are the art teacher. When talking to the student, avoid standing in front of windows that let in glare; in order to see to their maximum ability, some individuals with limited vision require just the right amount of light. During your presentations and demonstrations, encourage the student with limited vision to sit up close while you talk and demonstrate; even better for involvement, let the student assist in the demonstration by holding the art reproduction. A method always appropriate is to privately ask the youth, "How can we make it easier for you to do the work or see the materials?"

As an adult, the student's success will correlate closely with his or her mobility. The art teacher may wish to use art to promote the visually imparied youth's spatial understanding. The student's spatial understanding of his or her home, bedroom, neighborhood, or use of mass transportation can be depicted in relief maps. These can be made from cardboard, glue, felt, sandpaper, plasticene clay, moss, yarn, foil, plastic wrap, little boxes, and papers with different surface textures, and result in a project as useful for sighted students as for visually impaired students.

Don't give blind students unearned privileges. Don't indulge students and make them dependent on you. One must consciously avoid "babying" blind students in the mainstreamed classes. You must overcome your tendency to do for the student what he or she is capable of doing.

Hearing Impaired Youths

Most teenagers suffer from insecurity and fear of being considered different from their peers; hearing impaired teenagers are likely even more self-conscious and shy. Their feelings of difference may be increased by their lack of peer verbal feedback, as well as by the physical apparatus of their hearing aid. You can help them gain security in your mainstreamed class by your attitude fostering acceptance of individual differences. One art exercise is to have the whole class draw side-view or three-quarter-view portraits; encourage the hearing impaired student to show how he or she thinks his or her hearing aid appears. These portraits can then be combined with other students' portraits into a quasi-group mural, showing the students side-by-side, perhaps mounted in pairs facing each other. In subsequent class discussion, work to foster the acceptance of "how each of us has a different appearance;" discuss the shapes of our faces, the color, nature, and cut of our hair and how we might think about changing it, and our distinctive features and how we feel about them. Another way to promote hearing impaired students having satisfactory peer relationships is to have the student, along with one or two classmates, draw a cooperative design on the blackboard or have the student and a companion decide on a joint project. For example, a couple of students, one disabled and one non-disabled, might work together hooking a rug at a card table from which the top has been removed. Since hearing impaired youths may tend to be overly dependent on the teacher, have the student get help from a peer rather than rely on you.

A second problem affecting hearing impaired youths is rigidity. You can help to "loosen up" all your students, non-disabled and disabled, by incorporating gross motor activities and body movement songs and games into your art classes. Rigidity may be ameliorated by art activities involving gross motor activity: finger painting while standing up, painting at an easel with large brushes, puppet plays, body movement art motivations, and acting out pictures. Another approach is warm-up exercises. Prior to their actual drawing, have your class stand up while you lead them in arm swings, push-pull motions, and oval motions, involving their whole arm and upper torso. Have them draw the objects "in the air" first, then onto their paper using no marker but just their bare finger, and, after that, have them draw objects with the drawing instrument. You will probably get better drawings from all the students.

When hearing impaired students are academically behind, it is often only in the areas of speech, language, and reading. You can use discussions of the art projects going on as well as art criticism, art history, and aesthetic issues, as vehicles to develop these youths' desire to speak. However, since hearing aids readily pick up background noise and can prevent the student from hearing, hold art discussions in the classroom's quietest area as far as possible from ventilation, fan, and air duct noise. Art history reports on famous artists can develop abilities in speaking and reading as well as acceptance of one's handicap. Cite the great achievements of Beethoven and the great Spanish painter Francisco Goya, who did their greatest masterpieces after becoming deaf. Being deaf need not limit an individual's artistic expression.

Orthopedically and Neurologically Disabled Youths

One of our students was so bent up with scoliosis that she was scarcely able, and even less willing, to lift a pencil, yet she was so motivated by a string art project that she kept up with her non-handicapped peers and pounded a hundred nails into wood using a one pound hammer.

Rather than risk a spill by dipping into a jar, let the student press the sponge onto a paint-laden tray which has been covered with a paint-saturated, spongy layer of plastic foam. You may need to clamp down this paint tray using C-clamps. Grasping the thin handle of a paint brush may be difficult; the wider handle of a one-inch housepainting brush may be easier to handle, or the thin handle can be thickened with plaster of paris or tape. A little brayer can be rolled on the paint-saturated sponge tray and then rolled onto paper; this requires both hands, one to hold the piece and one to manipulate the tool. This two-handed activity is especially useful for persons with "a lazy hand." Since carving with knives can be dangerous, carving with rasps is recommended. Rasp carving on blocks of balsa wood requires considerable exertion of muscular energy, an important goal for cerebral palsied individuals, who tend to hang back and let others do things for them. Other recommended activities are printing patterns, painting, papier-mache work, and rug hooking. Since cerebral palsy is a neuromuscular disability causing deficits in rhythmic movement, your art curriculum for these youths should emphasize activities entailing rhythmic movements. A good project for persons with a spastic condition is making moulded shapes from wheat paste and two-inch squares of newspaper, which have been soaked for about an hour, and then pressed into or onto a greased form such as a bowl, plate, or mask. The subsequent bowls produced can serve as "Gifts for Special People in My Life;" thus the individual is helped to think of himself or herself as a caring, giving individual who can bring joy and pleasure to others. Some students have such frequent epileptic seizures that, during their waking hours, they have to wear plastic football-type helmets to protect their heads; we make a special effort to include in our class motivations helmeted topics, such as football, motorcycling, construction, and astronautical flight, for youths who must wear helmets.

Even for an individual who is considerably paralyzed, you can devise fulfilling activities. Individuals who are unable to use their arms can paint and draw with the brush held between their teeth; a biteable mouthpiece can be constructed from a cut-off rubber spatula. A light touch with a finger is all that's needed to make patterns in salt, sugar, flour, or millet sprinkled on a colorful tray. Perhaps the individual can press macaroni and seeds into clay. Working with a peer, the student can point to illustrations in magazines, and may even be able to help tear them out, and perhaps help in gluing the illustrations into a scrapbook of his or her interests. The student and a peer can make a mobile at eye level; the student can help select items to be attached, such as shiny pieces of aluminum foil and colored cellophane, and a string can be used to make the mobile move.

Sarah was one of our orthopedically involved students, a very shy twelve year old girl who had rarely spoken. Her withered arms plus her vision deficiency contributed to her withdrawn condition. One day we found a box turtle crossing the highway and brought it to class for the students to draw. We hoped that the subject matter of the turtle, which, when fearful, physically withdraws its head, would communicate an important message to the shy children, who have their own ways of "going into their shells." We talked about Mr. Turtle's shyness, fear, and need for safety as he lumbered across our big art table and periodically withdrew into his shell. Sarah responded beautifully, with the most sensitive and detailed drawing we had ever seen her make. Afterwards, we were thrilled by her eagerness to tell the whole class about how the turtle felt when he walled himself off from the world.

Mildly Mentally Challenged Youths

One out of every ten persons in our country has a mentally challenged person in the family. The magnitude of this statistic indicates the importance of developing among the regular students attitudes of acceptance toward their mentally challenged peers. Of course, acceptance comes from within; it's hard for a person to feel good about another person if one doesn't first feel good about one's self. Art classes, to a much greater extent than most other classes, are places where individuals feel good about their personal achievements. Mentally challenged persons can create art with as much or more feeling than non-disabled youth. As teachers, we should not only accept, but actively encourage, diversity. Seize upon individual differences in representations; for example, say, "Bill's bird looks tough because of its big claws and jagged feathers; Mary's bird looks gentle, because of its big eyes and smooth body." Thus, you can help the mentally challenged students learn to accept their art representations as worthy and honest expressions of their thoughts and feelings. Through this, they can accept themselves as individuals of unique worth.

Art projects involving learning a sequence of steps can help these youths to be able to do out-of-school, entry-level jobs involving sequences of steps. When working on group projects along with non-disabled students, mildly mentally challenged students can find pleasure in doing some of the project's more repetitive aspects, of which non-disabled youths would more readily tire. Often confronted by so much that is confusing, mildly mentally challenged students get satisfaction from doing over and over something repetitious in which they have achieved mastery. One of our students, who misbehaved during long bus trips to and from school, found much peace and satisfaction in repetitively stringing beads. What was even more remarkable was that this teenager had severe vision problems as well and had to hold the bead and telephone wire on which he strung the beads two inches from his good eye; yet, in overcoming the visual-motor challenge of repetitively stringing the beads hour after hour during the jostling bus trip, he gained great satisfaction and pride.

In your art class, through your expectations of normal behavior, you can, Pygmalion-like, help the mildly mentally challenged student overcome feelings of being inferior or different. The way you address the student can make the student feel either the same as the others or different. Don't use the diminutive, childhood version of his name (Tommy rather than Tom). Treat the student as maturely as you do your regular students. Help the student to maintain a normal appearance, for society has subtle ways of giving negative messages to individuals who seem to be different in dress and appearance, and the mentally challenged person has enough inherent difficulties without society's creating more. Praise the student when posture and grooming are good. Talk to the class about fashionable hair styles, as seen in fashion magazines. When the student wears appropriate clothing combinations, praise the student for good judgment.

Make opportunities for cultural enrichment available to the mentally challenged student. You may be the only person in the individual's lifetime who will take the student to an art museum, who will listen and take seriously his or her verbal responses to art. You may be the only person who will teach the student how to act at an art reception. Without your actively making cultural experiences open to these students, they may develop feelings of fear and inadequacy about going to museums, concerts, art fairs, and art receptions. You can involve the mildly mentally challenged youth in the exhibitions, performances, and receptions in your school. Help these students invite friends to a reception for an exhibition in which their art is displayed. Because cultural events are an important part of normal life, persons with developmental disabilities deserve to be equipped with the skills, etiquette, and experiences to enable them to participate.

Moderately Mentally Challenged Youths

You will probably find Down's Syndrome students to be your most cheerful and easily amused disabled students. They make your teaching a delight. Their affectionate nature makes them willing students, eager to try, and eager to please. The Down's Syndrome students we work with are memorable for their extreme good nature, attentiveness, eagerness to learn, and desire to please. They use their time effectively and need little direction. They willingly give encouragement and assistance to their peers. Building functional clay objects, such as mugs, and construction activities with styrofoam, toothpicks, and blocks have helped them develop their fine motor skills. Acting in our skits gave the students a chance to express themselves before their group. In spite of limitations in ability, our Down's Syndrome students have been delightful and a joy to teach.

Helping the student who is moderately mentally challenged to be able to live independently in the community is a major goal. If the students are equipped with the skills to live independently in the community, they can achieve for themselves a quality of life much more normalizing then they would find in an institution. Art projects that can help students function in the community include lettering their name and creating personal maps to find their way around the community. You can promote managerial skills by enlisting students' support in the collection and inventory of supplies. To help students deal with ever-present language problems, we emphasize their saying words, not only during the motivation and working periods, but especially during the sharing period. We treat withdrawal by projects in creating puppets for plays, making valentine cards and autograph books, and by the happy sharing time and play at the end of the lessons. Feelings of failure, destruction, and rebellion are dealt with by giving the student specific help in getting started, by encouraging accomplishments no matter how slight, and by dividing tasks into easy steps.

Autograph books proved popular with our moderately mentally challenged teenagers. Social interests are paramount for all adolescents, and although these challenged students could just barely write their first names, yet they delighted in assembling the book and collecting autographs from peers and teachers. Valentine-shaped clay ash trays with the initials of self and friend in a square appealed to their interests in boy- and girl-friends. Moderately mentally challenged youngsters enjoy constructing with building blocks and take great delight in making the highest tower or the most intricate construction. A clay activity useful for promoting three-dimensional visualization is making bird nests filled with eggs; the nest is a pinched-out concave form; the eggs are balls of clay. Some youths might be able, with the teacher's direction, to build a "mother bird." "Snakes" of clay, i.e. linear rolled-out cylindrical forms, might help people overcome a fear of snakes. Lots of dancing and play-acting about birds and snakes added to our art lessons for these playful youths.

Emphasizing the vocational usefulness of art activities is highly effective for students who are moderately mentally challenged. For example, as students are involved in pounding nails into wood or styrofoam, we emphasize the value of this training in learning to build houses in which to live; we discuss how successful one of our acquaintances is as a carpenter, and we stress the good feeling he gets by helping people to have a home. When we make paper boats or planes, we tell of someone we know who makes a living fueling and repairing these vehicles. When we make containers of clay, we describe our friend who makes a living creating ceramics. The youths love to feel that they are involved in activities related to work of real value in the world. As teachers, we believe that we can sow the seeds for these students' future occupational satisfaction, as they see themselves as "good workers."

Our theory is that once the drudgery of work has been elevated into something joyous and fulfilling, the intrinsic satisfaction of doing a job well and of receiving rewards for work well done will continue to reinforce the students. But first they must be enticed into feeling that work is something better to do than to pout, mess around, or loaf. You can lead students to this awareness of the satisfaction of work through art's appealing materials and the pleasure of imaginative creation. For students who are moderately mentally challenged, you can fuse the joy and playfulness of artistic creation with the success of completing a step-by-step process. Your art program can help the student realize how the human spirit can be expressed with the hands, and one's soul with the work of one's body.

Severely Mentally Challenged Youths

The high school art teacher may wonder how to teach art to severely mentally challenged youths. Those we have worked with have been, in their artistic representations, at the scribbling stage, and most have been in the earliest scribbling stage, that of disordered scribbling. For the most part, they have attained few concepts of directionality, such as horizontality and verticality. This presents a major challenge to a high school art teacher who is not used to working with individuals at this stage. In the public schools, students with severe mental impairment will probably be placed in mixed classes with moderately impaired and with multiply physically disabled youths. Thus many in this class will be functioning at a rather early stage of artistic representation. On occasion, one may find a severely mentally challenged student who can draw a geometric shape or a figure at the tadpole stage, but such individuals are of atypically high art ability. A few may have grasped the concept of circularity and will take pleasure in going round and round.

Getting youths with severe mental impairment to attend to any activity, even an art activity, can require one-on-one constant attention. Many will refuse to direct their attention to the task at hand, choosing instead to willfully direct their gaze elsewhere. A few will diligently work at ripping the plastic cover-up sheets from the table; they will eagerly seek out the opportunity to grab and rip up a neighbor's art, or to push the clay and paints off the table onto the floor. A few will have idiosyncratic rituals in which they persist, such as grabbing at the teacher's or nearby students' hair, jewelry, or clothing. One special problem is that the severely mentally challenged youngster may not be able to differentiate construction from destruction. A student may be just as likely to rip up the drawing or disassemble the collage as to create or assemble it. A common problem among severely mentally challenged brain-damaged individuals is the persistence of self-stimulatory behaviors, such as slapping one's head, making clucking noises, or wringing one's hands. The teacher can try to use art activities as a bridge to more constructive activities. Thus, slapping a block of moist clay may be attempted as a substitute for slapping one's head, using a clucking noise-maker could substitute for making the noises oneself, and waving a homemade banner can substitute for hand wringing. Painting and finger-painting, pressing assemblage materials into clay, and pressing and touching clay and smoothing it with water may help develop in the student an interest in handling art materials.

You can feel, at the end of a day's work, that you have helped this individual come closer to what he or she is capable of becoming. Perhaps some ability you have taught the student will help him or her be able to live at home with parents rather than in an institution. At the public school, maybe the student will be able to attend classes in which there is more mainstreaming; after leaving public school, perhaps the student will be able to live in a less restricted setting. It could be that the attitudes of pleasure in cooperation gained in your art class will transfer into progress in feeding and toileting, and in living with others. Because of the pleasure and sense of accomplishment gained through your art program, the severely mentally challenged individual may be helped to acquire skills and a mental attitude to enable him or her to have a higher quality of life.

Gifted Youths

Lay people, for the most part, tend not to think of giftedness as a handicap; most tend to think it more blessing than curse. Yet most teachers who have worked with gifted youths will probably agree that gifted youths have their special learning problems, which may include lack of motivation, boredom, mischief-making, and class disruption. There will be times when gifted youths' playfulness will get on your nerves. Yet try to be patient and nurture the playfulness of your gifted students, for their imaginative play precedes and catalyses their cognitive development. Brainstorm during all three parts of a lesson: during the motivation period and working period, ask "What other ways can we use this media; how else can we show space?"; during the sharing time, ask "How else have we shown perspective and space? Can anyone think of a way that no one used?" Whereas, for mentally retarded and hyperactive youths, structuring tasks and time was essential, don't over-structure the time and task for your gifted students; they need time to mull things over and the freedom to come up with an individual solution.

While your encouragement is essential, praise, especially global praise, such as "That is good," is not usually helpful. It is better to exhort your gifted students to put themselves into their work, "How can it be good if you dabble unconcernedly with it? I want to see blood, sweat, and tears. I want to see love and caring and thought and involvement." Demand effort and feeling. Lead them to appreciate the joy of losing themselves in their work. Encourage your students to use metaphors, which can let them put together thoughts and feelings about things that are taboo or frightening or just too powerful to be stated directly. Help the student to abstract, to boil down the size of the problem. Say to the student, "What is the big idea, the main idea, the essence, that you want to show?" By simplifying, they can be helped to find a way through the vast maze of possibilities the fertile mind opens up.

174

Establishing a chapter of the National Art Honor Society or National Junior Art Honor Society in your school is an effective way to recognize those with special ability. Advanced placement (AP) art history and studio art courses for college credit while the student is still in high school are still another effective means by which high school teachers keep gifted students motivated. To help them merge a rich imaginative life to the real world, help your gifted high school students to enter real world competitions such as Scholastic Art Awards, county art fairs, state Governor's Honors Programs, state school art exhibitions, PTA art competitions, poster contests, art school portfolio review deadlines, and the National Arts Recognition Talent Search. Those gifted in writing can be encouraged to submit their art reviews which demonstrate their abilities in art criticism and aesthetics to school publications, area newspapers, and national magazines which publish young people's work. Put the student into situations in which he can receive approbation, such as school and community exhibits, demonstrations, and competitions. Let the student be your representative at art meetings you cannot attend. Foster the student's growth through your phone calls and letters of recommendation to gain his admission into special enrichment situations. When he wins an award or gets accepted into a notable program, write the newspaper article, take the student's picture, and send it in to the local newspaper.

Show the student quality works by others. Don't let students be content to compare their work with that of peers. Henry Moore's high school art teacher, Alice Gostick, had Henry and two or three other students come to her apartment on Sunday afternoons for an art-honor-society-type meeting where they would look at and discuss the new art and aesthetic ideas in issues of *Studio Magazine*. To involve them in real world concerns, she had the students design the program for the school plays and carve a wooden bas-relief war memorial for those who had gone off to the First World War.

Hyperactive Youths

When working on a picture, hyperactive youths often rush through, going overboard, perhaps completely painting over the objects in the picture and pasting too many things on the page, then getting into trouble with classmates. Because hyperactive youths have plenty of social interactions, and especially too many that are not constructive, social activities, group learning, and sharing periods should be de-emphasized. Art activities for these youths should be teacher-directed, with little variation or opportunity for student choice. Lesson components, for example, the motivation, working procedures, clean-up and sharing time, should be done at regular times each period. Structure lessons by breaking long assignments into several shorter ones. The hyperactive child is not a good "waiter", so avoid long waiting periods. Give the student one object at a time, and clear the table of everything else. Some projects such as mosaics or printing which have repetitive steps may have a soothing effect.

When faced with too trying a situation or pushed too far, the hyperactive child may erupt, screaming, kicking, and throwing things. The teacher should watch for the point of loss of control, which sometimes has early warning signs, such as a change in breathing, flushing, pallor, or perseveration. Art teachers have observed perseverative pencil tapping, foot tapping, pounding of clay, and repeated opening and closing art closet doors just before hyperactive youngsters have had tantrums. Such tantrums by the hyperactive child make the student disliked, rejected, and ignored by peers, teachers, and parents. Whether the student is on or off medication, has taken it, or has forgotten or avoided taking it recently, further affect concentration ability. Thus, the individual's social world is radically different from that of the non-disabled child. The large size of regular classrooms, filled with peers who reject the student, are not the best milieu for this student, who works best alone, or in very small groups. Seating the student with a calm model student has been an effective method we found to help the student. Seek to limit, rather than to extend, opportunities for choice and stimulation by peers and environment.

Most likely the walls of your art classroom will be adorned with beautiful colored patterned art works and visually stimulating still-life arrangements. Yet hyperactive children function best in rooms with drab walls, devoid of distracting stimuli. (Of course, displays, while stimulating, can nevertheless convey a sense of order, e.g. by using similar size mats and symmetrical displays, one can combine excitement with order.) The hyperactive child can be seated so that his or her line of sight rests on a calm, ordered view; the student can be seated up front, facing an empty chalkboard, or in a corner, facing blank walls. (An analogous situation in the art world is that many art galleries have a special sales room with walls and floor carpeted in plain gray carpet, a couple of plain chairs, and a light to shine only on the one art work to sell; the room is devoid of stimulus except for the item singled out for attention.)

To help the student to use time wisely, emphasize that quality is more important than speed. "There is plenty of time. Do what you do well and carefully. That's what is important." Help the student to plan and show how to make transitions. Checksheets or instructions on the chalkboard spelling out each step of the art process can help. Say to the student, "Now, how will we begin? Then what will we do? Then what?" Structure both the time and difficulty so that with each step the child finds success. Also, to ease the student over the difficult transitions from one lesson stage to another (for example, from clean-up to sharing time), prepare the student by making announcements ahead of time about when and how the transition will occur. You can help the hyperactive student achieve in your art class by teaching the student to slow down, to reflect on his or her work, to use all the time available, and to execute plans.

Youths with Behavior Disorders

Behavior disordered students, especially when they look around the main-streamed class and see the work of peers, are often overwhelmed by a sense of being no good at art. Some of these students seem perversely bent on acting out over and over again a life script of their own inferiority. Occasionally we, as art teachers, inadvertently contribute to the problem by setting goals too high; more often it is the students who set their own goals unrealistically high. They will make a satisfactory piece, but then remember their self-appointed "loser" role, and suddenly paint over it or crumble it up, loudly proclaiming, "Aw — I messed up." They will then turn their frustration outward onto their classroom peers and attempt to discourage others as well, "Why you makin' that piece of junk, man?" Just as inferiority problems lead to behavior problems, so conversely those with behavior problems develop inferiority feelings. Resolving one problem often resolves the other.

In order that all students, both non-disabled and disabled, will feel satisfaction in their accomplishments, the teacher should emphasize how "we each make it in our own way." Accept divergent work with accepting statements like: "Sue has shown a completely different way of thinking about the problem. She uses blues and greens that feel to me like a picnic on a windy day and a field of blowing grass. Of what does it remind you?" If the teacher

177

can encourage and remind the student of past successes while the student still feels good about the work, inferiority feelings can be lessened. However, some behavior-disordered youths who are in conflict with the educational system dislike being singled out for verbal praise. For them, the more effective reinforcement is a quiet word which other students cannot hear, or a silent nod, wink, or smile.

Behavior disorders in the classroom can come not just from those labeled BD. Students with other disabilities may exhibit behavior problems as severe as those of the behavior disordered youths. Their behavior problems can impede their learning as severely, if not more so, than the physiological problem of their specific primary disability. Even gifted students can be behavior problems in high school classes, sometimes playing a role as "the brains" behind the mischief.

Art media which offer active resistance can be effective. Just as in our lives, we sometimes want to punch a punching bag to relieve the tension someone has caused; likewise, your BD students can find, through physical exertion, relief from their emotional hangups. Carving wooden totem poles from donated telephone poles, carving in plaster, or sand cores, stained glass work, nail art, metalwork, linoleum or wood block carving all require their energetic activity. Manual arts tools carry real world authority. Chisels, mallets, gouges, knives, and hammers are valued instruments for their reality, adultness, and vocational utility. The teacher can enhance this attractiveness with enthusiastic statements such as, "My uncle uses this kind of knife in work as a cabinet builder." Real world tasks can be great motivators; we have seen delinquent youths develop into more socially responsible individuals through the group's working together in painting a mural and creating a school totem pole.

Other kinds of materials may also have a calming effect. Opposite to the hard resistant materials, viscous and plastic materials may also have a calming effect. For example, smoothing creamy wheat paste onto newspaper for papier mache constructions has a calming effect. This use of viscous wheat paste by BD youths has been highly effective for their making large scale Red Grooms or Claus Oldenberg type papier mache constructions, and these projects have received much approbation in the school. Other materials which can be soothing for some students are those which require a great deal of repetition in their use, such as the materials of weaving. Weaving a "God's eye" worked for Butch, who had always been in some kind of trouble. When Butch was bad, which was frequently, his family used to lock him in a closet. One day while making "God's eyes" with yarn and sticks, the mentally challenged teenager looked up at me and said, "The next time, instead of gettin' mad at somebody, I'll do this." Butch had learned the value of replacing destructive, hateful, and self-destructive actions with more satisfying, constructive, artistic actions.

If a student comes up with a way of working with a material which is plainly unacceptable or dangerous, rather than to say, "No, no, no, don't do it that way," a better way is to say, for example "Let's try it this way, so that the paint won't splash." If the child perversely persists in abusing the material, the teacher should quietly substitute a different material without the offensive properties, emphasizing how much the student will like the new material and how it will make his piece special. Obviously it is in the teacher's best interest to avoid dangerous confrontations in the classroom. Giving the student a chance to cool off protects you, the teacher, from verbal abuse and physical danger. The reality of this danger is documented by the average of 1500 teachers assaulted in each state each year. Upset classes lead as well to the loss of large amounts of scarce art supplies and equipment, scissors, brushes, and hand tools.

To short circuit disturbances in your classroom before they become major, consider setting up a quiet corner in your classroom. As you design it, consider soothing features for the student's body, eyes, and hands. A beanbag chair or a rocking chair facing into the corner or just pillows on the floor can also create a comfortable sheltered reading place. For the eyes, a feeling of peace and containment can be achieved by something calming to look at: an aquarium, plants, posters with tranquil scenes and mottoes, quiet colors on the walls, a small carpet, and a divider just so high as to block out the student's view of classmates.

Rather than a physical corner of the room as a quiet corner, an art object of the child's creation can serve much the same function. Creating a terrarium, a restful miniature gardenscape, was effective for Sammy, a big violent psychotic sixteen year old boy who would fly into terrible rages. Once, in a fury, he threw a rock and smashed the face of our school clock. But in art class, Sammy was a different person. He loved the terrarium he made with such care, scrubbing off the label from the plastic liter cola bottle, cutting it apart, and filling it by thoughtfully and imaginatively placing moss, earth, rocks, plants, and a little fired clay frog he had made. He carried it around with him for weeks, taking it back and forth to home to show to his mother and even taking it with him on repeated admissions to the mental hospital. Sammy's art product became an extension of the ego, a reinforcing comforting object, a source of peace and calm.

Verbal encouragement alone may not be sufficiently strong to motivate the student with a behavior disorder. He may need tangible rewards and privileges. "When your design is complete and I approve it, then you may go on to transfer it to your tempera engraving paper." "Those who get 80 or better on the color test may work on their soda straw weavings." Contracts can clearly specify quantity, time, conditions, and quality, as well as reward. "Using rug yarn, I will weave a piece 1' x 2' of acceptable quality to my teacher, by April 1st, in exchange for which I shall receive the privilege of using the ceramic wheel for two weeks." Rewards such as giving a student access to special tools, arranging for the display of a student's work, or letting a student help before school by sorting pictures or arranging the supplies cost the teacher nothing. No cost is involved in having a student listen to a radio or cassette with an earplug, run an errand, or arrange a still-life, yet these free privileges can be used as effective rewards. Some privileges you can give are:

Having one's art work displayed in the hall or principal's office.
Being artist of the week or month.
Listening to a radio or tape recorder with an earplug.
Reading valuable art books.
Being allowed to move on to another activity, a free activity, or the "hardest, biggest, brightest."
Choosing a new seat.
Having access to special tools, equipment, art books, and a special art study corner.
Having art work selected for the school or town newspaper, art contest, yearbook.

Another type of contingency is to assist the teacher in some way: Teach another student. Work on a bulletin board display. Make direction cards for younger students. Operate the kiln. Operate the slide viewer or photographic developing equipment.

The above described alternatives should be introduced only gradually into the class in order to avoid confusion at the beginning of school in the Fall.

At the beginning of school, alternatives should be few, procedures simple, and art supplies minimal. Creating an appearance of order is most important; count or pretend to count all supplies. Make all directions as simple and few as possible, and write them on the blackboard. Have a student volunteer orally read each rule. While the students work, make your seating chart to give an atmosphere of order. After order has been established, then the teacher can introduce projects involving more alternatives, freedom, and fun.

A fun project combining viscous materials and macho smashing with a bat as well as a built-in reward is papier-mache pinatas. It is always a great success, "a smash hit," and it has resulted in memorable lessons. Group cooperation in the careful application of layers of paper, attention to qualities of dryness and strength, and artistic skill in designing and decorating the piece are worthy goals, to be rewarded by the object's destruction, spilling its candy and trinkets. To develop the students' sense of societal stewardship, their lovingly created pinata might be given to a group of even less fortunate youngsters, for example, for a party at a retardation center or day care center.

Conclusion

Practical suggestions have herein been described by which visual art can contribute to the quality of disabled students' lives and help them to be a part of the mainstreamed high school art classroom. By participating in a mainstreamed art class along with non-disabled youths striving to develop skills, the disabled youth is presented with a range of student models from which to choose to model response. The student is challenged by the varying levels of high achievement to put forth his best efforts to develop skill. In this article, art activities have been described to develop skills, projects that have helped those who would not speak to develop the will to speak, those without sight to feel part of the world of visual art, those with little strength to have the will to make, and those who are discouraged to feel confident about their creativity. The problems and methods pertaining to each particular disability have been presented herein one at a time. In reality, disabling conditions share many common problems, such as discouragement, fear of failure, feelings of shyness and of being different. These common problems can be well addressed by adapting the regular art curricula components of discussion, perception, creation, and emotional expression. Discussion activities help clarify feelings and develop speaking abilities; perceptual activities develop cognitive and observational skills; psychomotor activities develop perceptual, cognitive, and coordination skills. Artistic production activities develop the student's perceptual, cognitive, and psychomotor skills. Creating *any* object exerts a unifying, healing influence on its maker; even more so does creating an object when its maker strives toward expression of feeling, organization, and beauty.

Bibliography

Alkema, C. (1971). *Art for the exceptional.* Boulder, Pruett.
Anderson, F. (1978). *Art for all the children. A creative sourcebook for the impaired child.* Springfield: Charles C. Thomas.
Art Educators of New Jersey. (1984). *Insights, art in special education; educating the handicapped through art.* Reston: National Art Education Association.
Blandy, D., Pancsofar, E., and Mockensturm, T. (1988, January). Guidelines for teaching art to children and youth experiencing significant mental and physical problems. *Art Education, 41* (1), pp. 60-65.
Clements, C. and Clements, R. (1984). *Art and mainstreaming: Art instruction for exceptional children in regular school classes.* Springfield: Charles C. Thomas.
Clements, R. (Winter 1980). Contingency management in art class discipline. *Art Teacher, 10,* (1), pp. 12-13.
Copeland, B. (1984, November). Mainstreaming art for the handicapped child; resources for teacher preparation. *Art Education 37* (6), pp. 22-29.
Dalke, C. (1984, November). There are no cows here; art and special education together at last. *Art Education, 37,* pp. 6-9.
Gould, E. and Gould, L. (1978) *Arts and crafts for physically and mentally retarded.* Springfield, Illinois, Charles C. Thomas.
Karlin, M. and Berger, R. (1972). *Discipline and the disruptive child.* Englewood Cliffs, Prentice Hall, pp. 35-36.
Kingsley, L. (1974). *Teaching art to the deaf.* Gorden Press.
Lindsay, Z. (1972). *Art and the handicapped child.* New York: Van Nostrand Reinhold.
Lovano Kerr, J. and Savage, S., (1972, November). An incremental art curriculum model for the mentally retarded, *Exceptional Children, 32,* pp. 139-199.
Lowenfeld, V. (1950). *The nature of creative activity.* New York: Harcourt Brace.
Madeja, S. (1983). *Gifted and talented in art education.* Reston: National Art Education Association.
Mourreau, L. and Anderson, F. (1986, January). Task analysis in art: Building skills and success for handicapped learners. *Art Education, 39* (1), pp. 52-54.
National Art Education Association. (1989). Mainstreaming exceptional children. *NAEA Advisory,* reprinted from Council for Exceptional Children.
Olsen, M. (1977). *Art activities to encourage perceptual and cognitive development.* Ann Arbor, Florida.
Peterson, C. (1989). *Visual arts and the physically challenged person.* Videotape, DePere: St. Norbert College.
Rubin, J. (1977). *Child art therapy, understanding and helping children grow through art.* New York, Van nostrand Reinhold.
Rubin, J. (1987). *Approaches to art therapy: Theory and teaching.* New York, Brunner Mazel.
Sherrill, C. (1979). *Creative arts for the severely handicapped.* Springfield: Charles C Thomas.

Silver, R. (1978). *Developing cognitive and creative skills through art*. Baltimore: University Park Press.

Susi, F. (July 1989). The physical environment of art classrooms; a basis for effective discipline. *Art Education, 42*, (4).

Uhlin, D. and Chiara, E. (1984). *Art for exceptional children*. Dubuque: Wm. C. Brown.

Voigt, R. (1977). *Art and the exceptional child*. Atlanta: Metropolitan Cooperative Educational Services Agency.

Wadeson, H. (1988). *Advances in art therapy*. New York: Wiley.

Williams, G. and Wood, M. (1977). *Developmental art therapy*. Austin: Pro Ed.

183

14

Preparing to Teach Art to Secondary Students from All Cultural Backgrounds

ENID ZIMMERMAN

Indiana University

Art teachers across the United States continuously face the problem of how to educate students to learn about art in all its cultural contexts. They also must adapt teaching strategies, curriculum content, and learning environments to best meet individual students' needs. Solutions to these problems involve issues such as changing ethnic and cultural forces in the United States, debate about elitist and populist views of art education, value of an 'aesthetics' or 'cultural' approach to studying art objetcts, and appropriate, equitable strategies art teachers can take to educate students from a variety of backgrounds.

A Changing Population

In 1982, 80% of the population in the United States was white. By the year 2050, the white population will drop to 50% (Kellogg, 1988). In the 1988-1989 school year, there was no dominant ethnic group among the students in California; the number of non-Hispanic white children fell below 50% (Olsen, 1988). It is not difficult to conclude that the most recent influx of immigrants to the U.S. will have profound effects on schools in which these students are educated. It is significant that the "clearest difference between the latest immigration and earlier ones is the shift to third world nations as sending countries" (Kellogg, 1988, p. 203). How new immigrant students, non-white students whose backgrounds may go back many generations in the United States, and the present majority of students with Anglo-European backgrounds should best be educated is not amenable to easy solution.

Providing an equitable education for *all* students who study art is no less problematic.

Is Multicultural Education a Solution?

In the United States, the predominant culture, developed from Anglo-European roots, has determined to a great extent the dominant institutions, social values, language and other communication systems, and many other aspects of life. How students who are or are not members of this macro-culture or core-culture should best be educated has prompted many problems and some solutions. Bennett (1979) cast beliefs about educating students from diverse backgrounds into three categories: *suppression, assimilation,* and *pluralism.* Suppression takes a form of cultural racism in which non Anglo-European peoples are believed to have no distinctive culture worth preserving, all contributions of minority cultures are suppressed, and ethnic minority groups are viewed as basically inferior and a threat to the dominant culture. Cultural assimilation is viewed as a process in which persons from a variety of racial and ethnic backgrounds give up their original culture and become absorbed into the dominant core culture. In cultural pluralism, persons of different ethnic groups are permitted to retain many of their cultural traditions as long as they are able to adapt practices that "are necessary for society as a whole" (Bennett, 1979, p. 37). Within this view, ethnic diversity is respected and appreciated; a person can develop an ethnic perspective and still identify with the general policies of a nation.

Cultural Racism

Current stances about incorporating a pluralistic point of view into school curricula vary from no support (in the form of cultural racism) to full support and promotion of intercultural understanding. Members of a growing schoolbook protest movement have advocated suppression of what they term *secular humanism* and *globalism.* These schoolbook protestors fear that their children are being brainwashed into believing in a one world religion or government (Jenkinson, 1986, 1988) and that they are being taught in ways that break with and challenge key elements of Western thought and values. Among topics that are being protested are ethnic studies, themes that ask students to examine their own backgrounds,

186

portrayals of harsh realities of life, and negative representation of the United States and the American tradition (Rogers, 1988). Reform efforts to correct Anglo-European bias in curricula, therefore, may meet formidable opposition in communities across the United States. Now that the field of art education is seen as a viable market for textbook publishers, art materials and books distributed for use at elementary, middle, and secondary levels may be forced to become more ethnocentric as pressure is put on publishers to be ever more conservative.

Cultural Assimilation

Cultural assimilation has become the focal point of a debate between art educators who believe in cultural assimilation and those who espouse cultural pluralism. Smith (1981) contended that excellence in art education demands that experts choose what art is considered worthy of study and attention (Smith, 1982, 1986). Smith (1982) represented what he termed 'egalitarian elitism' in that the majority of people are capable of attaining excellence and should be offered opportunities to do so. The notion that art should be used to effect social change, for Smith, is contrary to appreciating art for its own sake (1982). In defending "the egalitarianism of Discipline-Based Art Education (DBAE)", Silverman (1988), posited that there are great works of art that should be used for study based on their aesthetic, social, and innovative significance and that there are "lesser works" that should not be used for instruction. Responding to Hamblen's criticism of DBAE as overemphasizing Western art, Eisner (1988) maintained that Western art should be emphasized "given our culture" as long as exclusive attention is not paid to Western art (p. 13).

Cultural Pluralism

In reaction to cultural assimilation in art education, a number of voices have been raised from a cultural pluralist point of view in respect to teaching art. In the early 1960s, Gardner (1961) asked "can we be equal and excellent too?" Hamblen (1984), like Gardner, concluded that a dynamic tension exists between concepts such as universalism and relativism as competing educational belief systems. A universal, elitist approach focuses on art concepts in terms of commonality of human experience; art objects are viewed in terms of formal qualities. A relativistic, egalitarian approach

187

focuses on art concepts in terms of differences in human experience; art objects are viewed in terms of the specific context and culture in which they were created. Hamblen concluded that differences between these sytems cannot and should not be resolved. It would seem logical that both can and should be incorporated into a cultural pluralist concept of art education.

Chalmers (1978) stressed that a past ethos in the teaching of art has led to inequities, omissions, and stereotyping. His solution is to emphasize economic, political, and social issues and the educational context of learning. Other art educators also have written about the desirability of achieving "a pluralistic society, rather than a well-managed stratified society" (Nadaner, 1981). Art often has been viewed too narrowly and London (1988) suggested attending to personal, political, spiritual, and social functions of art such as art for healing, celebration, social protest, personal transformation, meditation, spiritual growth, and play. According to these art educators, popular conceptions of studio art, art history, art criticism, and aesthetics are bounded by Western or Anglo-European cultural standards. A limited range of art objects are included, and these are viewed as aesthetic works of art capable of improving aesthetic experiences instead of scientific or cultural artifacts capable of imparting knowledge about the functions of art in society (Chalmers, 1984; Clifford, 1988). McFee (1988) advocated an emphasis on socio-cultural study of art along with study of studio art, art history, art criticism, and aesthetics. Learning about the arts in a curriculum with a socio-cultural emphasis would include study of fine arts, crafts, folk and ethnic arts, women's art popular arts, and electronic and mass media (Chalmers 1978, 1984; Chapman, 1978, 1982; Collins and Sandell (1984): Congdon, 1985a, 1985b; Feldman, 1970; Lanier, 1976; Lederman, 1988; McFee & Degge, 1977; Nadaner, 1981; Rosenblum, 1981).

Art, therefore, can be taught from a cultural pluralist point of view and can be studied as a means of understanding (1) concepts expressed in a culture, (2) how mores of a culture affect art, (3) how art both maintains status quo and effects changes within a culture, (4) roles of artists in different cultures, (5) different subcultures within a core culture, (6) the society in which students live including dehumanizing effects, (7) interaction of envionmental needs, resources, techniques, and culture, and (8) financial and educational support for the arts within a culture (Bersson, 1983; Loeb, 1983; McFee, 1988). Chalmers (1978) advocated an interdisciplinary focus for studying art from a cultural pluralistic point of view organized around themes such as art and religion, politics, social status, technology, economics, and decoration. The focus of such a program for art study would emphasize both *what* art is and *why* it was made.

Teaching Art to Middle and Secondary Students from Diverse Backgrounds

How then should secondary art teachers approach teaching students in their art classes who often, but not always, come from a variety of racial and ethnic backgounds? We as teachers, Bersson (1986) contended:

> always find ourselves caught in the dialectical middle between the high culture of the art world and the multi-cultural life-worlds of the population we serve; a balance or integration of these different art worlds in our teaching is essential. (p. 43)

A synthesis of these competing concepts has been demonstrated to be questionable; it remains to be resolved how the dynamic tension created between these concepts can be harnessed and the energy produced used to turn educational gears productively. Results might include equitable education of all people within our society, a celebration of diversity of individuals and cultures within that society, and increased understanding of similarities and differences among cultures.

Secondary art teachers need to examine their own attitudes and beliefs about teaching art and what objects and concepts they consider belong to the world of art, what art objects they prefer and why, what cultures' arts and what periods of art are most appealing, and why they have developed these positions (McFee & Degge, 1977). Teachers' aesthetic values often are not similar to those of their students because they may be from different ethnic, racial, socio-economic, and educational backgrounds. This is especially true for secondary art teachers who are teaching adolescents whose popular cultural referents may be very different from the teacher's even though the students and teacher may share similar cultural backgrounds.

Nadaner (1985) advocated that art teachers use art criticism to decide which media images and other contemporary art forms are of value and worthwhile for art teaching. The art teacher must also be what Nadaner termed *ethnographer* as well as cultural critic "to help a group ... negotiate a path

189

between home culture and dominant culture" (p. 53). For different students, solutions to which aspects of their sub-cultures and the core culture should be emphasized will differ; a recent immigrant, a native rural student, and a North American urban minority student all have different cultural and social needs. Teachers should decide what is the best art education for *all* students in their classes. Should all students be taught in traditional ways that do not take diversity into account? Should they be helped to develop better self concepts through learning more about the art of their own sub-cultures? Should they learn about art in a variety of cultural contexts different from their own? Should they learn how to use art as a means of social action and protest? These and other questions challenge teachers to individualize their art curricula, meet each student's needs and competencies, and educate students to understand and appreciate art of other cultures in a broad social context.

It is more common for elementary art teachers to use cultural pluralistic concepts and projects and to integrate art with other subjects than middle and secondary art teachers. Secondary art teachers tend to follow a more prescribed curriculum in which past art traditions are maintained and study of contemporary art is rare (Mason, 1986; Sletter & Grant, 1987). One reason may be that many more materials for teachers exist at the elementary than at the secondary level. Developing culturally pluralistic art curricula for secondary levels, therefore, would demand much original research and be very time demanding. While it is not possible for teachers to know in depth about the myriad cultures around the world, it is possible for them to help students develop a penetrating look at the art of some selected cultures. There are a number of resources that can help secondary teachers prepare to teach students from diverse cultural backgrounds.

Multicultural Approaches and Programs for Educating Art Students

Sletter and Grant (1987) observed that during the 1960s and early 1970s, the civil rights movement produced a number of educational policies and reforms such as special needs education, desegregation, bilingual education, and multicultural education. The original movement focused on concerns about racism and schooling; presently these concerns have been extended to issues about gender, class, and handicaps. Contemporary educators writing about teaching students from a cultural pluralistic point of

190

view have termed the resulting form of education *multicultural, multiethnic, multiracial, bicultural,* or *intercultural.* Sletter and Grant (1987) examined education literature for definitions and contributions to theory and practice of what they broadly term *multicultural education.* They categorized these into five approaches that emerged from the literature.[1] I will use their categories and descriptors to report and critique some examples of resources for preparing art teachers to teach middle and secondary students in a pluralistic society who come from diverse racial, ethnic, and cultural backgrounds.

Culturally Different

The first category, *teaching the culturally different,* is an approach in which "students of color" (Sletter & Grant, 1987) are assimilated into the cultural mainstream and existing social structure. Their own cultural backgrounds are used as building blocks so that they are better equipped to compete with whites in the core culture. A shortcoming of this approach is that often different sub-cultural groups are massed together under one heading such as Native Americans, Hispanics, or Asians. This type of education is offered for students of color only and not for integration into the entire school population. The onus is put on students and teachers to effect change rather than the core groups and institutions within the community.

In the middle 1970s, I worked on a project, The Arts in a Multicultural Society: Aesthetic Experiences for the Disadvantaged Child, designed to prepare pre-service elementary teachers to teach "children from economically, socially and educationally disadvantaged groups" from target populations of the poor, Black-Americans, Appalachians, Spanish speaking Americans, and American Indians (Lovano-Kerr, Shiel, & Zimmerman, 1974, p. 1). Pre-service teachers were to become knowledgeable about the arts from these cultures to prepare them to teach economically disadvantaged students from such cultures. Contributions of these cultures in the arts were used to encourage pride in the students' sub-cultures and to give them opportunities to become less disadvantaged and better able to operate in the core culture. Curriculum units were developed around concepts about art and culture, media and resources, and self-image and around art projects such as making pots, musical instruments, printmaking, tie dye and batik, weaving, stitchery, jewelry making, painting, and photography. In one lesson, for example, making weavings is related to studying weavings from

191

the target cultures and then adapting techniques and styles from these cultures to students' art work.

Human Relations

A second approach focuses on *human relations* as a mode of helping students from various cultural backgrounds cooperate with one another and build strong self-concepts. Integration is the thrust of this approach in which students, who may be different socially, economically, and/or ethnically, learn to appreciate each other's cultures. This approach usually lacks long term goals; if better understanding between groups is accomplished, it is not clear what the teacher is to do next.

Art education strategies and projects in the human relations area are generally found at the elementary level. This may be explained because emphasis is more on good feeling than learning art content, which generally is stressed more at the middle and secondary levels. Nadaner (1984) described a project in British Columbia in which students in one part of a city exchanged paintings they made about their daily lives with a partner class in another part of the city. The students who exchanged paintings described and interpreted each other's works to gain information about peers with whom they normally would not have much communication. Knowledge, in the project, was used to enhance social understanding. At the secondary level, projects similar to this one or a cooperative group art project, such as a wall mural painted at a school or community site, would serve to enhance intergroup dialogue and understanding. Using this approach, Taylor (1987) reported that students from different home circumstances and backgrounds can come to understandings and reach agreements in ways that would have been impossible if they had been working on individual projects or teacher dominated lessons.

Single Group Studies

A third approach, *single group studies,* focuses on experiences of a particular cultural group. Contributions of the group's culture are designed to be studied by students with similar backgrounds or by a group of culturally different students. Often groups such as Blacks, Asians, or American Indians are studied separately without attempts to show differences and similarities within these groups or with the white core culture. Also, although teaching about material culture is discussed and studied, current issues relating to racial oppression, social stratification, or social action are not. Often, step-by-step, stereotypic art projects such as making imitations of West African textiles, Japanese kites, or Indian molas are mistakenly labelled as a multicultural approach to teaching art.

Young (1985) described an art program that was operated by volunteers to improve and supplement art education of black students in their community. There was a human relations component in this program that served as means of social interchange and helping students adjust to school and community environments. Classes were conducted in a workshop and discussion format in which students learned about Afro-American art and history and created their own art products based on these experiences.

Another example of a single studies approach was A Tibetan Pilgrimage: Exploring the Arts of a Nomadic Culture, a project I helped plan and execute (Clark & Zimmerman, 1985). The theme of this exhibit was a pilgrimage by nomadic Tibetans at about 1900. Related materials were included that emphasized cultural similarities and differences of people in rural Indiana at the same time. This exhibit represented stops on the route of a pilgrimage and featured cultural and aesthetic aspects of family celebrations, regional festivals, and lifestyles of peoples in both rural Tibet and rural Indiana. Middle school students were the target audience for this project, and a group of 60 students of this age helped develop prototypic exhibition and participatory art materials. The exhibition was placed in eight school or community sites around Indiana, and pre-service and in-service teachers participated in educating docents to use the exhibits at each site.

Multicultural Education

A fourth approach, *multicultural education,* promotes cultural pluralism, cultural diversity, and social equity for all students. Contributions from many different groups and cultural values are integrated as integral parts of a multicultural curriculum. Goals for multicultural education include celebration of diversity, emphasis on respect for a variety of life styles and human rights, and equal distribution of power among members of all groups. Cultural values often become the main emphasis, and issues such as racism, social class, or gender issues are not discussed.

Several multicultural art education textbooks and projects, related to teacher education and targeted for secondary level students, have been developed.[2] *Art, Culture and Environment: A Catalyst for Teaching* (McFee & Degge, 1977) is a text relevant to the area of multicultural art education. The purpose of this book is:

> *to extend the range of what is considered to be art, to study art as cultural communication in our lives, and to make this material relevant to teachers in training so they can put it into practice in their classrooms.* (p. xvii)

Suggested activities are designed for early, primary, late primary, intermediate, and secondary school levels. The book is divided into chapters about observational drawing, designing and creating art, environmental design, cultural meanings of art, theory and research, and teaching and assessment. A section about individual differences is included for each chapter that offers a variety of means to extend student art abilities and understandings. Activities are organized at four levels: comparing similar art objects from different cultures, studying cultural effects on art in society, exploring differences in art of a variety of cultures within the student's own society, and investigating the diversity of art within one culture. The emphasis in this book is upon arts and crafts from non-western cultures and a wide range of examples of contemporary art.

Grigsby's (1977) *Art and Ethics: Background for Teaching Youth in a Pluralistic Society* is a textbook designed to provide art teachers with background knowledge to better understand and teach their students who come from diverse ethnic backgrounds. The focus is upon three ethnic groups: Afro-Americans, American Indians, and Spanish-speaking Americans. In this text, although *single group* and *culturally different* approaches are evident, the main thrust is to present a variety of art and life styles of specific ethnic groups and sub-groups within these groups and to discuss issues such as religious understanding, racism, and art used as social protest. Included also are discussions about resources appropriate for art teachers who wish to know more about minority group artists, ethnic and cultural differences between groups, how to use representative role models for art teaching, and the spectrum of "ethnic art" including "folk, academic, and intercontinental art" (p. 111).

194

Blandy and Congdon (1988) described a symposium, Multicultural Approaches to Understanding and Appreciating the Arts, the goals of which were to expand multicultural perspectives and enhance the concept of cultural pluralism. Students from a university art education and art therapy program attended this symposium. Emphases were upon expanding participants' abilities in designing art curricula to include expressions by various art groups; communicating with students, teachers, and community members; exploring alternative methods for teaching about the visual arts; and understanding the cultural and historical backgrounds of various social groups. Artists, educators, and community leaders from several different ethnic groups were featured speakers and workshop leaders. Topics such as racism, stereotyping, and social stratification were discussed.

Rodriguez and Sherman (1983) developed a project, Cultural Pluralism and the Arts: A Multicultural Perspective for Teacher Trainers in Art and Music, which was limited to three ethnic minority groups: Black Americans, American Indians, and Hispanic Americans. Although this project contained many elements of the *single group* and *culturally different* approaches, it went beyond these conceptions by emphasizing traditional to contemporary interpretations of art from these cultures. It focused upon different subcultures within these targeted groups and stressed that students are different in all classrooms and *all* students live in a pluralistic society. Twelve example activities were organized around both traditional and contemporary concepts related to each subcultural group. In this program art works were explored both as aesthetic and cultural objects; for each concept many classroom activities were presented that involved looking and talking about art and art making. Most of these are appropriate for junior high and high school levels.

World Views Through the Arts (Hough & King, 1979) was a project that used the arts as organizers to study how and why people in different cultures have a need to create and express themselves through the arts. Materials developed in this project were designed to be used by teachers in a variety of secondary school subjects including social studies, language arts, music, dance, and the visual arts. Readings and suggested arts activities were developed for each topic, including: (1) people's needs to create as viewed from different cultural perspectives, (2) comparisons between different societies' world views about the earth and nature and how these views change over time, (3) similarities and differences between style and design of various cultures and specific decades of American culture, (4) different ways cultures respond to change and express feelings about change, and (5) how society develops a sense of community through traditional and contemporary arts. Of special interest is the use of primary resources from many cultures in the form of poems, songs, interviews with artists, stories, diary excerpts, speeches, magazine and newspaper articles, and writings by scholars, art critics, and artists. Although the visual arts are not always the central focus, topics and concepts presented definitely exemplify a multicultural education approach.

Multicultural and Social Reconstruction

A fifth approach, education that is *multicultural and social reconstructionist*, is a social action position in which racism, sexism, and inequity are stressed and attended to as much as the cultural dimension of education. Students are taught to recognize and take action to effect change both in their schools and in society as a whole. This fifth approach is least developed and is the area that is most in need of research and development; presently there are no available instructional models or curricula developed that can be easily accessed in areas of both general education and art education.

Conclusion

Solutions about ways to teach art to secondary students from all cultural backgrounds demands that art teachers attend not only to universal, formal aspects of art work, but to relative issues as well. As an example, when writing about an exhibit of contemporary Australian Aborigine art work, art critic Robert Hughes (1988) concluded that:

> *Tribal art is never free and does not want to be. The ancestors do not give one drop of goanna spit for "creativity". It is not a world, to put it mildly, that has much in common with a contemporary American's — or even white Australian's. But it raises painful questions about the irreversible drainage from our own culture of spirituality, awe and connection to nature.* (p. 80)

Doug Boughton (1986), an art educator from Australia, discussing the art work of a contemporary Aboriginal-Australian artist and its relation to art teacher education, raised some difficult pedagogical questions:

If, through art programs, we produce teachers who believe that in contemplating the Aboriginal artist ... it is possible to respond only to the subtle unity of colour produced by the glorious richness of earth tones, the intriguing patterns and rhythms of lines and textures, and the asymmetrical balance of forms, we have not succeeded in developing cultural understanding. We have only succeeded when our graduates are able to understand that the formalist view is only one of many from the western tradition, all of which are inappropriate here. (p. 99)

Sletter and Grant (1987) concluded from their study of multicultural education literature that most materials in multicultural education were developed for the elementary level and teacher guides were usually single lessons rather than units or comprehensive courses of study. They also found that there were very few research studies at the elementary or secondary levels; most of the literature was still merely advocacy. If secondary art teachers desire to make multicultural education a goal of their art programs they must be concerned with issues of diversity, prejudice, and equity. They must be prepared to develop teaching strategies appropriate to learning styles and cultural backgrounds of their students and at the same time foster an intercultural understanding, both aesthetically and culturally, of an entire range of art objects. To accomplish these ends, programs, resources, and text books need to be developed that address these issues. The research skills and time needed to accomplish culturally pluralistic art education for all middle and secondary students are prohibitive. This task should not rest solely on the shoulders of art teachers but should be supported by local, state, and community resources; there remains much work to be done to successfully teach art to secondary students from all cultural backgrounds.

References

Bennett, C. I. (1979). *Comprehensive multicultural education: Theory and practice.* Boston: Allyn and Bacon.
Bersson, R. (1983). For cultural democracy: A critique of elitism in art education. *The Bulletin of the*

Caucus on Social Theory and Art Education, 3, 25-32.

Berrson, R. (1986). Why art education lacks social relevance: A contextual analysis. *Art Education, 39* (4), 41-45.

Blandy, D., & Congdon, K. (1988). A multi-cultural symposium on appreciating and understanding the arts. *Art Education, 41* (6), 20-24.

Boughton, D. (1986). How do we prepare art teachers for a multicultural society? *Journal of Multicultural and Cross-cultural Research in Art Education, 4* (1), 94-99.

Chalmers, F. G. (1978). Teaching and studying art history: Some anthropological and sociological considerations. *Studies in Art Education, 20* (1), 18-25.

Chalmers, F. G. (1984). Art education as ethnology. In R. N. MacGregor (Ed.), *Readings in Canadian Art Education* (pp. 103-115). British Columbia, Canada: Development Group Faculty of Education.

Chapman, L. (1978). *Approaches to art in education.* New York: Harcourt Brace Jovanovich.

Chapman, L. (1982). *Instant art, instant culture: The unspoken policy for American schools.* New York: Teachers College Press.

Clark, G., & Zimmerman, E. (1985). A Tibetan pilgrimage: Exploring the arts of a nomadic culture. *Journal of Multi-cultural and Cross-cultural Research in Art Education, 3* (1), 44-50.

Clifford, J. (1988). *The predicament of culture: Twentieth century ethnography, literature, and art.* Cambridge, MA: Harvard University Press.

Collins, G., & Sandell, R. (1984). *Women, art, and education.* Reston, VA: National Art Education Association.

Congdon, K. (1985a). A folk group focus for multicultural education. *Art Education, 37* (1), 13-16.

Congdon, K. (1985b). The study of folk art in our school's art classrooms: Some problems and considerations. *Journal of Multi-cultural and Cross-cultural Research in Art Education, 3* (1), 65-73.

Eisner, E. W. (1988). Discipline-based art education: Its criticisms and its critics. *Art Education, 4* (6), 7-13.

Feldman, E. B. (1970). *Becoming human through art: Aesthetic experience in the school.* Englewood Cliffs, NJ: Prentice-Hall.

Gardner, J. W. (1962). *Excellence: Can we be equal and excellent too?* New York: Harper Colophon Books.

Grigsby, J. E. (1977). *Art and ethnics: Background for teaching youth in a pluralistic society.* Dubuque, Iowa: Wm. C. Brown.

Hamblen, K. (1984). The universal-relative dialectic in an international perspective on art. *The Journal of Aesthetic Education, 18* (2), 99-102.

Hough, L., & King, D. C. (1979). *World views through the arts.* New York: Global Perspectives in Education.

Hughes, R. (1988, 31 October). Evoking the spirit ancestors: The ancient, mythic world of the Aborigines comes alive. *Time,* pp. 79-80.

Jenkinson, E. B. (1986). *The schoolbook protest movement.* Bloomington, IN: Phi Delta Kappan.

Jenkinson, E. B. (1988). The new age of schoolbook protest. *Phi Delta Kappan, 70* (1), 66-69.

Kellogg, J. B. (1988). Forces of change. *Phi Delta Kappan, 70* (3), 199-204.

Kerr-Lovano J., Shiel, T., & Zimmerman, E. (1974). *The arts in a multicultural society: Aesthetic experiences for the disadvantaged child.* Bloomington, IN: Arts in a Multicultural Society Project.

Lanier, V. (1976). *Essays in art education,* New York: MSS Information Corporation.

Lederman, A. (1988). Art for the real world. In J. Burton, A. Lederman, & P. London (Eds.), *Beyond DBAE: The case for multiple visions of art education* (pp. 78-86). North Dartmouth, MA: University Council on Art Education.

Loeb, H. (1983). The visual arts in multicultural education. Occasional papers VIII. London, England: School of Oriental and African Studies. (ERIC Document Reproduction Service No. ED 248 153).

London, P. (1988). To gaze again at the stars. In J. Burton, A. Lederman, & P. London (Eds.).*Beyond DBAE: The case for multiple visions of art education* (pp. 26-41). North Dartmouth, MA: University Council on Art Education.

Mason, R. (1986). Helping student-teachers broaden their conceptions of art curricula. *Art Education, 39* (4), 46-51.

McFee, J. K. (1988). Art and society. In *Issues in discipline-based art education: Strengthening the stance, extending the horizons* (pp. 104-112). Los Angeles, CA: The Getty Center for Education in the Arts.

McFee, J.K., & Degge, R. M. (1977). *Art, culture, and environment: A catalyst for teaching.* Belmont, CA: Wadsworth.

Nadaner, D. (1981). Art and cultural understanding: The role of film in education. *Art Education, 34* (4), 6-8.

Nadaner, D. (1984). My new friend painted that: Developing social understanding through art criticism. *Art Education, 36* (5), 24-26.

Nadaner, D. (1985). The art teacher as cultural mediator. *Journal of Multi-cultural and Cross-cultural Research in Art Education, 3* (1), 51-55.

Olsen, L. (1988). Crossing the schoolhouse border: Immigrant children in California. *Phi Delta Kappan, 70* (3), 211-218.

Rodriguez, F., & Sherman, A. (1983). *Cultural pluralism and the arts* (Contract No. 008104518). Washington, D.C.: U.S. Department of Education Ethnic Heritage Studies Program and the University of Kansas.

Rogers, T. (1988). The schoolbook protest movement: A warning for art educators. *Art Education, 41* (5), 6-7.

Rosenblum, P. (1981). The popular culture and art education. *Art Education, 34,* (1), 8-11.

Silverman, R. (1988). The egalitarianism of discipline-based art education. *Art Education, 41* (2), 13-18.

Sleeter, C. E., & Grant, C. A. (1987). An analysis of multicultural education in the United States. *Harvard Educational Review, 57* (4), 421-444.

Smith, R. A. (1981). Elitism versus populism: A question of quality. *Art Education, 34* (4), 4-5.

Smith, R. A. (1982). Elitism versus populism: The continuing debate. *Aesthetic Education, 16* (1), 5-10.

Smith, R. A. (1986). *Excellence in art education: Ideas and initiatives.* Reston, VA: National Art Education Association.

Taylor, R. (1987). *Educating for art.* London, England: Longman.

Young, B. (1985). Visual arts and black children. *Art Education, 37* (1), 36-38).

Notes

[1]Sletter and Grant's (1987) review was limited to books and articles published in the United States about American schools grades K-12. They conducted an Education Resources Information Center (ERIC) search and identified a total of 89 articles and 38 books. No visual art resources were included in their review. Using the same descriptors in the ERIC system, I was able to locate eleven references specific to art and multicultural education.

[2]Both Chapman's (1978) and Feldman's (1970) teacher education textbooks present cultural pluralistic approaches to teaching art and are recommended as resources for teaching students from all cultural backgrounds. They are addressed, however, more toward teaching art to elementary rather than secondary students and, therefore, are not included in this discussion.

15
The Role of the Researcher in Secondary Art Education

LINDA S. BRADLEY

Duval County Public Schools,
Jacksonville, Florida, and
University of North Florida

The role of the researcher in secondary art education is of special interest to me because I returned for one year to the secondary art classroom to do research about the young adolescent. I returned to the public schools as a middle school art teacher in an inner city school in one of the largest school districts in Florida. This year allowed me to re-examine my views on art teacher education, particularly in regard to curriculum and instruction, learning styles, motivation, and discipline. After having been an art education professor for several years, I found this return to the secondary school provided me with an opportunity to determine whether beginning teachers are being adequately prepared to teach secondary school art, especially in urban or inner city schools. Since I was returning to the art classroom after an absence of 10 years, this experience gave me the opportunity to compare and contrast secondary art, students, administrators, facilities, and schools in general, to determine how things had changed in a decade.

Research Partnerships Between Universities and School Districts

More research is needed in secondary art education. For research to be applicable to situations in secondary art classrooms, researchers must work more closely with school districts. Researchers have to become more aware of the actual needs of students, teachers, and administrators at the building, system, and state levels with regard to art education research, and then they need to help address those concerns. Researchers are beginning to examine the research problems teachers face in their classrooms. In the past, rewards

Conte crayon.

for doing school-related research were not an incentive for many reseachers; consequently, many chose to pursue more theoretical problems in their discipline (Duckett, 1986a, p. 463). In addition, the problem was compounded because teachers perceived university professors as "lacking a realistic understanding of what goes on in classrooms" (Duckett, 1986b, p. 162).

In the United States, school districts and universities have recently begun to work cooperatively on common goals of teacher education in research and teacher training (Ishler and Leslie, 1987). In some states as part of omnibus education acts, legislative mandates have been enacted which will require professors to return to school classrooms for periods of time in order to remain current with what is occurring in the schools (Wisniewski, 1986, p. 291; Warshaw, 1986).

What Does the Teacher Need From the Researcher?

One area which needs to be studied is learning style. When providing instruction, teachers need to understand and relate teaching style to the student's individual learning preference. It is important for teachers to know how students personally analyze and interact during the learning experience in order to motivate them. In addition, within secondary classrooms the teacher will find a wide range of learning abilities within the grade level, with the range of differences in ability increasing with age.

Learning style indicates how a student learns and likes to learn. Style characteristics reflect genetic coding, personality development, motivation, and environmental adaptation, and cognitive and affective elements (Keefe, 1988). Since students will have different learning styles and abilities, one method of instruction will not apply to all students. McFee's (1961) Perception-Delineation Theory in the field of art education is similar to one aspect of current research on learning style.

McFee's writings, especially the Perception-Delineation Theory, provided ways for teachers to accommodate individual student differences found within their classrooms. The Theory provided teachers with ways to obtain information about their students:

as you assess their readiness; ... create a classroom psycho-

logical environment that is encouraging and supportive of children from different cultures; ... select things to stimulate their interest in art and create with them a workable physical environment; ... help them use the new information in terms of their readiness; ... provide means for them to express and create through art or critique art and environments, and ... assess what they have learned, how their readiness has changed and so you can plan with them their next activities (p. 147).

The Perception-Delineation Theory deserves to be re-examined and/or extended by researchers as it relates to current literature on learning style found in educational literature. Art education researchers need to examine the adolescent's cognitive development, individual differences in information handling, and the cultural diversity found in public schools today.

Learning problems frequently are not related to the difficulty of the subject matter, but rather to the type and level of the cognitive proceses required to learn the material. Research has determined that individual influences on a student's ability to apply specific cognitive skills may be attributed to environmental preferences, for example, the level of light, heat, or noise present during learning; the amount of active, hands-on learning allowed; a need for mobility; the size of the work group; and the time of day (Keefe, 1988, p. 23). Since students come to school with enormously different interests, aptitudes, and background experiences, it is difficult for them to adapt to a uniform curriculum.

A second area where research is needed deals with teaching in urban schools. One criticism of higher education is that"current university programs are not adequately preparing teachers for work in urban schools" (Haberman, 1987, p. 6) or to work with the diverse student populations often found in urban settings. To help resolve this, some universitities are beginning pre-service training programs to train teachers for urban schools by placing them in classrooms under the supervision and leadership of successful master teachers. Beginning teachers working in urban settings need to be knowledgeable about multi-cultural education, especially methods of effective curriculum and instructional planning, organization and management, how to communicate with students who speak non-standard English, ways to motivate these students, and methods in student and teacher evaluations.

The role of the researcher. Secondary drawing from the Duval County
Public Schools, Jacksonville, Florida.

Educational research of this type is currently being done, with teacher education departments providing courses about teaching in urban settings; however, art teacher education needs to conduct similar research which is applicable to the field of art. Cross-cultural art education is one such area where much study is needed (Lovano-Kerr, 1983). More ethnographic research needs to be done regarding practices of experienced inner city art teachers to determine how they motivate students to achieve success in art.

Third, current trends indicate that increasing numbers of students, especially those from minority groups, are at-risk of not graduating from high school. These at-risk students who have not succeeded under current standards generally are already alienated from formal schooling. Frequently they have been retained and are older than their classmates: are underachievers; and have personal problems such as drug abuse, pregnancy, and poverty-related difficulties (Barber and McClellan, 1987, p. 264).

Some states have come to realize that school programs need to assist these at-risk groups; consequently, state art education associations have been asked to assist state departments of education in resolving these problems.

In art education, much research has dealt with the production areas of painting and drawing with very little research into the other production areas such as crafts (Chapman, 1982, p. 105). However, at the secondary level, the drawing and painting development of the middle school and senior high aged adolescent still needs further study (Bradley, 1986). Research such as child drawing development studies by Lowenfeld (1987) needs to be extended to include the entire adolescent period.

Art education researchers need to work with state departments of education to compile surveys dealing with "basic census data" (Chapman, 1982, p. 108) about the facilities, teaching responsibilities, training, and resources provided to secondary art teachers nationwide.

More research is needed in administration and public opinion about art in secondary schools. Chapman (1982) states that more research needs to be done about art teachers' beliefs and preferences as they influence what students learn. There is a need for public school art administrators and universities to work with state departments of education to strengthen the quality of art instuction provided. The goals of secondary art education need to be established, with the rationale for art in the school curricula firmly established (Clark, 1986, p. 4).

Along with what students learn, research into assessment instruments of learning in the arts will be of importance because "they are the tools teachers will use to detemine whether the pace of instruction is appropriate or whether their instructional objectives have been met" (Stiggins, 1988, p. 363). Art education researchers have a responsibility to ensure the quality and appropriateness of these assessment instruments as used in the art classroom.

Conclusion

Even though psychologist G. Stanley Hall, who initiated the Child Study Movement, urged teachers to recognize the importance of the adolescent years in development, this age group has been overlooked in much art education research.

In the area of curriculum and instruction there needs to be an examination of how and what to teach and when to present the material (Smith, 1986). This is an area in which researchers can provide much needed assistance. Each of these questions could be used to determine how adolescents acquire knowledge and skills in the four areas of art curriculum: art production, criticism, aesthetics, and art history.

Eisner (1972) states that "The major contribution of research resides not in its ability to provide directives but in its ability to provide perspectives, ways of looking at educatonal phenomena, and ways of asking new questions" (p. 254).

Michael (1983) sums up the need for art education research about the adolescent very clearly by stating, "After teaching art for many years at all levels, I have found the secondary level to be the least understood. Perhaps this is a result of — or is reflected by — the meager amount of research and writing which has been done in this area" (p. xiii). He continues by saying that secondary art teachers need research because they tend to "approach the teaching of art at the junior and senior high school either from an emphasis on creative child art or an emphasis on professional adult art" (p. xiii).

Researchers in art education need to focus on the secondary level. They need to realize that students in the final years of their secondary school education are the ones upon whom we need to impress the importance of art in today's society. These students are the nation's future leaders, and they will determine the level of importance placed on art education in the school curriculum in the years ahead.

References

Barber, L. W., & McClellan, M. C. (1987). Looking at America's dropouts: Who are they ? *Phi Delta Kappan, 69* (4), 264-267.
Bradley, L. S. (1986). Graphic development of the early adolescent. *Visual Arts Research, 12* (1), 55-67.
Chapman, L. H. (1982). *Instant art, instant culture: The unspoken policy for American schools.* New York: Teachers College.
Clark, G. (1986). We need all the help we can get. *Art Education, 39* (2), 4.
Duckett, W. (1986a). An interview with William Cooley: Improving the public schools through decision-oriented research. *Phi Delta Kappan, 67* (6), 462-466.
Duckett, W. (1986b). An interiew with Robert Eaker: Linking research and classroom practice. *Phi Delta Kappan, 68* (2), 161-164.
Eisner, E. W. (1972). *Educating artistic vision.* New York: Macmillan.
Ishler, R. E., & Leslie, E. C. (1987), Bridging the gap between a public school system and a university. *Phi Delta Kappan, 68,* 8, 615-616.
Haberman, M. (1987). *Recruiting and selecting teachers for urban schools.* Reston: Association of Teacher Educators.
Keefe, J. W. (Ed.). (1988). *Profiling and utilizing learning style.* Reston: National Association of Secondary School Principals.
Lovano-Kerr, J. (1983). Cross-cultural perspectives on cognition and art: Implications for research. *Journal of Multi-cultural and Cross-Cultural Research in Art Education, 1* (1), 77-87.
Lowenfild, V., & Brittain, W. L. (1987). *Creative and mental growth* (8th ed.). New York: Macmillan Publishing Co. Inc.
McFee, J. K (1961). *Preparation for art.* San Francisco: Wadsworth.
McFee, J. K., & Degge, R. M. (1977). *Art, culture, and environment: A catalyst for teaching.* Belmont: Wadsworth
Michael, J. A. (1983). *Art and adolescence: Teaching art at the secondary level.* New York: Teachers College Press.
Smith, R. A. (1986). *Excellence in art education: Ideas and initiatives.* Reston: National Art Education Association.
Stiggins, R. J. (1988). Revitalizing classroom assessment: The highest instructional priority. *Phi Delta Kappan, 69* (5), 363-368.
Washaw, M. (1986), Return from the tower, *Phi Delta Kappan, 68* (1), 67-69.
Wisniewski, R. (1986). The ideal professor of education. *Phi Delta Kappan, 68* (4), 298-292.

16
Theory-Practice Schisms of the 1990s

KAREN A. HAMBLEN

Louisiana State University

The often-cited statement by Santayana that we are fated to repeat the past if we don't heed the lessons from our history can be extended into predictions for the future. Predictions for the future may serve as warnings of events that should be reshaped, if not completely avoided. By the same token, predictions can imply a certain inevitability and become self-fulfilling. It is with these pitfalls and possible pratfalls in mind that predictions for art education in the 1990s need to be framed and qualified.

Just as we continually reassess and revise the meanings we give events of the past, so also, predictions need to be understood within the framework of reassessments and readjustments that are continually subject to revision and updates. It is tricky, if not foolhardy, to predict the future with a sense of inevitability. There are, however, some characteristics of our field and of society — and, one might even suggest, characteristics of human nature — that allow us to predict some possible future events with a modicum of certainty. One such prediction is that there will be theory-practice schisms in art education.

The purpose of this chapter is to describe the configurations that theory-practice schisms may take in the next decade. The history of art education and current theory-practice schisms provide some powerful clues as to the shape art education may take in the 1990s. For example, some current difficulties with and objections to the implementation of discipline-based art education (DBAE) can be extended into the near future. In this sense, prediction is thoroughly grounded in the past and in the present. Just as taxes and death are inevitable, in art education the existence of differences between theory and practice has been more or less a constant. Laments by university researchers on the gulf between theory and practice bring on yawns of *deja vu* or resentment on the part of already overly burdened classroom teachers. Classroom teachers find that theories and research results often bear little resemblance to the realities of instruction.

In art education, theory-practice schisms have existed, do exist, and, in all probability, will continue to plague both university researchers and classroom teachers. The only thing in question would appear to be the exact characteristics such schisms will have in the future. Therefore, the purpose of this chapter is to discuss possible characteristics of 1990s theory and practice differences based on (1) the history of our field's theory-practice schisms, (2) factors that inhibit classroom implementation of theory, and (3) theories that are now being presented to the field.

History's Theory-Practice Differences

In many respects, the history of art education is a history of the two parallel developments of theory and practice that only occasionally deviate from their courses and intersect. Even our written histories of the field are most often the histories of theory and not of what actually occurred in the schools. The Owatonna Project has come to characterize the 1930s, although its impact beyond the small community of Owatonna is questionable. The 1960s and 1970s are discussed as a series of movements in environmental design, aesthetic education, art education for social responsibility, aesthetic literacy, and so on, although the extent to which any of these were formerly implemented was probably minimal.

That historians tend to chronicle theory to the exclusion of the daily, concrete experiences of teachers and students dates to the inception of our field. From a review of nineteenth century Massachusetts school records, Bolin (1988) found that Walter Smith's ideas on art education were not as widely implemented as we have been lead to believe through our written, formal histories (Logan, 1955). Our written histories, in this sense, both document and proceed from differences between theoretical prescriptions by researchers and the actual practices of classroom instructors. In our professional journals, we read about one world, and, in our classrooms, we encounter another. This is not to say that theory and practice are necessarily antagonistic. The child-centered approach of Progressive Education and later of Lowenfeld embodied theory that was highly compatible with studio production and art teachers' perceived roles as nourishers of creativity (Doerr, 1984). However, the persistence of Lowenfeldian principles of

212

instruction may not so much attest to the implementation of theory per se or to Lowenfeld's unique vision of art education as much as how his vision fits within the studio model of instruction and the characteristics, values, and assumptions teachers have brought to the classroom. Theory and practice primarily converge when theory is compatible with or adjustable to the realities of practice and require minimal adjustment of the latter.

Classroom teachers are well-aware that what they do in their instructional settings often bears little resemblance to the prescribed programs that appear on the pages of research journals and in the hefty tomes published by state departments of education. Theory and its supportive research provide a formalized and consistent explication of rationales underlying proposed practice. In contrast, teachers' actions are governed by the practicalities of the classroom; their practice is based on tacit knowledge and an intuitive sense of "what works."

Although for purposes of clarity and brevity, theory and practice will be discussed in this chapter as two separate and integral entities, such, of course, is not really the case. Theory and practice are each multilayered and often self-contradictory. Regarding practice, Efland (1976) notes that teacher intent and actual practice may be sharply divergent. We have numerous instances in which defenders of Lowenfeld discuss how his ideas have been misinterpreted and misapplied (*Art Education,* 1982). One might cogently argue that Lowenfeld's theory of art education has only rarely been pristinely implemented. Programs purporting to teach for creativity are usually pale imitators of truly creative enterprises inasmuch as school activities must be compatible with rules imposed by school administrations, time requirements of school schedules, and social definitions of good taste. Degge's (1976) study of a junior high art class revealed numerous levels of meaning, interpretation, and contradiction co-existing among the teacher's stated theory, her actions, the students' behaviors, the students' interpretations of their behaviors and the teacher's statements, and so on. There is, therefore, no mere singular theory-practice relationship, but rather a series of fits and misalignments, with practice, at best, approximating the broad-based intent of a particular theory.

Sources of Theory-Practice Schisms

Erickson (1979) attributes theory-practice schisms in art education to our proto-discipline status. Although we can trace our history to well-established programs of art instruction in the last century, we do not have a well-formulated body of research or theory development to support practice such as more mature disciplines have. Erickson also finds the feminization of the field to be an impediment to the development of theory and the conducting of supportive research studies. Female art educators, who have predominated in the field, have tended not to see themselves as researchers or as dealing with the abstractions of theory. Feminine characteristics have also been applied to the field of art education in general and to the role of the artist in particular (Doerr, 1984). Recent research on gender issues would tend to bear out Erickson's contentions, inasmuch as females in various professions either do not perceive themselves as researchers and creators of meaning or, through decades of discriminatory practices, have been prevented from exercising those roles (Rush, 1985).

According to Erickson (1979), women art educators have tended to place a high value on their roles as artists. Again, this value has often been shared with male art educators. In a similar vein, other studies have found that teachers, male and female, tend to value classroom activities for their own sake rather than for what these might accomplish, let alone how closely such activities adhere to stated goals or some underlying theory (Lortie, 1975). Personal and practical knowledge based on the requirements of specific classroom contexts take precedence in the value system of most classroom teachers. Lortie (1975) finds that for teachers the present takes primacy, and there is a resistence to changes that are not based on experience, i.e., are based on abstract principles and statements.

In surveying the history of art education, Lanier (1975) was moved to write that the more art education changes, the more it stays the same. Essentially, Lanier was pointing out that while art education theory varies over time, classroom practice is surprisingly consistent and resistant to theory proposed by academicians. Much of the apparent variations within art education have remained on paper — as journal article publications, as conference discussions, or as content for graduate level seminars. Classroom art instruction, since its inception, has consisted primarily of studio activities. Although the rationales for studio production vary over time, since the Progressive movement of the 1920s and 1930s and later Lowenfeld's widespread impact on the field, there has been a certain amount of consistency in the belief that studio activities tap and promote creativity, self-expression, personal growth, and a general appreciation of art. The concrete, focused nature of studio work coincides with teachers' reliance on

214

personal and practical knowledge, on activities that are context specific, and on short-term outcomes. The studio model of art instruction has provided continuity to practice and resistance to alternative models.

Traditionally, each art teacher has been more or less responsible for developing his/her own curriculum. Just as studio activities have often been devised to elicit differences among student outcomes, art teachers have, likewise, acquired an independence not often seen in other subject areas. Mathematics, science, and language teachers strive for a commonality within their respective fields. Conversely, art teachers, in their own teaching and in their students' work, search for ways to create differences. Art teachers can be fiercely independent and are particularly resistant to theory unless it is amenable to their value system.

The values of teachers in general and the character of art instruction in particular are but two sources of theory-practice schisms. Not to be discounted is the lack of time and opportunity for teachers to implement theory, to pursue research interests, and to have the administrative support to make major changes. Also, as teachers often mention, much theory and research in art education is difficult to understand and to implement, and much is simply inappropriate to the classroom or of little significance for practice.

Various motives and values enter into the production and utilization of theory and research, not least of which is academia's admonition to the professor to "publish or perish." Classroom teachers are rightly skeptical of academic ivory towerism and of studies needing major translation and adjustment if they are to be made classroom "friendly." This is not to suggest that researchers and theorists only work for job security. Theory can be proposed with an optimistic idealism of what should/might be and also with an acknowledgement that major adjustments would be needed for implementation. After a decade of proposing ways art study could be focused toward understanding human relationships for social responsibility, Lanier acknowledged that, while this was still a good idea, it had very little chance to be implemented in the real world of classroom instruction. Likewise, in discussing approaches to aesthetic study and proposing an emphasis on critical consciousness, I have stated that this latter approach is incompatible with current educational practices and has little chance of success (Hamblen, 1988). Nonetheless, I believe that it is important that this option for aesthetic study be explicated and available to the field.

215

Various movements are underway to overcome some of the more blatant theory-practice incompatibilities. The Holmes Group's report on teacher education reform specifies that a special level of career professional be established consisting of individuals trained to translate theory and research for the classroom teacher's use (Holmes Group Executive Board, 1986). Career professionals would bridge the gaps between theory and practice and between academia and the classroom. The recent funding of research institutes by the National Endowment for the Arts is another attempt to generate theory and research that has more-or-less direct classroom application ($800,000 National Arts Education Research Center, 1987).

Theory development and research in art education can serve a function similar to that of basic research in the sciences, i.e., the generation of new ideas, the examination of current ideas and practice, the exploration of possibilities, etc. In this sense, basic theory and research have much in common with the value placed on divergent thinking in the studio-based art classroom. If a field only has applied theory and research, it will stagnate. Conversely, when most theory and research is idealistic, esoteric, or self-serving, classroom teachers are either unable to understand it and translate it into practice, or it is just plainly seen as being of no value. It is not my purpose to propose what proportion of researchers' efforts should be devoted to basic or to applied theory and research, but rather that a dictatorship of either basic or applied be avoided. To that extent, some degree of a theory-practice schism is unavoidable and, in fact, healthy.

Predictions for the 1990s

Undoubtedly, in the 1990s, we will continue to see a variety of theories such as we have seen in the past, many of which will come and go without creating hardly a ripple in classroom practice. The strong focus on studio production will, in all probability, continue in art education, with this prediction contingent upon teacher education retaining its focus on studio courses for art content. Technique, formal qualities, and media will probably remain strong contenders for curriculum content and organization. Any changes will, to this extent, be slow and incremental to the studio model of instruction. Art study will mean, in most instances, the making of art. Art teachers on the secondary level will continue to exhibit an independence and pride in differences among their students' work and in the strengths of their individually developed curricula.

In most respects, these predictions can be made for the short-term future of art education, and, in broad outline, these characteristics will probably be evident for some time to come. There are, however, some indications that art education may undergo some major changes in outward appearance, if not in substance. The 1990s could portend some differences due to several crucial factors. The back-to-basics movement in general education has caused a reassessment of some current practices in art education, such as the "nonacademic" nature attributed to studio and child-centered instruction. This movement and the aesthetic education model dating from 1965 have been embraced by the Getty Center for Education in the Arts in its support of discipline-based art education (DBAE) (The J. Paul Getty Trust, 1985). Any prediction for the 1990s must take its major configurations from the infusion of grant monies, curricula developed within the DBAE model, and the consortium supportive of DBAE that has been formed among national arts organizations, governmental agencies, and philanthropic foundations.

In the past, philanthropic attention given to art education was neither programmatic nor national in overall scale and thrust. The Getty Center for Education in the Arts, as part of The J. Paul Getty Trust, combines money and influence with a theory that is specifically focused toward eventual classroom implementation. DBAE theory differs from previous theory and research in that it is not piecemeal, esoteric, or regional. It is national in scope, has its roots in the twenty-year old aesthetic education movement, and conforms to the characteristics of general education.Combining the Getty's influence, prestige, and political acumen, not to mention a generous budget, one might think that the 1990s would see a major convergence between DBAE theory and classroom practice. That may be the case. A number of factors, however, indicate that the marriage of DBAE theory and practice may be less than blissfully compatible. When the Rand Corporation (1984) was hired to conduct a study of school districts having an aesthetic education curriculum, only two districts in the U.S.A. were found to have programs approximating such instruction. Moreover, at the time of the Rand study, instruction in aesthetics was not part of the criteria for assessment, as it is now. From what the Rand Corporation found regarding the status quo in 1984, it is evident that DBAE theory, if pristinely adhered to, would represent a major change in art instruction.

According to published literature sponsored by the Getty, the distinguishing characteristics of DBAE theory are as follows: art instruction is to consist of content in the four areas of aesthetics, art criticism, art history, and studio production; instruction is to be sequenced within and between grades; student outcomes are to be evaluated; and the DBAE curriculum is to be implemented district-wide (Clark, Day, & Greer, 1987). Given the Getty's prestige and the national organizational support of this interpretation of DBAE, one might think that an alignment of theory and practice would be inevitable. DBAE theory, however, already shows signs of erosion, with significant changes having been made from initial theoretical pronouncements. Some of these changes are due simply to misinterpretations of DBAE theory. Others are due to concessions being made in response to objections, to difficulties in implementation, and to vehement criticisms.

Misinterpretations and Other Erosions of Theory

Many teachers already believe they are teaching a DBAE curriculum inasmuch as they have studio activities which upon completion are discussed in group critiques, art historical reproductions are used to expand upon studio lessons, and formal qualities are studied to foster aesthetic appreciation. Among such teachers, there may be little perceived reason to change substantially their curricula.

A major problem with implementing a DBAE curriculum has hinged on the need to teach in the four content areas. A simultaneous sequencing of content in four areas is no mean feat. Initially it was believed that equal instructional time would be devoted to each of the four areas; later, this was changed to the proposal that the four areas would be treated equally in substance, if not necessarily in actual time. In many instances, this has come to mean that studio activities act as the core and integrator for the sequencing of content, with the other three areas as major components of each studio lesson. In this respect, DBAE theory has been adjusted to the value system and expectations of the status quo.

In art classes taught by nonspecialists, such as is common in the elementary grades, practice will perhaps most closely approximate original DBAE theory in terms of content, sequencing, and evaluation. Nonspecialists will more closely follow prepared curricula and will not have the strong personal and professional commitment to the studio model of instruction. Nor will they necessarily object to a tightly focused program dealing with content that some critics of DBAE believe inhibit creativity and self-expression.

218

(Burton, Lederman, & London, 1988).

However, in implementation by nonspecialists, much of the diversity and richness of content envisioned by the original DBAE theorists may be lost. For example, Day (1985) believed that evaluation of outcomes constitutes a major difference with previous art programs. Day went on to cite numerous ways to evaluate art outcomes. Subsequently, however, evaluation has most often come to mean objective pencil — and — paper testing and standardized tests (Greer & Hoepfner, 1986). Art content amenable to such testing has usually been factually based, dealing with formal qualities and technical information.

Teacher education is, perhaps, the starting point for future theory-practice convergence and for the implementation of dramatic curriculum changes. One might argue, however, that preservice art teachers have never really been adequately educated in studio instruction, let alone in the other three areas of DBAE. Rarely are preservice art teachers schooled in all the art techniques they will be required to teach, let alone schooled in the research findings that support content and methods of studio instruction. For DBAE, prospective art teachers will need to have content and methods courses in all four DBAE content areas. Even at those universities in which major course requirement revisions have been made, only studio and art history requirements show any hints of parity. Usually one or two classes in aesthetics and art criticism constitute study in those content areas.

How change or, more specifically, the implementation of theory can be interjected into a pre-existing system has been a major concern of philanthropic, governmental, and academic institutions. The Artist-in-the-Schools program of the 1970s that was sponsored by the National Endowment for the Arts was successful to the extent it adapted instruction by artists to elementary schools with few or no existing art programs and to secondary schools where studio instruction was already provided by an art specialist. The status quo, anywhere in a system, can sabotage major change. The Holmes Group Executive Board (1986) report on educational reform indicates that student teachers who bring new approaches into their field experiences are often reprimanded or redirected toward existing practice. For DBAE theory and practice to converge in the next generation of teachers, student teachers with a DBAE background will need to be supervised by master teachers likewise schooled in DBAE content and methods. Major institutions that are promoting change are finding that even if a theory is perceived as positive and worthy of implementation, change must be interjected within numerous areas of a system and, optimally, implemented in time as closely as possible.

To bring some type of fit between theory and practice, the following factors, institutions, and constituencies need to be considered: existing instructional practices, high school graduation requirements, university entrance requirements, teachers' value systems, teacher training, administrators' expectations, inservice for master teachers, preservice experiences, and art students' expectations. Student expectations that art study consists of making art and a subsequent loss of student interest for other types of instruction are major concerns of secondary teachers who wish to implement DBAE, but who are aware of the need to maintain enrollment figures in elective classes. Of course, requiring such classes for graduation and/or university entrance would lessen this problem.

Opponents of DBAE Theory-Practice Alignments

Schisms between DBAE theory and practice in the 1990s will not only be due to misinterpretations and difficulties inherent in implementation. Major criticisms of the Getty's interpretation of DBAE will also play a role. Various criticisms are developing, with the most vocal and strong critique emanating from those who believe that DBAE theory ignores creative expression, minimizes studio production, and negates what has made art a valuable area of study (Burton, Lederman, & London, 1988). In essence, this critique maintains the values of the status quo.

Others fault DBAE theory for being excessively narrow in focus, and they call for instructional content that is inclusive of nonwestern art, ecological considerations, collaborative art and folk art, and is responsive to the way anthropologists and sociologists construct artistic meaning (Blandy & Congdon, 1987). A third critique of the Getty's interpretation of DBAE theory faults it for too closely resembling the characteristics of general education, limiting ways DBAE could be interpreted and implemented, and not allowing for the development of critical consciousness (Hamblen, 1987).

Summary

DBAE theory has already, for various reasons, undergone modification as it has become part of practice. DBAE theory and practice may be closest when implemented by nonspecialists and when specific programs are funded by the Getty Center for Education in the Arts. Along with DBAE theory-practice schisms, the 1990s will continue to see art instruction as it has been traditionally taught. As noted earlier, some instructors of the studio model of instruction will assume that they have embraced DBAE principles, again indicating that practice embodies layers of meanings and inconsistencies — which could very easily be seen as indicative of a schism between practice and goals.

For various reasons, art education researchers will undoubtedly continue to formulate theories that have little chance of wide-spread implementation. Some of these theories will be distinguished by their idealistic nature, others by their obscure nature, and still others by their attempts to provide alternatives to DBAE and/or traditional studio instruction. Kuhn (1970), in his discussion of how change occurs in the sciences, stressed the role that dissident researchers play by causing a consolidation among the status quo as well as by providing insights and debate that may foment change. Given the practical requirements of classroom instruction, the emotional security provided by the status quo, and the differing values of researchers and classroom teachers, there will always be theory-practice schisms. Differences between theory and practice should be anticipated, and, as long as they do not rigidify the field, they should be valued.

References

Art Education. (1982). *35* (6).
Blandy, D., & Congdon, K. (Eds.). (1987). *Art in a democracy.* New York: Teachers College Press.
Bolin, P. (1988). Theory and practice: An historical examination of research and change in art education. Paper presented at American Educational Research Association Conference, New Orleans.
Burton, J., Lederman, A, & London, P. (Eds.). (1988). *Beyond DBAE: The case for multiple visions of art education.* North Dartmouth, MA: Southeastern Massachusetts University.
Clark, G. A., Day, M. D., & Greer, W. D. (1987). Discipline-based art education: Becoming students of art. *Journal of Aesthetic Education, 21*(2), 129-193.
Day, M. (1985). Evaluating student achievement in discipline-based art programs. *Studies in Art Education, 26*(4), 232-240.
Degge, R. (1976). A case study and theoretical analysis of teaching practice in one junior high art class. (Doctoral dissertation, University of Oregon, 1975). *Dissertation abstracts international, 36*

5750-A.

Doerr, S. L. (1984). If you want to get stroked, talk to your mother: Art education as the discipline it deserves to be. *Art Education, 36*(5), 31-34.

Efland, A. (1976). The school art style: A functional analysis. *Studies in Art Education, 17*(2) 37-44.

$800,000 national arts education research center created by department of education/ arts endowment. (1987, December). *NAEA News, 29*(6), p. 4.

Erickson, M. (1979). An historical explanation of the schism between research and practice in art education. *Studies in Art Education, 20* (2), 5-13.

The J. Paul Getty Trust. (1985). *Beyond Creating: The place for art in America's schools.* (1985). Los Angeles: The J. Paul Getty Trust.

Greer, W. D., & Hoepfner, R. (1986). Achievement testing in the visual arts. *Design for Arts in Education, 88*(1), 43-47.

Hamblen, K. A. (1987). An examination of discipline-based art education issues. *Studies in Art Education, 28*(2), 68-78.

Hamblen, K. (1988). Approaches to aesthetics in art education: A critical theory perspective. *Studies in Art Education, 29*(2), 81-90.

Holmes Group Executive Board. (1986). *Tomorrow's teachers: A report of the Holmes Group.* East Lansing, MI: Author.

Kuhn, T. S. (1970). *The structure of scientific revolutions.* Chicago: University of Chicago Press.

Lanier, V. (1975). Objectives of art education: The impact of time. *Peabody Journal of Education, 52* (3), 180-186.

Logan, F. (1955). *The growth of art in American schools.* New York: Harper and Brothers.

Lortie, D. (1975). *Schoolteacher: A sociological study.* Chicago, IL: University of Chicago Press.

Rand Corporation. (1984). *Art history, art criticism, and art production: An examination of art education in selected school districts, Vols. I, II, and III.* Los Angeles, Author.

Rush, J. C. (1985). Male and female: Patterns of professional behavior in the university. Paper presented at the National Art Education Association Annual Conference, Dallas, TX.

17
New Approaches to Secondary School Art Education — A Program for the Artist of the Future

GEORGE SZEKELY

University of Kentucky

Introduction

You enter the classroom through portholes cut into silver sheeting. At center stage, a student is focusing a video camera on a miniature "rolling" movie set — skateboards made up of dominoes and Legos. In another area, a student is busy searching through a microscope, discovering simple organisms whose shapes inspire elaborate images, transposed onto an Etch-a-Sketch. While some students play video games in one corner of the room, others are discussing art on an imagined "talk show." Over play phones, a teenager is "ordering" art, envisioning and fabricating images to be interpreted by someone else on the receiving end.

These are high school students? This in an art class? Where are the materials — the crayons, the paper, the paints, the still life? And where is the teacher?

The teacher is there, and the teacher is talking — but this teacher's "talk" is considered a "lecture to make art by." Students are whispering, plotting pictures, putting on disguises, and investigating a wide variety of materials in the room. Post-it papers carry a student's poetic messages stenciled to select parts of the room: "Art is the public confession of a secret," "Art arrives in a dream." Other stenciled memos are stuck on windows and aligned on doorsteps in public areas of the room.

Can you make art this way?

In an experimental secondary school art program established for the third year in the Kentucky Public Schools, sixteen classrooms have become laboratories, rehearsal halls, and play spaces where serious investigations are taking place — through the process of active play — in search of original clues to creative art making.

In this university-sponsored demonstration project, secondary school students are encouraged to turn to their own experiences and observations in discovering art. They explore environmental and natural materials, technological "toys," and collectibles. They are expected to touch, select, arrange, take apart, and discuss. Dancing, performing, and role playing are part of the "syllabus." Lights, sounds, and space are avenues used to discover every aspect of a classroom's surfaces and furnishings. Everything is potential material or inspiration for the creation of art.

The undergraduate art education classes are held in "host" schools where graduate students are employed as associates in these innovative programs, so they can learn about this project's philosophy, content, and emphasis. The "host" school is actually a laboratory site for secondary school art teachers and future teachers to cooperatively participate with university faculty in developing and implementing art programs. The program was started in 1985 with four schools. Approximately two new schools have been added each semester, selected from regional middle schools, and junior and senior high schools. Since 1985, sixteen schools and over 500 students have participated in the program. Ongoing evaluations and open dialogues are scheduled regularly as part of the follow-up process.

The basic premise behind the creation of these programs is that art students must be on the forefront of new discoveries, not handed ready-made solutions or directed by an art teacher's own inspiration. The inspiration must come from the student, if it is to have significance as art.

In the last decade, enormous changes have occurred in the public world of art, art making, and the art process. School art must respond to these changes, by challenging the young artist of the future to learn independence, to question, and to face uncertainty creatively. Art programs for students must provoke and challenge both teachers and students to rethink what art is. Students should be able to conduct their own art investigations, experiment and make decisions, as well as plan and improvise from their own art actions and experiences, not just silently receive information. Students who can learn in this way, and who can incorporate contemporary experiences into their own creative output, have the best chances of becoming contributors to the new art world.

In order to foster this new kind of thinking in art education, we must rethink our methods for creating art classroom "instruction."

The Problem with the "Traditional" Art Class

In a typical art classroom, the teacher comes to school with ideas and lesson plans. He or she brings materials and tools, which may be distributed to an unsuspecting class. The teacher demonstrates a technique, work places are assigned, and the art "project" begins. The bell stops student activities, and grades are critiques, pronouncing judgment on specific solutions to the assignment. At this point, the art work has essentially been completed.

Whose art is this, anyway? Where is the opportunity for students to experience the process of creation in its most preliminary formative state? If students do not discover their own art and learn how to plan and execute an idea, how will they ever learn to function as independent artists? And if artistic search, inspiration, decision making, moments of discovery, collection, and rehearsal are omitted, how will the students' art have any personal relevance? If the source of artwork is not authentic, the work is doomed to fail in its attempt to communicate anything to anyone.

Each class must involve students in a search for ideas so that they see themselves as art sources, generators of invention. Art always has recognized new ideas, with each generation searching and finding the answers to the same essential questions. Facing the unknown is central to the artistic challenge.

School art is too often presented in simplified answers and tried-and-true methods culled from the experiences of others. Secondary art lessons, in particular, have a responsibility to the student who often sits through long school days desperate to come alive, to breathe freely, and to think independently.

A chair wrapped as a canvas depicting a California Raisin peformance inside a lunchbox.

The Art Room and the Art Teacher: A New Perspective

If students and their art are to come alive, art rooms must become lively settings that invite movement and participation. Students must be permitted — and encouraged — to look into their own contemporary world — favorite videos and culture heroes, fashion and musical styles, and private fantasies — to locate inspiration for their creative vision. They must come prepared for art class, armed with memories and recollections of meaningful observations; they must be encouraged to search anywhere and everywhere for ideas and materials; they must maintain collections of every conceivable sort; and they must keep notes, seeking clues to their own ideas about art.

The art room must become a play space where students' collections can be displayed, where their playful actions, explorations, treasure hunts, rock concerts, light shows, dances, and performances can be given a stage. An art teacher should encourage personal styles and statements in dress, music, writing, films, video games, or any other area that helps a student discover his or her own interests and, thereby, defines a direction for his or her art.

Simple props — a pool of water, a stack of blocks — encourage the imagination to roam. In one class, students created a beach environment, using a plastic children's pool (the lake), a slide projector (the sun), and blankets and towels to add a touch of realism. They took great delight in the exploration of a new toy — special bathtub blocks that bond together when wet in gravity-defying configurations. Students observed as the sculptural monuments floated and bumped into each other, tilting over to new positions and balancing in fresh ways. This became an important lesson to the student as artist discovering and testing a new material.

Students select their own materials in the laboratory — classroom — and the classroom setup of these materials is influenced by the students' own interests, rather than the teacher's. Students are able to browse through what appears to be a flea market, a junkyard, a hidden treasure, or a secret container — but the search is an active one and opportunities abound to try out, try on, take apart, rearrange, and gather clues and experiences to begin art works from a significant and personal response to the environment.

Secondary school students have unique interests, concerns, and experiences from which their art should emanate. The particular dreams, fears, and hopes of teenagers today leads to a singular art, with its own voice and its own images. Students must be permitted to review and connect their own lives to their art — through vehicles as diverse as hairstyles, hangouts, button graphics, video arcades, and new products. Teens may exhibit art on hand painted shoes, jeans, or on glittery or brightly colored shoelaces; the tools, stencils, and imagery of customized cars, too, have brought powerful statements to school art. Interest in new technology, such as remote control, have produced images that mirror the rhythm of robotics; contemporary sounds are explored through synthesizers and experiments with tape recorders. Fears — of nuclear war, in particular — have been expressed through Halloween masks and graffiti. Students' shared conversation, and even show-and-tell sessions are valuable ways to encourage young artists to look to themselves and their own community for ideas and feedback.

The art teacher in this kind of classroom should be seen by students as a special person who welcomes student discoveries and inventive performances which bring the art room to life. He or she is a trusted person one can play in front of, share secrets and ideas with, and browse freely with, not a person who tells students to "leave all your junk at home." When students' favorite objects and collections are contraband in most other places in school, the art room must continue as the place where play is preserved and students' individual possessions are valued and inventiveness is encouraged.

The Notion of "Play" in Secondary School

In my alternating visits between elementary and secondary school art classes, I am always struck by the silence in the high school classrooms. If elementary art education is more likely to make imaginative use of play activity to introduce and inspire art, secondary school art instruction is too much like college studio instruction.

When lifeless, obedient, joyless bodies follow mechanical paths, with few exciting things in the room to see, few fun things to do, experiment with, or try out, art works tend naturally to be less inventive, less lively in spirit, material, and form. As students become further removed in time and mental set from invention, environmental experimentation, and self-initiated playing, they become more immobilized when asked to work without a teacher's specifications.

The fewer the opportunities for older students to "practice" playing, the more necessary play is in order for them to see or create art from a fresh perspective, and to be capable of generating original art problems and solutions. Even though they may have "been away" for a long time, students of any age don't need much prompting to return to the world of imaginative activity. The simple pleasures of playing in the water, digging in the earth, or piling up rocks are never forgotten — even after toys are long discarded at home and playing has been rejected in the classroom as students reach the upper grades.

If art is to be fresh and experimental, those eager pots and pans players in all students must be revived. Some students may be shy at first, or feel awkward playing within school boundaries, but a playful teacher or a challenging setting can draw in participants. No one is too old to enjoy the fun of confetti, the trying on of hats from a 1930's collection, or inventing hairstyles of the future. The joys of clapping and snapping hands, drumming bodies, parades, circuses, and light shows are alive and well in even the most frozen souls. Playing "house" is a natural prelude to the design and decoration of private spaces.

As play becomes a part of every art class, students regain their ability to see everything in a playful light — a natural and necessary preparation for the creation of new art. Activities may move freely in space, from tables to floors or even under tables — remember Michaelangelo, working on his back with his canvas above him? Windows can become observation decks to the streets, or to the heavens; they can become control towers or mystical mirrors. Furnishings become not just chairs and tables, but armatures, easels, airport runways, or stages. A painting may start with the arrangement of flowers, a salad bar display, or a table setting of brightly colored dishes. Faces are not exempt from the fun — mirror play, mouth sounds, and makeup all extend our notion of what is an art canvas. The classroom becomes larger than itself by the bringing in of earth, snow, parts of trees, leaves, rocks — what better way to produce a landscape than to become a part of it first? Students may create their own still-life — or not so still still-life — with dominoes, potato chips, marbles, or random pocket collections. An art "space" becomes created or "marked" by movement through or across and above or underneath. Students themselves become "art" by using their own bodies — making shapes, dancing, imitating forms, pretending to be rock stars, leaving footprints on new surfaces, or creating shadows on the

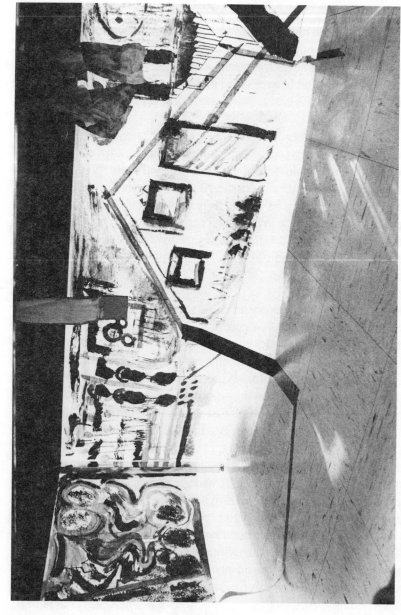

This drawing is under a classroom table and wrapped around its legs to create an environment.

wall. Art classes may draft their own "manifestos" or create avant-garde art groups. Theater, music, performance — students need to be aware of and part of the interdisciplinary world of art as it is being shaped today. They must look to themselves and their own environments to ask and answer their own individual questions.

After 25 years as a painter — I often confess to students — I *still* don't know what a painting is. Yet I begin each day fueled by the challenge of finding new answers. Secondary school students of art are capable of play, and they require play to be artists and to create art. Art requires excitement, and constant reinvention.

Classroom Activity: A Sampling

Below are some descriptions of typical classroom activity in the Adopt-a-School program. Included here are play and performance activities, and experimentation with media, space, and technology.

We believe that the activities described here are a means to incorporate higher-order thinking in our students, so that they will be able to generate unique solutions, come up with multiple approaches, and deal with uncertainty in an art program

• Students *wear* their canvasses and twirl to the beat of La Bamba. Some students wear "sandwich boards," some high-fashion paper "clothes." But all are away from their desks, experiencing "drawing" as performance. This is somewhat different than the lifeless marks usually made by students sitting at tables, whether they are writing their school work or "writing" their art. The mechanical movement of mechanical tools — ball-point pens — constrain the freedom we first knew when we began to scribble as children. In dancing their art, students reawaken that feeling — joyfully leaving a "mark" on an art surface or in space.

In this class, pencils become drum sticks tapping a beat, or batons conducting the music. Lines are drawn across a terrain of gliding partners; students can feel the bounce of a mark on a human canvas.

• The art room becomes a ski slope or an ocean floor, as students negotiate the terrain with art tools in hand.

The teacher, wearing an official Olympics hat and carrying a stop watch, coaches the "art" team. Drawing tools may be taped to shoes as students slide across plastic sheeting on the floor or angled white paper reaching from table to floor. Sticks with drawing attachments become "skis" and unusual tracks are created from sponge sleds.

Playful use of classroom space can create speedways or runways to take off from or parade through. Closets may be transformed into elevators or time machines. Students experiment with new body stances, considering all actions in the environment as a possible springboard for a new creation.

• Transforming the classroom into a restaurant becomes a challenge in color and design. A waitress walks around taking orders using a simple pad as her prop. Breathtaking color spreads are possible, in the setting of a table or the creation of a salad bar. Art room tables become places to "cook" and mix new "sauces" and "soup" colors. A pizza box invites students to invent new toppings; an imagined ice cream store begs for the creation of new flavors. Students use blenders, mixers, spatulas, feather brushes, funnels, and ziplock bags, patenting new color mixes, trying out new surfaces.

Turning the art room into an imaginary test kitchen helps students perceive their role as "inventor." They are encouraged to utilize daily experiences and search their environment, which engenders a greater willingness to explore and experiment.

• If art classes are to be at the forefront of art invention, they must revive the performance instincts of student artists. All of us as children loved to try on clothing, try out different roles, and envision ourselves in various settings.

Turning the art room into a delivery room is simple: a doctor's mask, a watch, a few toy animals, and a lunchbox of art tools (labeled "Doctor's Bag") will do. In one classroom, the birth of a baby (stuffed elephant) was a memorable event, and the emotional event was "captured on film" as drawings on long strips of plastics.

A hanging clear sheet of plastic easily becomes an x-ray screen, with "patient" and "doctor" facing each other and drawing each other from opposite sides of the screen. Art tables covered with white sheets become "operating tables," and students can "perform surgery" by drawing inside a tracing of their own body.

One is never too old to dream, play, or participate in expressive fantasies. Students who have "climbed the craters of the moon" when walking over chairs and tables, "collected moonrocks" by painting sponges, and "traveled on a roller coaster" through a line of chairs have participated in fantasy journeys that have made them richer as individuals and therefore, better artists as well. When the Challenger occurred, students tilted chairs and climbed into a "rocket" in order to hear the countdown and relive the sounds of national tragedy; thus, they were able to share the sounds of a national tragedy and take part in contemporary myth-making. Art best derives from such personal journeys, moments of meaning which can be touched and transformed in the art classroom.

• Technology is as much a contemporary art tool as a paintbrush, and there are many ways to tap into its power — to enhance, inspire, or transform a work of art.

In one class, a mysterious black box was placed on the floor with a "Danger" sign attached. Different colored wires sticking out of its belly engendered even more curiosity as students were asked to "wire up" their works by tying their selected drawing surface to the box. Artists were instructed to proceed with great caution as mysterious "charges" emanating from the box (caused by the teacher's repertory of sound effects and background noises) caused drawing surfaces to lose gravity and sent artists' tools and hands afloat. As things happen to "cool and freeze," artists were given gloves so they could continue. When a red button was "activated" on the back of the box, students were warned to begin timing the drawing, moving in only one direction or the other so as not to shake or disturb the explosive timer.

Perhaps the greatest revelation of some of these experimental play activities for adolescents is the degree to which this age group responds — a group that reportedly has "forgotten" how to play, or at least, has not recently been permitted to do so.

Technology continues to inspire students when art tools are imaginatively electrified, motorized, supercharged, laser-powered, computer-activated, or remote-controlled. Students can be encouraged to apply what they know about modern instrumentation to what they don't know, or can only imagine; for example, computer tomography scan gives a three-dimensional picture of the inside of the human body. Students can "use" this equipment to "look" beyond the wrappings of Egyptian mummies and discover the faces and costumes not visible to the naked eye. Their imagination is their only limitation.

• The pleasure of being scared can open the way to art both by bringing students closer to their basic emotions, and by acting out and overcoming the "scared" feelings of making new art.

When I brought my "dangerous pet, Bobo" into class inside a burlap sack, under the heavy security of a motorcycle chain, students were urged to stand back as lights were lowered to "calm the beast." Young explorers tried to unravel his identity as they listened to the growling noises and examined the evidence: his glowing footprints (dayglo stickers), fur, and even smell (shaving lotion). Altering the class mood also contributes to the creation of a playful spirit among classmates.

With the same thrill of discovery, the young artists hunted for buried treasure, excavating school grounds, and were delighted to find (in a planted chicken bone) "the oldest horse bone in Kentucky history." Mapping and modeling the horse, trying to answer basic questions about its origin, became an exercise in creative documentation. Such active searching, investigating, imaginary wondering should not diminish in art classes as students progress from the lower to the higher grades.

• It is not necessary for a teacher to paint in class to demonstrate his or her creativity. I have practiced magic, juggling, and robot-like performances before my classes, proving through my actions that the art room is our canvas, and each art lesson is our art "work." Art teaching must be creative performance which invites fantasies, licensed playful searching, and open investigation. As teachers, we must be both trusted audiences and playful partners in invention.

This is the way to experience the magic in art, to feel our power as artists, to know our ability to visualize and transform objects and spaces in our world. These are the experiences that give students a sense of mastery, of competence, of confidence in their own creative and artistic identities. These are the experiences that will give them the courage to search through their own experiences for material, so that they will make an authentic art, a personal art.

If invention is the norm, students will feel that they can become anything or anyone, that they can travel anywhere and view anything — even beyond the limits imposed by ordinary eyes or by classroom walls.

Guiding Students to Uncover Personal Influences

Traditional art instruction typically offers the same art history to all students — preselected and preclassified by the teacher. But the Adopt-a-School program challenges young artists to discover personal heroes and mentors, taking clues from their own interests. Seeing artists as people begins an important process that begins with admiration and progresses to connection. Collecting portraits or old photographs of the young Matisse, or Degas in his later years, as well as research into the stories, anecdotes, and recorded conversations of artists helps students think of artists as real people which may be lost when only looking at the work. Imagined conversations between artists and students can take many playful forms — students may look into mirrors and imagine themselves as their favorite masters; make-up and costumes can be utilized to "awaken" the master inside the student and have him or her speak to student audiences.

As a child, Manet walked through the Louvre and selected a spot for his future paintings to hang; he chose the artists and influences he wanted to "be next to." Students, too, can imagine what it would feel like for their work to hang next to a piece they admire by actually hanging their work next to a reproduction in a student exhibit.

Picasso spoke eloquently of the stirring moment when he "discovered" African art. Matisse spoke of the hands of other artists he admired, and Miro talked of seeing through the eyes of the Spanish painter El Greco. How often are our students stirred or moved by an art history slide lecture; how often do they have the opportunity to act on their own responses by effecting changes in their own art?

Students may benefit from preparing their own slide shows, instead of being shown slides with explanations. The technical task of learning to make slides has its own rich creative potential, as students select, sort, and sequence works to be photographed and presented. The opportunity to review a selected body of work by an admired artist helps build expertise

235

and confidence as a student sorts through and examines in detail an artist's lifelong production. Every artist speaks through his or her work to an aware and conscious listener-viewer, so these "encounters" are valuable for students who are beginning their own personal search for their own individual art history.

Students need to discover their own unique pleasures, insights, and influences, and they should be encouraged to define these influences through their own work, to write and talk about their exciting discoveries with one another.

As an alternative to slide shows, which is how art history is usually studied, students can examine actual objects: old hats, Fiesta dishes, old buttons, comics, or radios — these familiar objects all can provide clues to historic forms, fashion, and styling. Art of the past can be uncovered in a personal way through the examination of family heirlooms, photo albums, and collections such as greeting cards and photographs. Studying our past is important; it helps us feel a part of an evolving art history, and know that we are also contributors to it.

In addition to studying artists as our forebearers and our colleagues, students should be encouraged to see *themselves* as having an artistic history. Art history does not begin with European art, or Egyptian art, but with *children's* art, and each person's own creative past. Students' memories of their early scribbles, their forts and imagined shelters under tables, their first struggles to form letters of the alphabet are all memories that should be fostered. Recognition of our own creative past helps us have a perspective on adult invention: children's imaginary sand structures allowed adults to consider the earth as a canvas for "earthwork art" for the first time; Lego structures and fashion play may very well be for some professionals the foundation for architectural and fashion inventiveness.

What we ourselves have built or discovered forms the basis of important historical memories of ourselves as players and as inventors — and it permits a visualization of ourselves as creative artists of the future.

The Art Student as Critic

Art criticism depends on the ability to see and describe visual worlds in special ways. In the school programs we examined while forming the Adopt-a-School project, we noted that final judgments over art works were too often left to the teacher. Students dutifully filed completed works into portfolios and awaited grades from the more "knowledgeable" adult. Final critiques were rarely conducted, and when they were, they were usually led by the teacher, and were carried forward according to the lesson's original objectives.

Individual searching cannot fare well under such circumstances. If students are to experience artistic roles first-hand, and progress in their own work from one project to the next, there must be a greater emphasis on understanding of their own art. What the student him- or herself has learned should be considered more important than the teacher's evaluation of the work.

Making artwork is a creative chain; only the artist is in a position to direct a work, alter it, or harvest ideas from it. Each artwork is a personal journey of promises and possibilities, sometimes — but not always — revealed to outsiders.

In the Adopt-a-School project, we encourage keeping artwork out of storage for as long as possible. Through playful activities, criticism can become an active search — as art making is. In our view, students must be provided with the time and the opportunity for *in-depth seeing*, which is not done by approaching art objects on walls with a checklist of what to look for.

Presenting one's work before an audience, playing with it, not being afraid to handle it helps build the student artist's confidence and strengthens critical abilities. Being a member of the audience is an equally valuable experience. Below are some suggestions, based on experiences in our classroom laboratories, on how to help students gather clues from art, and how to become their own best critics.

Move art from the desks where the piece was made to a new space; see it in different poses, from different distances and from various angles, and in relationship to other objects.

Use the whole body to investigate and explore one's physical relationship to a work of art. "Touch" the work with eyes and fingers, imagine hugging it, squeezing it, pulling its lines or tasting its colors. Works can be imaginatively held, held up, or hung. We can drop works and observe their fall, spin it on platters, turn it on angles, prop it up or lean it against our body, wear it, or pose with it. It is important to freely handle finished art, brush up against it, brush over it with make-believe brushes, re-experiencing its strokes and markings. All art works can be imitated in imaginative ways: draw it in the air with a flashlight, become a shape conforming to the shape of the piece. Even talking to a piece of art or interviewing it can be revealing for students.

Exhibiting, Viewing, and Dissecting Art: Inventive Approaches

Even when work is being exhibited in a conventional manner, we can relate to it in unconventional ways. Note the difference in the ways adults and children normally enter an exhibit hall: adults walk from work to work in a regular pattern, but children enter with a rush of excitement, sweep their eyes over the entire space which itself captivates their interest as much as the work being displayed in it.

Playful walking can help us learn about space and how art is accommodated to space. Students may want to try moving about the room in different ways: crossing the space in unusual patterns or at different speeds; taking close-up and panoramic views; moving about randomly, or backwards, or in circular patterns.

Focusing is important, and students can experience their art — and their classmates' art — in different ways by zooming in nose-to-nose with an artwork (without actually touching it), or moving back into the farthest space possible while still keeping the work in sight. They can imagine themselves as a slow-motion camera with a zoom lens. Students may sit down and look up at the work from different levels, or lie back and stretch out, relaxing the muscles while viewing the art. They may stretch to see the picture from a giant's point of view. They can tune in with creative move-ments — twisting and turning, and rotating the body to look at a work upside down, or from an odd angle. They may dance before the artwork, spreading their arms to feel its boundaries and its scale, crossing the space the work occupies.

Another way for students to look at a work of art in a creative manner is to pass it by, instead of confronting it directly, just as we so often pass by our environment in cars, on bikes, on foot.

The point is to recognize the active nature of seeing. The student should learn to see art from different approaches, experiencing first-hand how those different perspectives to a work can change or enhance our understanding of it.

Placement of art is another area students can experiment with: art can be hung in different corners, draped, placed on clotheslines, or hidden for special controlled viewing inside a closet. An artwork can be isolated or placed in the company of other works; it can be set against a window, a checkered floor, patterned wallpaper, or on wheels. Each placement provides new views of the art. The depth, height, angle, or lighting all contribute to an artwork's revelation of its many sides.

Students can also explore the possibilities in reproducing art works, for example, through simple tracing, xerox, video, Etch-a-Sketch, or through computer graphics. Artworks can be projected onto a paper screen and viewed in different scales, drawn on, mapped out, or diagrammed. The surface of a three-dimensional form can be wrapped or rubbed; its shadows can be traced; it can be videotaped from different angles. Imaginative "restructuring" with scissors and paper, clay, or wire can help students see how shapes and forms fit together, allowing students to learn about their art in retrospect and illuminate decisions they may have made intuitively at an earlier stage.

Writing About Art: Its Value for the Student

Artists have always made use of diaries and notebooks, in conjunction with sketchbooks, as a format for working out ideas and plans. Often ideas generated and recorded before or during the creation of one work can be helpful or inspiring on another, later piece. Such private notations and public writing is a useful part of classroom work in the Adopt-A-School project. Whether it is a simple "artist's statement" or an art journal, or students' preparation of publicity and exhibition materials, writing is an important means for students to conceptualize and share their ideas.

Computers in the classroom are useful for creating professional-looking news releases, art catalogs, art reviews, and so on. Students may be encouraged to model their own "reviews" on movie and rock and roll critics they admire.

Preparation for an Art Show: The Gallery Owner's Program

Students in the Adopt-a-School program study the process of preparing for an art showing in order to learn about the art being shown. They visit with artists preparing for exhibitions to learn about the many choices and the various steps that go into selecting works and "dressing" them for a show. They visit galleries preparing for an exhibit, and in one particular project, the student "becomes" a gallery owner with an assigned school space and a mandate to prepare a series of shows. The student must design, curate, and install the exhibitions, which may include preparing for one-person shows, group exhibits, opening reception plans, and publicity writing. This project helps the student become an "insider" to the art world and extend the creative process: unusual exhibits devised by students in the program have included upside-down art; hidden artworks; collaborative works; and tours where audiences are blindfolded.

Students bring their role-playing activity to their exhibition work as well: in one exhibit, a "janitor" with a mop sat in a darkened (student) gallery, admiring the show. A "thief" snuck up to him and asked advice on the best works to steal. Students have posed as younger and older people, members of various professions in the arts, and visiting dignitaries who speak no English. All of this imaginative playing fosters a knowledgeable exchange of ideas about their work, and fresh ways of perceiving their creations.

Young children make art for their parents and teachers — a loved and trusted audience. Secondary school students begin to wonder more about the fate of their art as it journeys beyond the family and goes into the hands of strangers. The role playing of gallery owners, auctioneers, and art sellers generates significant discussions about artists' rights, the preservation of art, and trading practices in the art market.

When students are able to learn from their own art, and make decisions based on what they learned or experienced in the creation of their work, they are truly learning to be independent practitioners of art; if they depend on assignments and the ideas of others, they will remain students, not artists.

Bibliography

Battock, G. (1973). *New ideas in art education*. New York: E. P. Dutton Co.

Eisner, E. (1987, September). The role of discipline-based art education in American schools. *Art Education, 40* (5).

Guilford, P. (1971). Creative thinking in children of junior high level. *Psychological Lab Reports*. University of California.

Leiberman, N. (1977). *Playfulness: Its relationship to imagination and creativity*. New York: Academic Press.

Michael, J. (1983). *Art and adolescence*. New York: Teachers College Press, Columbia University.

Palmer, F. (1970). *Art and the young adolescent*. Oxford, London: Pergamon Press.

Resnick, L. B. (1987). *Education and learning to think*. Washington, D. C.: National Academy Press.

Szekely, G. (1988). *Creativity in art lessons*. New York: Teachers College Press, Columbia University.

18
The Next Generation: Initiative or Inertia in Secondary Art Education

GUY HUBBARD

Indiana University

In 1965 a watershed meeting occurred at The Pennsylvania State University. The Seminar in Art Education for Research and Curriculum Development, better known as the Penn State Conference (Mattil, 1966), led art educators to acknowledge that they were part of an enterprise that not only included art professionals but also scholars from the social sciences, as well as curriculum generalists. They also acknowledged the need for a more systematic attack on the design of art curricula.

The years since the Penn State Conference have been marked by significant changes. The number of art teachers has increased. Continued school district consolidation led to the development of larger secondary schools staffed by teams of art teachers, usually working in better equipped facilities than formerly. Informational resources to help teach art, such as books, instructional packages, prints, and slides have also become more accepted and as a consequence more plentiful, to the point that art curriculum textbooks are now found increasingly at all levels of art education. Above all, however, the period has been marked by a growing recognition that art teaching embraces all dimensions of visual arts and is not confined to studio practice.

In spite of apparent improvement in art education, the 1980's have been marked by numerous outbursts calling for reform in education as a whole. Perhaps the best known was published as *A Nation At Risk: The Imperative for Educational Reform.* (National Commission on Excellence in Education, 1983). This document addressed educational issues in relation to world competitiveness; needs for advancement in technological innovation, commerce, and industry; as well as improved standards for teaching.

Closer to home and more recently, Brent Wilson confronted the profession with sobering statistics about its actual health. In an address to the National Art Education Association (Wilson, 1988), he summarized the findings of his research for the National Endowment for the Arts (National Endowment for the Arts, 1988) and concluded that "arts education in America is characterized by imbalance, inconsistency, and inaccessibility." For example, only slightly more than half of America's 7th and 8th graders enroll in art classes; twenty one percent enroll in grades 9 and 10; and sixteen percent enroll in grades 11 and 12. Moreover, within those classes taken, little, if any, attention is given to our artistic heritage.

The 1980's: The educational circumstances of the late 1980's are very different from those in the 1960's, and yet certain elements remain the same. Unlike education in most countries around the world, American schools are governed locally and not by a centralized bureaucracy. One pronounced result of the U.S. model is great diversity. Wealthier districts generally provide better space, equipment, and supplies — not to mention better student-teacher ratios and more extensive offerings — than poorer ones. Local autonomy goes beyond economics, however, and asserts itself in the form of the attention given particular areas of study. In some districts, for example, the arts are prized and supported generously. In others they languish. Legislation exists in all states in an effort to compensate for gross inequalities of resources as well as curricular imbalance across districts; but these measures have only modest influence. These differences are certain to become even more pronounced in the future if the separation between rich and poor school systems follows its present path and if the nation's economic troubles as a whole are not addressed satisfactorily.

Demographic factors are also affecting education vitally. More people are coming to the United States in this decade than at any time since the peak immigration years at the turn of the century (Kellogg, 1988). But instead of coming to work in factories and mines, immigrants are entering a nation that is rapidly abandoning many of the primary industries that were its original sources of wealth. The country is rapidly being transformed bimodally into an information and a service economy, and comparatively few people are needed to operate increasingly automated industries.

In order to satisfy these needs, education is being called on to play a complex and potentially contradictory role. From a vocational perspective, workers in business and industry — the informational industries in particular — are required to have comparatively high levels of education. Workers in service industries, on the other hand, are rarely expected to need high levels of formal education.

From a far different but equally important point of view, all people — regardless of vocational aspirations — need a general education. They must master basic intellectual skills and be able to respond intelligently to the flood of information they encounter in the course of their everyday lives. They also need to have a feeling of self esteem and a sense of belonging to American culture. Serious problems arise in a nation when people lack these values. The large numbers of young people who drop out of school, for example, set the stage for negative forces that if allowed to grow could destabilize the nation or, if nothing else, alter its character for the worse.

Yet another condition that is due to affect events in education, including art education, is the advancing age of teachers. A substantial proportion of all teachers will reach retirement age during the 1990's and will be leaving the profession. While enrollments in teacher education programs are gradually increasing after a period of considerable decline, some doubt exists that the numbers of qualified graduates will be adequate for the time when many older teachers are retiring and when the bulge of school populations now entering elementary schools advances to secondary education (Plisko and Stern, 1985). During the 1990's and beyond, teacher shortages could easily lead to larger classes, increasing numbers of two-shift days, and even to reductions of school offerings — with the worst conditions occurring in those schools that are least well equipped to handle them.

Technological change is also impacting on all areas of life, including education. Not very long ago, educational technology meant films, slides, projectors, tape recorders, and perhaps duplicators. Some, like film and slides remain useful; and yet videotape has engulfed the home market and offers many opportunities to teachers not possible with film. For example, television broadcasts can be recorded at home on VCRs for use next day in classrooms — something unthinkable in an earlier generation.

When microcomputers first appeared, they were seen as tools for mathematics and business. They have since found their way into most areas of the curriculum — including art. With the growth of computer memories — not to mention greater sensitivity by programmers to people's needs — computers have come to play an active part in school life, both as tools and as devices for accessing and manipulating information. And while such applications as databases and networking largely remain the preserve of business and industry, the rapid spread of these services, together with the potential of laserdisc technology to support teaching, suggest that profound curricular and administrative changes lie ahead for educators in all areas.

The primary challenge of secondary education is not so much technological as intellectual, however: how can teachers help students use tools that serve the mind to help solve problems? Such problems may call upon mathematical skills, but problems can just as readily call for analysis of artistic designs followed by actions to resolve those problems. Computers and related machinery are thus best seen as extensions of our minds, much as other tools — be they automobiles or chain saws — are extensions of our bodies. How then should these tools be used? How can art teachers prepare themselves to address the problems they face?

The Next Generation

Various proposals for reform have been published, one of the most recent being by the U.S. Department of Education, under the auspices of the then Secretary of Education, William J. Bennett (U.S. Department of Education, 1988) In *American Education: Making It Work,* Bennett and his staff propose strengthening the bonds between home and school and engaging in greater parental involvement in school life. They propose that efforts be made to lead toward an emphasis on excellence in academic and intellectual studies to match those placed on athletics. They also propose redefining curriculum and improving its content.

Lewis J. Perelman takes a much more uncompromising position when writing for the National School Boards Association (Perelman, 1988). He declares that educators, if not all of American society, are at a crossroads. Education, in Perelman's view, can be allowed to continue as it has been, that is, with "business as usual"; or it can be entirely restructured. He presents scenarios of each to dramatize his case, pointing to continuing rapid decay if we continue along the present path. As one might expect, his vision of a restructured education is extreme. He proposes deregulating schools and dismantling the entrenched bureaucracies that administer them and replacing them with school-based management where technologies

246

would be applied in every possible way to meet students' individual needs.

Whether Bennett's proposal, Perelman's, or some other, is likely to be instituted or not is less important here than to draw attention to the need for fundamental reform. One thing is certain, the dilemmas reported by Wilson are not likely to disappear as long as the system persists in its present form. The risk, of course, is that with major changes art teaching might be reduced still further or disappear altogether. A more positive viewpoint is to look ahead with optimism to a time when art finally occupies a substantial place in the educational scheme of things. And it is with this more positive point of view in mind that the following proposals are made.

Curriculum Changes

The momentum to introduce verbal, intellectual art content has gathered strength to the point that it is represented in state art guides, textbook adoption criteria, and pronouncements from professional organizations. The cafeteria of studio art offerings that characterizes many secondary art curricula is being challenged, although little action has taken place. The trend away from the study of art as creativity, therapy, and craft activity toward more intellectually substantial and comprehensive content learning is proceeding but only slowly, and much yet needs to be done.

Probably the strongest claim to increased attention comes from the history of art, where the dimensions of time and space make it a potential ally of history and geography. Thus far, however, art history has had too narrow a focus in secondary art rooms. The richness and diversity of American art, for example, is rarely addressed, largely because it is not emphasized in college art departments where art teachers are educated; and yet an important goal of education is to introduce students to their own culture. Regardless of personal inclinations and past training, art teachers can expect to have to give more attention to American art, including its Afro-American and Hispanic dimensions, in ways that have not occurred before. Moreover, the populous border states, with their ethnic diversity, are challenging traditional values in education much as they are in national politics. All of this will increasingly influence art instruction over the next generation, and art teachers should be redesigning their curricula now in order to meet this challenge.

While the arts of the Americas deserve attention, the extent to which people recognize the need to know more about world cultures, will cause art teaching to undergo still further modification. Since the Second World War, the United States has increasingly looked to the Pacific Rim nations of the Orient much as traditionally it looked to Europe. For the most part, however, art curricula continue to emphasize Western European artistic values. Wherever works of art are studied in art classrooms, French Impressionism and Post Impressionism are usually represented prominently. The arts of Africa made a start during the civil rights movement of the 1960's, but they still do not receive systematic attention. The study of Asian arts has entered the college curriculum, but little or nothing is included in most secondary schools. In sum, secondary art curricula have a long way to go before a world perspective on art can be said to exist. Interestingly, art curricula in numbers of Asian countries recognize American and European arts as well as their own art traditions.

Criticism and aesthetics is receiving increased attention, judging from recent and growing interest of both in the literature and in convention presentations. However, both are less well developed than art history, and much work is needed before they will be ready for full inclusion in elective art programs in high schools. It might well be that these studies will be more effectively handled by focusing on the more dynamic, contemporary art forms of film and television in contrast to art historical studies where the emphasis lies on static art forms.

From quite a different perspective, an area of art that deserves recognition is computer graphics. A handful of professional artists have embraced this new medium, and more can be expected to follow. And most commercial studios now use computers to generate images and lettering. For high schoolers who plan on becoming professional designers and architects, some exposure to specialized computer software is already proving valuable. For those who do not have professional aspirations, computers offer opportunities for expressiveness to a degree that is often denied them with traditional media because of lack of talent or experience. As computers become ever more powerful, as well as less expensive, these opportunities will increase. At one level, art teachers may instruct students to create expressive images by writing their own programs. Art teachers may also find themselves contributing to general computer literacy, since graphics programming is an excellent vehicle for learning how computers work. At another level, students may learn to make good use of specialized programs to create pictorial art, graphic design, and animations. Computerized images can be cropped, distorted, enlarged, repeated, and reduced at will. They can quickly be transferred to other programs as designs, illustrations, lettering, and movies. In effect, aesthetic problem solving in school can frequently be exercised more effectively by electronic means than with conventional art tools and materials.

A difficult task to be faced will be deciding which art forms are to be dropped from the traditional list of subjects found in school art curricula to make way for the new ones. Vested interests in one or other areas of art are sure to lead to passionate resistance to any suggestion of removing them; and yet that is exactly what will have to be faced if the verbal and intellectual needs of art teaching are to be addressed; and if computing is to be given its proper place. It is not far fetched to anticipate a future where much school art is conducted at computer workstations rather than on drawing boards. The visual arts, after all, have never been dependent for their existence on any particular medium; and a graphic generated by a computer is nothing more than an image created by a medium, albeit an extremely flexible one.

Working in an Information Age:

Art teachers guide their students with information that is visual, verbal, and manipulative. Recent transformations in the ways information is handled in much of society have not yet reached art education to any extent; but during the next decade access to information is likely to transform education, and art education along with it. Art teachers, unlike teachers in most areas, are only now beginning to acknowledge the usefulness of textbooks. Instructional texts for art have been available for over a century, but not until the last twenty years have systematically organized curricula in textbook form been generally available for secondary art instruction. Ironically, support for art textbooks comes at a time when other forms of information storage retrieval are emerging to challenge books as primary sources of classroom information.

Information is increasingly being stored in databases. A database may consist solely of text or it may include motion and still pictures ranging from animals to great paintings that can be displayed to inform students about an object, a concept, or a technique. Collections of information may also consist of research that can be put to immediate use in the art room. Books of lessons, and collections of prints and slides are sure to continue in use; but much of what they presently do will eventually be supplanted by electronic media.

Armed with such resources, together with specially written programs for using these materials, art teachers will be able to bring an array of images and supporting text materials to student attention on demand — all of which have the potential to open the doors on individualized instruction in undreamed of ways. The challenge for art teachers is not only to be ready for these changes but to be anticipating how to take advantage of the opportunities they offer. The National Gallery of Art, for example, published a videodisc of part of its collection (National Gallery of Art, 1985). It was a spectacular achievement. However, individual users had no help in how to organize the images to incorporate them into their teaching until a computer program was written that enables a user to search for a particular artistic quality from the several thousand images in storage and bring it to the screen (National Gallery of Art Laserguide, 1988).

At some time during the next few years, sequences of art lessons are also likely to be organized into comprehensive databases, complete with visual images, that will enable students as well as teachers to browse in search of useful or appealing activities. The development of art instructional databases will make useful information available to the poorest schools either for the price of a telephone call or the modest cost of compact disc (CD). Moreover, lessons and other materials acquired in this way will be easy to modify to suit local conditions. Instructional databases for art do not exist yet, but efforts have begun in science and social studies; and the availability of encyclopedias on CDs — which are themselves vast repositories of information — is evidence enough that the task is practical and will eventually be undertaken in all subjects.

The electronic transformation of education will have other ramifications as well. Teachers never have enough good ideas; and yet the task of sharing is difficult except at professional meetings. Networking, or the provision for people to communicate quickly and easily with one another by computer, is almost certain to become a regular part of an art teacher's life in the not too distant future. In some subjects, high school students are already communicating with each other in different communities and even other countries. And much as businessmen are presently sending pictures to each other by fax machines, art teachers will soon be able to do the same: they will exchange images of art works, diagrams of techniques, maps, charts, and even student work to help them with their teaching.

By means of such devices, the isolation that art teachers have often suffered in the past may be replaced by collaboration and the rich exchange of information. In fact, the more important changes are likely to emphasize human values rather than machine dependency; in the most effective situations machines will be so unobtrusive as to be virtually unnoticed.

Career Changes:

The kinds of curricular changes described above, not to mention preparing materials to make full use locally of information brought in from outside databases, are going to require considerable work. Local control of schools almost always leads to local modifications; something that is difficult when using mass produced textbooks. Variants of instructional materials may need to be prepared for students who are artistically talented or those who are mentally handicapped — or who need to see particular Hispanic or Afro-American artworks — to help emphasize a particular concept. These preparations cannot be expected as overload assignments, so art teachers should expect periodic reassignment outside their normal classrooms, perhaps in materials preparation serving all their colleagues in a school district or learning to use new instructional materials and teaching others to use them. In other words, much like professionals in other occupations that are rapidly changing, art teachers should expect their careers to include partial or complete shifts in direction from time to time.

Postscript:

If appropriate changes in secondary art education are to occur, then modifications in college preservice programs are urgently needed. The curricula of most college art departments, however, represent elite, traditional arts and disregard broader definitions of visual arts, such as motion pictures, television, and computing. Moreover, colleges and universities have historically not responded to the needs of elementary and secondary schools so much as expecting the responses to be the other way around. In view of the educational needs of rapid national and world changes, not to mention the expanding social and ethnic diversity of the United States, secondary art curricula need to be much more broadly based. It remains to be seen whether art teachers will be able to turn to their colleagues in higher education for assistance with the task that lies ahead.

References

Kellogg, J. B. (1988). "Forces of Change", *Phi Delta Kappan,* 70, 109-204.
Mattil, E. L. (1966). *A seminar in art education for research and curriculum development.* University Park, PA: The Pennsylvania State University.
National Commission on Excellence in Education. (1983). *A nation at risk: The imperative for educational reform.* Washington, D.C.: United States Department of Education.
National Gallery of Art. (1985). Videodisc Publishing.
National Gallery of Art Laserguide. (1988). Voyager.
Perelman, L. J. (1988). *Technology and transformation of schools.* Washington, D.C.: National School Boards Association.
Plisko, V. W. and Stern, J. (eds.). (1985). *The condition of education.* Washington, D.C.: U. S. Government Printing Office. p. 144.
Toward civilization: A report on arts education. (1988). Washington, D.C.: National Endowment for the Arts.
Wilson, B. (1988). *Art education, civilization and the 21st century: A researcher's reflections on the national endowment for the arts report to congress.* Reston, VA: The National Art Education Association.